JUVIE TALK

Unlocking the language
of juvenile justice

D1547615

Richard Ross

MacArthur
Foundation

Photographs and Introduction ©2017 Richard Ross
Theater: How and Why ©2017 Peter Sellars

Support for this project has been provided by the MacArthur Foundation.

For more information, to read the blog, get updates, or find out how you can take action and get involved, see the website www.juvenile-in-justice.com

Editorial: Claire Bredenoord
Production: Raymond Douglas
Design: Mariano Hernán Spina

ISBN: 978-0-9855106-2-6

Printed and bound in Portland, Oregon

10 9 8 7 6 5 4 3 2 1

Table of Contents

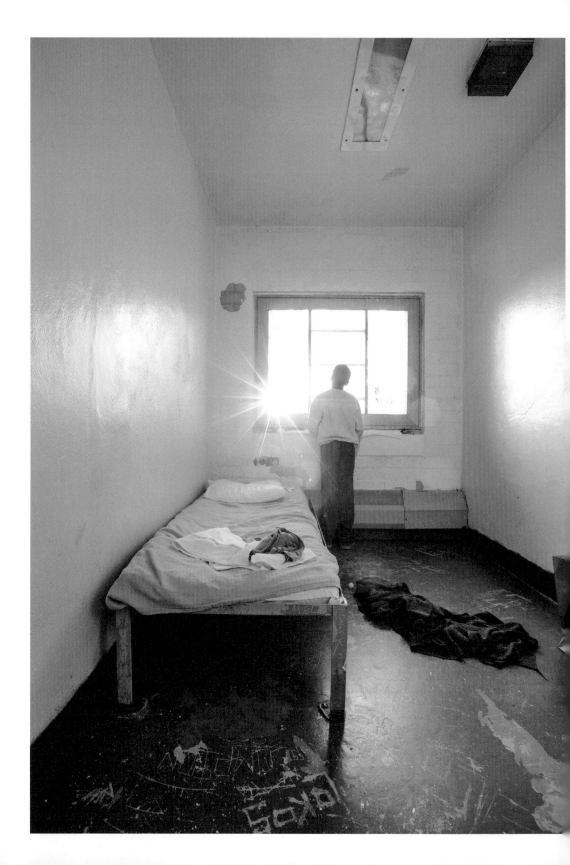

Introduction

by Richard Ross

"We are born into a box of time and space. We use words and communication to break out of it and reach out to others."

—Roger Ebert

"Stories matter. Many stories matter. Stories have been used to dispossess and to malign, but stories can also be used to empower and to humanize. Stories can break the dignity of a people, but stories can also repair that broken dignity."

—Chimamanda Ngozi Adichie

"Is it the performance or the part you liked?"

I thought I was just being kind to an actor friend when I praised her evening's effort. She wanted more. She parsed my words, "performance or part?" she insisted and explained theater to me in that one question.

The kids I have visited, interviewed, photographed and recorded this past decade have all be playing parts that have been written for them by society. Think of this world as a play; these children as actors. Stage direction such as "Enter stage left" can be equated with poverty, poor schools, privation. "Enter stage right" can define privilege, race and economic advantage. As an actor, a child may not have much latitude to play the role differently than written. Their binary world may be defined by their worst event rather than their highest accomplishment. Stage left, stage right—directions written before they are born. Success is decided by zip code rather than DNA. A white female born in Lafayette, Indiana will have a different life outcome than an African American male born in Liberty City or Miami Gardens.

This book and accompanying website were created to assist you: the student, the teacher, the actor and the director, to take these words and stories and empathize with these lives. Explore the language and see where it intersects with your own lives and experiences. Imagine and embrace the lives off-stage where the characters are formed.

The interviews are the opening to the backstory. Pages can be arranged and rearranged to create a play for classes in middle school to courses in university. It can be staged in a theater or classroom; with the audio, visuals and text, much of the raw material is here for a drama, and an opening into the world these kids inhabit and have come from. What is necessary is the ability to understand the circumstances that have brought these kids to these situations and a willingness to interject your own lives and experiences to bridge their world and yours.

The book—the play—is meant to be a curricular tool for a discussion of human rights, mass incarceration and the potential for children to succeed. While it is important to be able to empathize with these kids, it is also critical to realize there are multitudes of ways the words can be spoken, and even be rewritten.

We all grow with a language that defines our environment and who we are. Words both testify to and create our surroundings, families, relationships and attitudes. My vantage point is that of an observer. My limitations are of age, race, and education contrast with these kids. I don't want to over-rate or misrepresent my qualifications, nor do I want to minimize the importance of observation and careful note-taking. To quote the cartoon character Popeye, "I am what I am." The experience of working with the 1,000 kids I have met allow and demand of me to postulate a simple idea. The language of these children is defined by more than geographic dialect. It is not the southern drawl, nor the long Boston "a." In this world, the language is informed by poverty, trauma, violence and lack of opportunity as well as physical geography.

Language comprises more than chance nouns. In some areas of the US the geography of poverty is so broad that there is little opportunity for interaction between the cultures of haves and have-nots. One 14-year-old in Milwaukee grew up eight blocks from Lake Michigan and had never seen the water. For many of the kids telling their stories a few blocks encircle the sum total of their environment. Watts in Los Angeles is a 51 square mile area. There is little exchange in language between Watts and Beverly Hills. It is a chasm more than the 13 miles that physically separate these disparate worlds. As these communities become isolated, so does the communication. The result is the language turning in on itself, defining a very specific experience. Incarcerated children come from very limited geographical areas.

As these are anecdotal observations—and not qualitative, properly sampled data—I invite the reader to explore the patterns of this world, as well as their own experiences to form their own conclusions. You, as the reader, might investigate the structure and architecture of the language emerging from this pool of anecdotes, and measure it with your own experience and history.

The goal of this book was to visit young, incarcerated people and learn how their specific language gave insight into their past, present and future.

The majority of the stories on the following pages come directly from interviews with over 1,000 incarcerated youth during my visits to all types of juvenile placements— detention centers, correctional facilities, boot camps and beyond.

I knock on the door of a cell, ask to come in, take off my shoes and sit on the floor as we talk. The youth are told they can end the conversation at any time, but more often I listen to their stories for at least an hour, writing notes as I record. Throughout these interactions the most pervasive word is "respect." There is a myriad of ways that this word shapes, or rather fails to manifest in these kids' lives. What they want most is basic respect, and to be treated as a human being whose life has value.

Several stories included in the book came from Juvenile in Justice partnering with the Center for Education Excellence in Alternative Settings (CEEAS) on their Untold Stories Initiative. Teachers at schools in detention facilities across the US used the Untold Stories writing curriculum, culminating in a contest where we selected 13 stories for publication. Students were encouraged to tell their stories with their language, and they provided many of the definitions for the highlighted words in their writing. The quality of writing in all of the entries was remarkable, but it is the content of their stories that truly sticks to you. The scenes they share give us a valuable glimpse into their lives.

In defining terms, whether colloquial, legal or institutional, we have provided the most accurate definition possible. Despite our efforts, the nuances of what a "come-up" is vary from city to city. Just as what constitutes "assault" in Kansas law is different from "assault" in North Dakota law. Even the word "juvenile" varies from state to state; depending on jurisdiction it can be somewhere between eight and 24 years old. In other cases policies only exist in one state—such as Measure 11 in Oregon—or a few states— like "Romeo and Juliet" laws. Rather than create a static book, we wanted to foster an experience where students could share their own lives to find where experiences intersect, where their world is heard.

To more directly share this experience, we have partnered with Peter Sellars to offer ideas about the nature of theater and roles. These are not specific stage directions. The final production is left to the director/actor. Much of the stage direction will be suggested online and include images, audio and video that can be included in any production. Here we hope to create a curricular tool to allow students outside these institutions to understand more the lives of those tens of thousands of incarcerated children.

To protect the identity of the children, the faces are obscured, specific facts may be redacted and names are reduced to initials and then altered. In a few instances the child depicted is similar in age and race, but not the same child speaking. In no way does this alter the truth of these stories and hopefully, the power of these words, their words—Juvie Talk.

—

Acknowledgements

ac·knowl·edg·ment

ək'näləjmənt/
noun
plural noun: *acknowledgments*

> **acceptance of the truth or existence of something.**
> **"there was no acknowledgment of the family's trauma"**
> **synonyms:**
> **acceptance, recognition, admission, concession, confession**
> **"acknowledgment of the need to take new initiatives"**

Acknowledge the kids pictured in this book

Acknowledge the disorder in their lives

Acknowledge the instability of food and shelter

Acknowledge the failure of the education

Acknowledge the poverty

Acknowledge the privation

Acknowledge the discrimination

Acknowledge the abuse—emotional, physical and sexual

Acknowledge the violence

Acknowledge the trauma that brings them here.

We have to acknowledge our own part as a society in both causing the situation and curing the problem as manifested in these kids, their families and their communities.

It is these kids that have to be seen, appreciated, understood and acknowledged.

This work would not be possible without the intelligence and devotion of Claire Bredenoord who toiled through the endless manifestations of this work.

Peter Sellars is a visionary who can transform words into actions, silence into song and has helped in changing retribution into hope and redemption.

Raymond Douglas has worked diligently with Mariano Hernán Spina in bringing these stories to print, and collaborated with Alison Ho and Andrew Parnell in transforming the project for the web.

Haley Wolfe and Siavash Zohoori brought the voices of these kids to become an important audio component of this work.

Brandon Yadegari assisted in the compilations and simply keeping the studio humming. Margo Steurer keeps the books balanced and our world in a state of amusing imbalance.

Kat Crawford, Christy Sampson-Kelly and David Domenici at CEEAS for their collaboration in allowing us to utilize creative writing from incarcerated youth.

This publication has been supported by the John D. and Catherine T. MacArthur Foundation, and the University of California, Santa Barbara.

I am also humbled by the support of such friends in the field as Bart Lubow, Victor Rios, Liz Ryan, Frances Sherman, David McKune, Kim Tandy, Tony Johnson, Vincent Schiraldi and Laura Lindgren. The Annie E. Casey Foundation has always been a partner in my work and this book is the result of many journeys they assisted.

The encouragement of Nick and Leela is always important, as is the support and understanding of Cissy who has to field my babble and mood swings when I return from these interviews—these journeys into another world.

—

Theater: How and Why

by Peter Sellars

Theater is a way to try and enter someone else's life, and a way to let someone else into your life. Can you put yourself in someone else's shoes, in someone else's mind, in someone else's heart, in someone else's neighborhood, or in someone else's jail cell? Can you imagine what someone else is experiencing? Can you imagine how that experience would shape that person's choices, actions, attitudes, public behavior, and secret feelings and hope? How many ways are you like this person? Of course you are different. But how many ways is this person like you? The longer and the deeper you look, the things you share totally outweigh the differences. Maybe all that separates you is a cement wall and the fact that, for today, you are allowed to keep the shoelaces in your shoes.

The power of theater is that it gives us a chance to create the conditions in which we can really begin to try to see each other, hear each other, and find what makes us equal when the world around us makes us so unequal. It is a chance to realize how fluid your own identity is, and to recognize that neither you nor anyone else needs to be trapped in a single identity, a single situation, or a single scenario – because all of us are way more interesting, complicated, and hopeful than appears on the surface. And the same way you don't want someone else to judge you without understanding what you're going through, theater creates a space where you don't have to judge other people from the outside. Or judge them at all. Instead you can try to understand them.

So when you're acting, you have to learn someone else's words. As you do that, you might start to notice your own thoughts, feelings, and prejudices about other people. Suddenly, you have to think about and feel what they are saying, and notice things about them that you didn't notice before. Which will lead you to think about and feel what they are not saying. Everyone says certain things that we want other people to think or feel or notice about us. But other things, that we don't want people to notice or that we are uncomfortable with, or that we have mixed feelings about, don't get said. So start to observe and understand how the person you are playing moves. What is their music? What are their rhythms? How do they live in their body?

And how do they live in their mind, in their imagination? When you are 16 years old and locked in a steel and cement cell 23 hours a day, you are going to need your imagination. Every person is way more than what they look like from the outside; where they grew up, where they went to school, their test scores, what kind of job they have, or how many times they've been arrested. In theater, you try to discover what's inside a person that we have not seen yet. All human beings are changing every day. We have good days and bad days, and violent days and calm days, and we make mistakes and we get some things right. But that is always in play, moment to moment in every human life. There are no "good people" or "bad people" – there are just people with good and bad moments, qualities, habits, and tendencies, and the tension between all those things that plays out differently on different days, in different situations. Theater is about recognizing the minute-to-minute dynamic inside the tension of every human life. Everything is in play – like in sports. Every element that comes together to create "team you" wins some games and loses others.

But your life is not the scoreboard or the stats. You can be courageous and brilliant and lose the game, or win the game without playing well, or fairly. Life is about everything that doesn't appear on the scoreboard. The story behind the story. Not what the world thinks is going on, but what is really going on. Most theater is focused on crisis. Not because crisis is depressing, paralyzing, freaks you out, or is fun. Crisis is the moment where change enters our lives. The old thing doesn't work anymore. We need a new idea, a new approach. We have to imagine something better and then become that.

For example, some laws are unjust and they need to be changed. Just because something is legal doesn't mean it's right. And we all know plenty of things that are illegal but prosecuted differently in different neighborhoods. And surrounded by a lot of hypocrisy. So theater lets us create a space where we can enact both the legal and the illegal and, without risking anybody's life, try and find where justice really lives.

Some people have already made large mistakes. And you may be next. It's human. But mistakes are not just something to ruin lives. Mistakes are also one of the only ways that human beings learn something deeply. And the only way you can learn from a mistake is to revisit it, go back into the situation, look at everything again, and give yourself the chance to make some other choices and feel what that feels like. Theater is the second, third, and 150th chance for all humans. It lets us go back and do something all over again, like a rehearsal for life, and discover that we can create a different future with some new possibilities. There is no discovery without total commitment and risk. Really great theater takes you into the danger zone and needs courage and insight and skill and brilliance and humor and honesty. There is no place to hide. And there is nothing to wait for. The time is now.

Human beings are living contradictions. We are "of two minds" about most things, and our hearts are hurting so often in the crossfire. Each person is an infinite self living inside a limited body. Theater is about learning to live inside human contradictions. To take a simple example from acting – if you're playing a loud person at a party, the truth is probably that that person is very shy. Something is true if, and only if, its opposite is also true! You are usually telling yourself one side of your own story. But there are other sides. Learning to tell those other sides of the story is theater.

The only thing you need to make theater is human beings. Everything else you can imagine. The more you imagine everything, the more amazing theater becomes. The best theater is super specific, and very, very accurate about someone's feelings and situation. Keenly observed, through a microscope or a telescope, recognizing layer after layer of all the elements that are in play in a human life, in a family, and in a world. Which is why we call it "a play." And so, right next to all that accuracy and insight, theater adds freedom. Now imagine every other possibility, for yourself, and for everyone else.

And then step into the rest of your real life. And really act. And in real life, acting means action. Take action. Make change. Brilliantly. Because now you understand the situation from the inside, you know the forces at work, and you are equipped to enter the high level, high stakes sport of moving the ball down the field. That ball is the world.

—

Create Your Own Play

If your school, class, program or institution would like to construct a play using the content from Juvie Talk, visiting us on the web gives you the ability to do so. By specifying the number of actors, the key topics you would like to cover, and the amount of time available, our website will generate a customized PDF that you may use to direct a Juvie Talk performance:

juvietalk.com

For more information, please visit us online at the address above or send us an email:

studio@richardross.net

Stories Collection

juvenile:

/ˈjoŏvəˌnīl, ˈjoŏvənl/
adjective

- a young person; childish, immature;
a person below the age at which ordinary
criminal prosecution is possible

justice:

/ˈjəstəs/
n oun

- just behavior or treatment; the quality of being
fair and reasonable; the administration of the law
or authority in maintaining this

LEVELS- can refer to a number of different classifications depending on jurisdiction and context: levels as a hierarchy of privileges earned through good behavior; levels measuring how far you are in a program; levels as an indicator of a youth's mental health status; levels ranking how intensive the services are from facility to facility.

PROBATION VIOLATION- failure to obey the conditions of one's probation as set forth by the court, which may result in new charges and/or detention.

UA- short for urine analysis test, the most prevalent form of drug testing.

PROBATION- the status of a delinquent youth under court ordered supervision within the community, with specific conditions such as school attendance, the wearing of an electronic ankle monitor, refraining from interaction with other youth on probation, drug testing, etc. Failure to obey the conditions of probation may result in new charges and/or detention.

RUNNING AWAY- a status offense that can bring a child into conflict with law enforcement, juvenile court, detention, or dependency court, depending on the runaway's circumstances; running away often leads children to commit more serious crimes in order to survive.

ON THE LAM- on the run, avoiding contact with authorities; a term used for fugitives At the facility M.E. has been placed, points are a daily measure of one's behavior and dictate your progress in the level system.

IDENTITY THEFT- "the assumption of a person's identity in order, for instance, to obtain credit cards from banks and retailers; to steal money from existing accounts;... or to establish accounts using another's name."

STATUTORY RAPE- a general term for the crime of engaging in sexual activity with a minor. The age restrictions for reporting the crime vary widely from state to state.

FLEEING STATE- to leave the state in an attempt to avoid a trial or prosecution for a crime, making the person a fugitive from justice.

SUICIDE WATCH- a state of constant observation that may be ordered for a child if they are believed to be suicidal or are inflicting self-harm.

No one visits me here. Dad is a firefighter. I have a green shirt. I'm on the lowest **level**; it's an orientation shirt. I will be here for a year for **probation violation**. Ran away from a treatment center, failed a **UA** while on probation. The other kid that I got in trouble with is over at the adult facility. He is a year older than me. We did the crime together. He got jail; I got **probation**. There's lots of meth where I'm from. I was in treatment then **ran away**. I was **on the lam** for three months, getting high and drunk. Hung out with the wrong people. Had a girlfriend, but lost her when I was arrested. She sent me a Dear John on my birthday and I got less points than

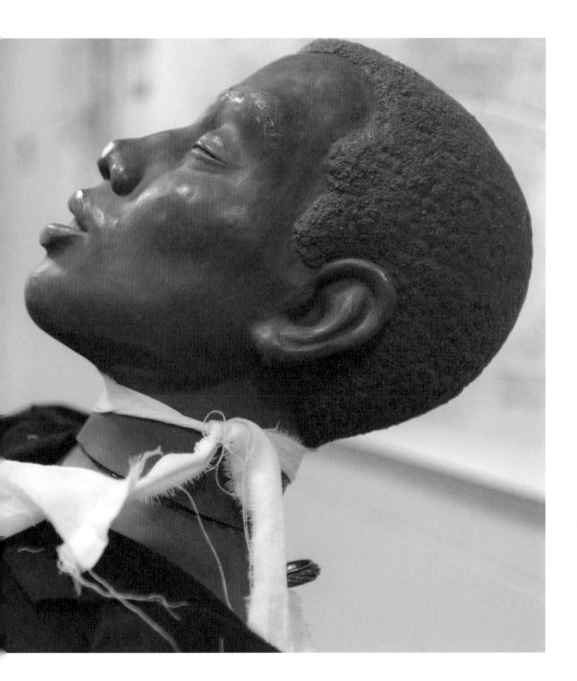

any other day. Tomorrow I get a blue shirt. One day I will get to level three and get to wear my own clothing. My family needs me a lot. My dad and brother are in jail. He is there for **identity theft**, **statutory rape**, **fleeing state**, etc. I have one brother who is a carpenter. When I get out I want to live in Juneau as a fireman. My mother lives at home with six siblings—three younger and three older. I live with four and my mother. I am on **suicide watch**. Everyone in my family is suicidal. My brother was in here and he tried hanging himself. My other brother was in here when he was 10 or 11 for stabbing me and another brother. It comes from my father who is bipolar.

- M.E., Age 18

I'm a freshman in high school... I should be a junior. I have four and a half high school credits when I should have sixteen of eighteen credits. I have ADHD... it's really bad. I got in lots of fights. I'd just be **scrapping** all the time. Eventually I joined a gang on the south side, the Projects Gang. I was in a **group home** for three months but I ran away from the home to live with my **homies**. I was the only white kid. They didn't trust me **putting in work, tagging**, it takes a while to earn your status. My family? Divorced. I was adopted when I was two. My mom's a special ed high school teacher. My dad worked at a kitchen and cabinet company then lost his job. He hasn't had a job for a while. I have problems with my dad. He has come to visit me twice. He got **DV** charges. He beat the shit out of me. I've been here 60 days. I'm almost halfway done. I'm here on level one in the **JIP**. It's sort of like **house arrest**... you can only be at one parent's for house arrest. My older brother is locked up for a **DUI** for two months. He's in Yuma now, but I can't write him because he's locked up. My younger brother is a straight A student. I've been getting into

trouble since day one. I was bad from day one. My brother would dare me to do things and I would do it. If I didn't **kick it** with him I wouldn't have been bad. I wish I never done that. I messed up so bad. This is my last chance. Here is my last chance. I have 19 charges on me, I'm glad I came here. My homies say this place is **whack**, but if I complete this program I can get my **felonies** dropped to **misdemeanors**. I wish I had a time machine.

- P., Age 16

SCRAP- to fight with hand-to-hand combat.

GROUP HOME- a form of out-of-home placement for kids who have been removed from their home "which provides 24-hour non-medical care and supervision to children, provides services to a specific client group and maintains a structured environment, with such services provided at least in part by staff employed by the licensee."

HOMIES- close friends who have your back and are there for you in times of need.

PUT IN WORK- to perform tasks (often illegal or dangerous) to gain respect in one's gang – for example, "marking territory, attacking members of a rival gang, participating in a drug run, etc.

TAGGING- the practice of quickly marking a signature, symbol, or sign in public spaces akin to graffiti, which can sometimes be used to mark territory.

DV- stands for domestic violence.

JIP- short for Juvenile Intensive Probation Supervision, assigned to juvenile offenders on conditional release or probation to provide structured and frequent contacts with an intensive supervision officer for youth who may otherwise be placed out of the home, as an alternative to incarceration.

HOUSE ARREST- "confinement to one's home or another specified location instead of incarceration in a jail or prison," most often enforced with an ankle monitor.

DUI- stands for Driving Under the Influence; the crime of driving while under the influence of alcohol or drugs.

KICK IT- to spend time with, to hang out.

WHACK- slang for uncool, undesirable, or unfair.

FELONY- a serious crime, characterized under federal law and many state statutes as any offense punishable by imprisonment in excess of one year.

MISDEMEANOR- "under federal law, and most state laws, any lesser offense other than a felony."

I flunked seventh grade... just moved onto ninth. I've been here one month. I was supposed to be in phase two but I'm in orientation because I got a **code of conduct**. Mom and dad are divorced. They don't talk. My mom is a housekeeper and my dad works at the car wash. He did time for **aggravated assault** and **assault with a deadly weapon**. My mom has a boyfriend and my dad has a girlfriend. I sleep on the couch. I've been in detention eight out of nine times. The longest was one year. Took the case to trial and lost. It was **drug possession**. I had a whole backpack full. This happened in 2007 after I was **on the run** for almost a year—I got caught for **burglary**. I pled intent to burglarize. Here's my last chance. I'm doing well here but there are some little bumps. There's a lot of people in here I know from **the outs**. Gang habits get in the way I **represent, throw up the hood, tag** on my schoolwork. No gang stuff is tolerated here. I have three older brothers—two in gangs and one in school—and an older sister. Older brothers have done juvie and jail time. One of them **dropped his flag** a long time ago... He has two kids and a wife now. Dad was from a hood where everyone was the same race. Everyone in my hood's a different race—but mostly Black. You get **jumped in** in the gang. I was 14, it was for three minutes and 11 seconds. You can put down your flag for a little bit but you are in for life.

-K.N., Age 16

CODE OF CONDUCT- a set of behavioral expectations for youth held in a facility, which varies by institution and jurisdiction; here K.N. refers to the infraction he got for the violating of rules.

AGGRAVATED ASSAULT- "when a defendant intends to do more than merely frighten the victim" by "threat of bodily harm coupled with an apparent, present ability to cause harm," including "intent to kill, rob, or rape."

ASSAULT WITH A DEADLY WEAPON- the charge of assault aggravated by the use of a deadly weapon, such as a knife or gun, to commit the crime.

DRUG POSSESSION- the carrying of illicit drugs on your person and/or property.

ON THE RUN- avoiding contact with authorities; a term generally used for fugitives, synonymous with "on the lam".

BURGLARY- "the criminal offense of breaking and entering a building illegally for the purpose of committing a crime".

THE OUTS- short for "the outside," often used by people in locked institutions when referring to life outside of institutional settings.

REPRESENT- to express loyalty to a place or group.

THROW UP THE HOOD- to show your gang sign, which is generally associated with a particular neighborhood or "hood".

TAG- to quickly mark a signature, symbol, or sign in public spaces akin to graffiti, which can sometimes be used to mark territory.

DROP ONE'S FLAG- to stop representing and participating in the activities of a specific gang.

JUMP IN- an initiation ritual for membership to a gang, which typically entails the inductee receiving a beating for a predetermined amount of time while remaining defenseless.

I'm 16 years old. I committed a **capital offense**. My goal is to join the military, but my **felony** might get in the way. But one of the **CO**'s told me the military is making a lot of exceptions for enlistment. My brother and cousin are here too. I get a lot of personal hygiene items as I am interested in my personal appearance. Also when we get a new inmate who is part of my community, we put together a package for him, so he feels welcome. I am allowed a portion of my money on these items at **canteen**. No, this is not excessive.

-F., Age 16

CAPITAL OFFENSE- a criminal charge that is punishable by the death penalty. Crimes punishable by death vary from state to state. These offenses may include first degree murder, murder with special circumstances, rape with additional bodily harm, and the federal crime of treason.

FELONY- a serious crime, characterized under federal law and many state statutes as any offense punishable by imprisonment in excess of one year.

CO- stands for correctional officer.

CANTEEN- a store within a confinement facility that sells hygiene items, snacks, paper, stamps, etc.; also known as a commissary.

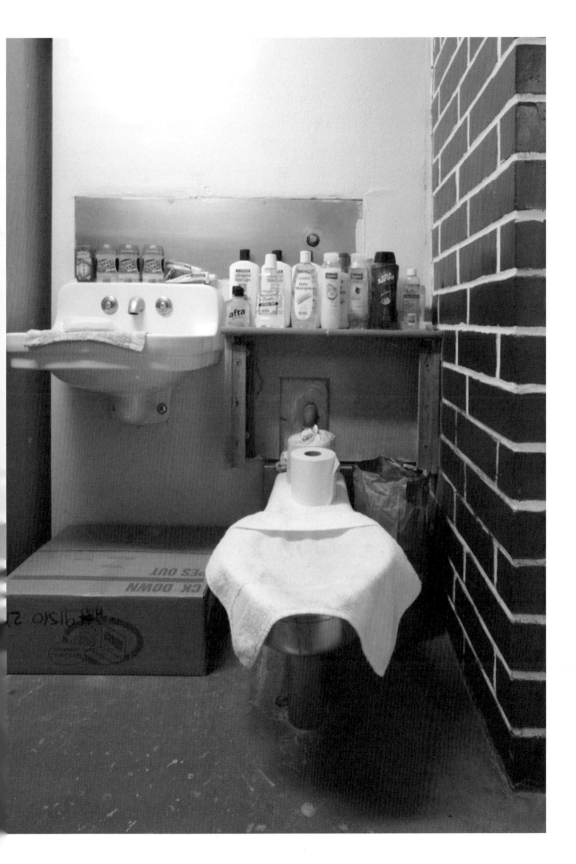

PETTY THEFT- theft of goods or money valued at less than a specific amount designated by the jurisdiction (e.g. less than $500).

FELONY VANDALISM- "the intentional and malicious destruction of or damage to the property of another," which causes significant damage of which the cost to repair is above a certain value designated by the jurisdiction (e.g. more than $1,000).

DISTURBING THE PEACE- a crime falling under the broader category of disorderly conduct, referring to conduct that compromises the safety, health, or overall peace of the public.

ASSAULT WITH A DEADLY WEAPON- the charge of assault aggravated by the use of a deadly weapon, such as a knife or gun, to commit the crime.

POSSESSION WITH INTENT TO DISTRIBUTE / SELL- the crime of not only being found in possession of a controlled substance, but intending to distribute the substance, which is determined by factors such as quantity of substance in question, presence of packaging materials, or large amounts of cash.

GANG AFFILIATED- to be part of a gang, friends or family with someone in a gang, or to act for the benefit of a gang; to be declared gang affiliated by law enforcement can result in increased supervision in the streets or gang enhancement charges added onto other criminal charges.

CAMP- a boot camp style corrections institution for boys.

EM- stands for electronic monitoring; see also "Ankle Monitor".

ASSAULT- though what exactly constitutes an assault varies by jurisdiction, it generally refers to the crime of causing another fear that "he/she is about to suffer physical harm," with the degree of the assault depending on how much harm was caused.

PEPPER SPRAY- "an aerosol spray that temporarily irritates the eyes and mucous membranes" used by law enforcement and correctional officers to incapacitate aggressive or unruly people.

ISO- short for isolation; solitary confinement.

I've been here five and a half months. This is my seventh time. First time, I was 15. I go to alternative high school. I have about 170 units. I'm about to graduate. I've been to three different high schools. I stopped going to school. I only do school work when I am here. My mother is a caregiver to an old lady. Dad is in prison on gang and drug related charges. I live at home with my grandpa, two brothers and my little sister. The first charges against me were **petty theft, felony vandalism, disturbing the peace**. Then I started getting some heavier charges like **assault with a deadly weapon, possession with intent to sell**, narcotics charges. Mostly marijuana. The police would call me **gang affiliated**. Nobody visits me here. I've been to

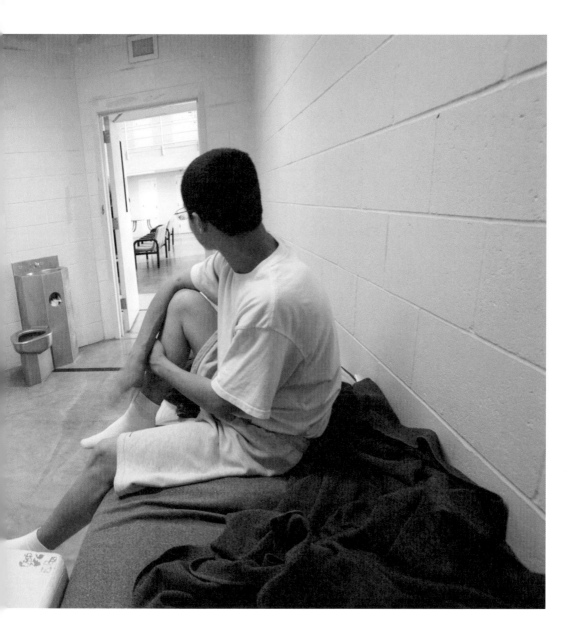

camp three times. Third time I didn't finish. I don't want to be there. I'm over it. Same shit over and over again. I'm here on new charges and I picked up two more. **EM** violation. I was with my homeboys and we fucked up this other guy's car. Also got an **assault** on a police officer here. Staff tried to put his hands on me so I hit him. I've been **pepper sprayed** here and once at camp. I'm inside the room because I am on **iso** for breaking a computer keyboard at school. I been here two weeks straight. I never really cared about my life. Then I got a girlfriend and I cared about her. She hasn't called or written since I've been here. She left me hanging. She was special; all the other bitches are just whores. They just be bitches man. I don't know how old my mom is. I think she may be in her 30's... maybe 37. I'm here. It sucks but I can't do shit about it. I just have to deal with it. Who am I? Not really anything beyond the gang, just my legal name.

-K.N., Age 17

WARRANT- "a written order issued by a judicial officer or other authorized person commanding a law enforcement officer to perform some act incident to the administration of justice... most commonly, police use warrants as the basis to arrest a suspect and to conduct a search of property for evidence of a crime."

PROP 21- a California measure passed in 2001 that among other things, makes youth 14 years or older charged with certain felonies ineligible for juvenile court, automatically transferring them to adult criminal court; makes detention mandatory for 30 specific serious crimes; and increases sentences for gang-related crimes up to 10 years.

FIRST DEGREE MURDER- "a premeditated, intentional killing, or results from a vicious crime such as arson, rape, or armed robbery," though exact definitions vary from state to state.

GANG ENHANCEMENT- refers to a set of laws allowing courts to increase the severity of a sentence due to a crime's perceived commission for the benefit of a gang. Gang enhancement charges can result in a youth's case being transferred to adult criminal court or time added to one's sentence.

GANG UNIT- a specialized unit with a group of officers assigned to deal chiefly with gang-related issues, with the goal of reducing gang activity in the community.

GBI- stands for great bodily injury, a charge of causing significant physical injury or injury that causes permanent damage, usually accompanied with another more general charge (i.e. assault with great bodily injury), and significantly increases the length of the sentence if convicted.

DJJ- stands for Department/Division of Juvenile Justice, can be used to refer to the juvenile justice system in general or more specifically the juvenile corrections facility of a given jurisdiction.

YOUTH AUTHORITY- refers for California Youth Authority, the former name of the California's Division of Juvenile Justice (DJJ).

PAROLE- though youth may use the terms "parole" and "probation" interchangeably, parole refers to the court-ordered community supervision of individuals who have been released from confinement prior to the end of their original sentence.

CODEFENDANT- "one of multiple defendants sued in the same civil action or formally accused of committing together the same crime."

COUNTY- short for county jail, adult detention facilities.

JUVENILE LIFE- short for Juvenile Life Without Parole, "A prison sentence that comprises a person's entire natural life, without possibility of release, for an offense committed before the age of 18".

SEVERANCE- the decision to try multiple defendants' cases seperately.

HOMIES- close friends who have your back and are there for you in times of need.

50-TO-LIFE- a life sentence with a chance of parole after 50 years.

JUVENILE LIFE- refers to a sentence lasting until the youth has reached the age limit for juvenile custody in a given jurisdiction (in some jurisdictions, youth can stay in a juvenile corrections facility until age 25); the maximum possible sentence in juvenile court.

My dad is on the run. There is a **warrant** out for him. He comes and visits sometimes. This place doesn't look that deep as to who you are. My mom visits all the time. She drives up. I have been here 33 months. I was 14 when I entered... charged **Prop 21**. They have me charged with **first-degree murder** with a gun and **gang enhancement**. Now I'm the longest kid here. I was here with a different case when I went to camp and the **gang unit** came up and I caught another case. Originally I was in for **GBI**. Gang enhancement adds time. I was 14 when I was **jumped in**—in junior high. That world wasn't so good for me... I got kicked out of every middle school. I was the class clown. I have three older brothers, one younger. All of them are in trouble. One in **DJJ**, one **Youth Authority**, younger one is in kids' prison... I think the other two just got out on **parole**, but I'm not sure. I am starting trial next month with **codefendants** in **county**. One is already sentenced to Youth Authority. He got **juvenile life**. He will be released when he is 23. There are five of them in County. I was the youngest. I was 14. Then there was 16, 17, 19 and some guy in his 30's—all waiting for sentence or trial. We got a **severance**. I was in the mindset I was running the show and I wanted to show my **homies** I was someone. Now I am the same guy but I have a different mindset here. I stay focused on the trial. I could be looking at **50-to-life**. I think a kid should be accountable somewhat... but not all the way. I was really young and didn't know what I was doing. It was too much for a 14 year old. It was night, we was doing all kinds of drugs. I've seen what drugs do to people. It makes them scandalous. My mom hired a private attorney. He wants to get me moved from adult to **juvenile life**. I would stay at the Youth Authority until I am 23.

-S.D., Age 17

I go to schools with the boys because I have a **non-contact** with another girl in my unit. We came in on the same charges this time so they have to keep us separate. The food sucks and we get three meals a day. I live with my mom. My parents are divorced. I don't communicate with my dad. He abused me. I have an older brother in **camp**. I was charged with **11550**. **Meth**. My mom couldn't believe it. They found a **doggie** when I was 14. Then I caught a **211—armed robbery, carjacking**... We would pretend to hitchhike and get picked up by **pisas**. Most of these guys were lonely and looking to hook up with a younger girl... "Oh do you want a ride?"... I was never armed, but I always had a knife. These guys never have papers. They asked me if I wanted a ride and then I took their money and then their car and threatened to turn them in. I was on meth. Then one of them called the cops. I have friends that hook up for drugs. A lot of girls are like that, no self-respect. They dropped a lot of charges and let me plea to the high level charge. It's a five-year charge. I've been here six months. I may end up going to a **group home** in LA or Lompoc or Ventura. They're not that fun—a bunch of drama girls. I was lucky I didn't get pro-cessed as an adult. Lots of time the guards play favorites. We get only one five-minute phone call a week. We get a three-minute shower with hand soap. No lotion. We get one hour of yard time, sometimes two.

-M.Q., Age 15

NON-CONTACT- refers to the status of two or more inmates who cannot come into contact with one another due to being co-defendants.

CAMP- a boot camp style corrections insti-tution for boys.

11550- refers to California Health and Safe-ty Code section 11550, which states that it is against the law to "use or be under the influence of any controlled substance".

METH- short for methamphetamine, also known as crystal, ice, etc.; an extremely addictive stimulant drug.

DOGGIE- a meth pipe.

211- refers to California Penal Code section 211, pertaining to the felony of robbery.

ARMED ROBBERY- the crime of theft "by force or intimidation" with a deadly weapon; depending on jurisdiction may be charged as aggravated robbery.

CARJACKING- "the criminal taking of a mo-tor vehicle from its driver by force, violence, or intimidation".

PISA- Spanish word meaning countryman, often used to refer to Mexican immigrants who make little effort to assimilate to the culture of the U.S.

The men M.Q. was robbing were not doc-umented citizens, which prevented them from contacting law enforcement to report her crimes.

M.Q. was given the option to plea guilty to the most serious charge she faced in order to get her other charges dropped.

GROUP HOME- an out-of-home placement for kids who have been removed from their homes "which provides 24-hour non-med-ical care and supervision to children, pro-vides services to a specific client group and maintains a structured environment, with such services provided at least in part by staff employed by the licensee."

Been here a year and a half. Just getting into trouble on **the outs**. I am identified as **VLP**. I am told I am gang affiliated. I am in 12th grade, a senior. I graduate in 2 weeks, but I still have the rest of my time. Three more months. I was sentenced to two years **orange** when I first came in on **Prop 21** charges. Then the charges were dropped to juvie. I can get out on probation when I am 18... but it's tough to do it right because I can get 15 years confinement if I mess up. It is hard to do it when you get out. I will live with my Mom. She is a nurse at a convalescent home. Dad is a landscaper. They are divorced. Mom visits me every Sunday. Dad will visit once in a while. My older brother is in prison for **attempted murder**. They are just doing their job by being in a gang. Court put me on a **gang injunction** when I was in sixth grade. You dress like a gang member. They look at you with a white t-shirt and you are automatically gang related because you wear cheap clothing. Group therapy is for people that are weak minded. I don't do **group**. The system doesn't care. I'm in the **MRT** program. They try to help me. I can get a job with my mother at a convalescent home. I have a certificate for culinary arts. The food here is nasty. My sister is

21 or 22. She's the good one in the family. She has a family of her own. I just want to stay out of trouble but you're never going to leave your best friends. Whatever they do you have to stay with them. Every time I am in here it is on a different charge—stuff like **gang-enhanced felonies**. I don't come in for no **baby time**. Least I've done is 60 days.

-B.N., Age 17

THE OUTS- short for "the outside," often used by people in locked institutions when referring to life outside of institutional settings.

VLP- a local gang.

Whether B.N. is actually a member of a gang or not, being labeled as "gang affiliated" or "gang associated" by law enforcement weighs heavy in the court system (e.g. gang enhancement charges). Many youths employ phrasing such as B.N.'s to refer to their status in the eyes of the court without revealing how they self-identify.

ORANGE- wearing orange, refers to the color of jumpsuit assigned to youth who have been tried in adult criminal court.

PROP 21- a California measure passed in 2001 that among other things, makes youth 14 years or older charged with certain felonies ineligible for juvenile court, automatically transferring them to adult criminal court; makes detention mandatory for 30 specific serious crimes; and increases sentences for gang-related crimes up to 10 years.

ATTEMPTED MURDER- the crime of attempting to kill another person without cause or justification, proven by substantial steps being taken towards committing the crime.

GANG INJUNCTION- "civil court orders that attempt to address organized crime... resulting in serious civil liberties violations. Law enforcement use them as a tool to label people gang members and restrict their activities in a defined area. Gang injunctions make otherwise legal, everyday activities—such as riding the bus with a friend or picking a spouse up from work late at night—illegal for the people they target."

GROUP- short for group therapy, "a form of psychosocial treatment where small groups of people meet regularly to talk, interact, and discuss problems with each other and the group leader".

MRT- Moral Reconation Therapy™, "a cognitive-behavioral counseling program that combines education, group and individual counseling, and structured exercises designed to foster moral development in treatment-resistant clients".

GANG-ENHANCED FELONIES- serious crimes for which the severity of punishment has been increased due to the defendant's alleged commission of the crime in relation to a gang.

BABY TIME- a short sentence.

COUNTY- short for county jail; adult detention facilities.

GTA- stands for grand theft auto; the crime of theft of an automobile, which is a felony in most states regardless of the car's value

PROBATION VIOLATION- failure to obey the conditions of one's probation as set forth by the court, which may result in new charges and/or detention.

PLACEMENT- court ordered residential assignments in both the delinquency and dependency systems, which may "be secure and prison-like or have a more open setting, like group homes or foster care".

GROUP HOME- an out-of-home placement for kids who have been removed from their home "which provides 24-hour non-medical care and supervision to children, provides services to a specific client group and maintains a structured environment, with such services provided at least in part by staff employed by the licensee." Some group homes have over 100 beds.

ISO- short for isolation; solitary confinement. In J.R.'s cell there is a black line painted about four feet from the door, which he must stay behind at all times.

THE YARD- the exercise area of a facility, generally outdoors.

TRUANCY- the status offense of repeated absence from school, which breaks compulsory education laws in the U.S.

PROBATION OFFICER- the public official supervising youth on probation, with whom youth have regular meetings.

ASSOCIATED- refers to gang affiliation.

GUARDIANSHIP- authority and responsibility held by a person who is legally appointed as the guardian of a minor, which grants the right to make decisions on the child's behalf including but not limited to residence, education, parental visitation, and medical treatment.

J.R. is not allowed to have schoolwork in his cell because he is in solitary confinement. This is a fairly typical practice and some facilities even prohibit youth from having books in isolation.

By "probation school," J.R. refers to alternative education high school, also known as continuation school: the learning institution many youth with behavioral challenges and histories of delinquent behavior attend in order to catch up on missed credits and receive a diploma.

CPS- Child Protective Services, the agency that in many states provides services in cases of child abuse or neglect.

PETTY THEFT- theft of goods or money valued at less than a specific amount designated by the jurisdiction (e.g. less than $500).

They move me to **county** next month at 18. I was 12 or 13 when I first came here. **GTA**. I was with a friend and we just wanted to drive his aunt's car around. I was in eighth grade. I saw the car with the keys in it. We put it in reverse and I wrecked it. It was in the parking lot. The farthest I've ever been from home is Six Flags (about 150 miles South). I have been on **probation violations** and in trouble in here ever since. Most are probation violations. I got into a fight here and I am looking at eight years in adult prison. I went to **placement**—a **group home**. There was a group of homes; each had about 10 to 12 kids in them. My behavior was not following their directions so they sent me back. I want respect. I don't usually get that here. I've been in iso for about seven going on eight weeks. I read anything, everything. Books about murders and mysteries. I have to remain behind the black line. Sometime I just scream... they don't like that behavior. When I have nothing to do I sometimes sing. I sing as loud as I want and I sing the same song over and over again. I can sing a song 10 times. No matter. I'm not allowed out. But I get out once a day to shower and then go to **the yard** for large muscle movement for one hour. When you are in iso you do a lot of exercise. You work out, sing, read. They bring my meals to my room. I've pretty much been here from when I was 12. Once I spent nine months out with my family. I got violated again so I got sent inside. I picked up a lot of charges inside juvie. Violations? Like once I was **truant**. I forgot to call my **probation officer** and she arrested me. They would say I am **associated** because of my tats, but I'm not. I even tried to get them removed. A group home is like probation but they don't have uniforms. It's four hours from here so my mom didn't visit much. Usually my mom visits every week. My grandparents have **guardianship**. My mom didn't have the stability to take care of me and my sister. She had a drug problem. Now she has a new baby. I don't know where my dad is. I have a year left of high school, but I won't be able to finish it. I have 163 units. I need 200 to graduate. I only get to do school work in the classroom. Maybe I can get a GED. I went to the probation school. I didn't really have a home. I was sleeping on park benches or with friends since I was eight. I didn't have no food to eat. My sister was at my grandparents. We were building a relationship with my grandparents. **CPS** never really knew who I was. I was out on the street and when they came to my house my mother didn't say anything about me. Mom was in custody I think for **petty theft**.

-J.R., Age 17

WEED- marijuana.

COKE- slang for cocaine, a highly addictive stimulant drug.

METH- short for methamphetamine, also known as crystal, ice, etc.; an extremely addictive stimulant drug.

SB 163- refers to California Senate Bill 163, which allows for youth who would otherwise be placed in a group home to remain in the family home with expanded family-based services that work with families to address issues.

WARRANT- "a written order issued by a judicial officer or other authorized person commanding a law enforcement officer to perform some act incident to the administration of justice... most commonly, police use warrants as the basis to arrest a suspect and to conduct a search of property for evidence of a crime."

BENCH WARRANT- a warrant issued by a judge when an individual fails to adhere to the rules of the court, e.g. not appearing to a court date or probation meeting, which enables an officer to immediately arrest an individual during a stop.

GPS- refers to electronic monitoring devices which must be worn by some probationers and parolees to monitor their whereabouts; see also Ankle Monitor.

Many states have laws prohibiting the congregation of individuals on probation, especially in relation to gangs. When applied to youth, this means that youth can be charged with violation of probation for simply being in the same room as another youth offender or a youth who has been labeled gang affiliated.

BRACELET- refers to the electric monitoring device worn around the ankle, which is used to track the movement of individuals on house arrest, probation, or parole.

I've been here a month and I have a month to go. This is my fifth time here. I'm in eighth grade, but I haven't been to school since I was in sixth grade. Yeah, drugs have been involved... I've been to rehab a couple times. We do mostly **weed, coke, meth** and alcohol. All my friends have guns. All the boys. The girls carry knives. Yeah they are gang affiliated. I was 13 the first time I came in here. This is my fifth time. I've been on **SB 163**, the program just before placement. I had to have sessions with

my parent. Me and my dad would meet someone twice a week. I was picked up on **warrants**. That means a **bench warrant** was issued because I cut my **GPS**. We can't go past a certain point but when I am with my friends like five out of six of us are wearing GPS so we are not allowed to congregate. So I cut my **bracelet** off. I live with my dad's second family—my dad's parents and brothers, their girlfriends and my cousins. The house is not that big. I sleep in the living room with my 19-year-old cousin, my 12-year-old cousin and my six-year-old cousin.

-N.R., Age 14

I have five years in **YOS** with 15 **adult hanging**. Before this I was in the detention center for 11 months... those count towards my five years. I was going to school there. There's no school in **OTP**. And the food was better over there. Today was **zero day**—hardest day I've ever had to do. I felt beat up at the end of the day. It took mental as well as physical perseverance.

-D., Age 16

YOS- stands for Youthful Offender System, the branch of the Colorado juvenile justice system that acts as a middle tier between youth corrections and adult criminal corrections.

ADULT HANGING- when a youth's sentence involves time in an adult facility that may or may not need to be served depending on behavior during juvenile sentence, as in adult time hanging over one's head. See also Blended Sentence.

OTP- stands for Orientation Training Phase in Colorado's Youthful Offender System; the first phase in YOS, which utilizes a militaristic, boot camp style approach to treatment.

ZERO DAY- a military-originating term for the first day of one's training, in which one must complete a series of tasks intended to physically and mentally challenge the person, usually with the aim of "breaking" them.

I have four years with 12 **hanging**. 10 months to go here, then the last year at phase three. I'm in for **vehicular homicide** and **vehicular assault**. I had gotten my license a month before. The accident happened at 8:30 PM. The only thing that happened before that was a **curfew ticket**. My mom lives in New Mexico... but I can't be paroled to there 'cause there's no **reciprocity** with Colorado. My mom visits once a month. Dad lives in Minnesota... he comes every five or six months. I wasn't a very good student. I would be **truant** and skip a lot. School wasn't my place to be, y'know? I switched places with a passenger after the accident, but confessed after about three days. I was **out on bond** for a year and went to an alternative school and was more successful there. Here I do well in school. I get A's and B's. I have to pay $17,000 in **restitution**. I get six dollars a month for going to school. My family sends me money. Some goes to restitution as well. I can't approach the family that I wronged to apologize. There is a **restraining order**. I will live in Denver with my mom and her boyfriend.

-O., Age 20

TIME HANGING- when a youth's sentence involves time in an adult facility that may or may not need to be served depending on behavior during juvenile sentence, as in time hanging over one's head. See also Blended Sentence.

VEHICULAR HOMICIDE- the killing of a person with a vehicle, whether inside or outside the vehicle, intentionally or unintentionally.

VEHICULAR ASSAULT- the causing of significant bodily harm to another because one is driving recklessly.

CURFEW TICKET- the summons given to minors found in public without a guardian after a certain time of night which varies by jurisdiction; see also Status Offense.

RECIPROCITY- in this use refers to states acknowledging a person's status in the justice system across state borders, such as acknowledging the terms of one's parole in a state other than the state in which they were convicted and allowing them to complete parole in that state.

TRUANCY- the status offense of repeated absence from school, which breaks compulsory education laws in the U.S.

OUT ON BOND- to be out of confinement due to one's bail being posted in the form of a bond, a guaranteed payment of bail that must be paid if the defendant fails to return to court for trial.

RESTITUTION- the payment of money and/or donation of services to the victims of a crime or society, with the intent of the restitution being to compensate damages caused by the crime.

RESTRAINING ORDER- "a command of the court issued upon the filing of an application for an injunction," which prohibits individuals from performing certain acts, such as carrying out threats or coming within a specific distance of an individual who feels threatened.

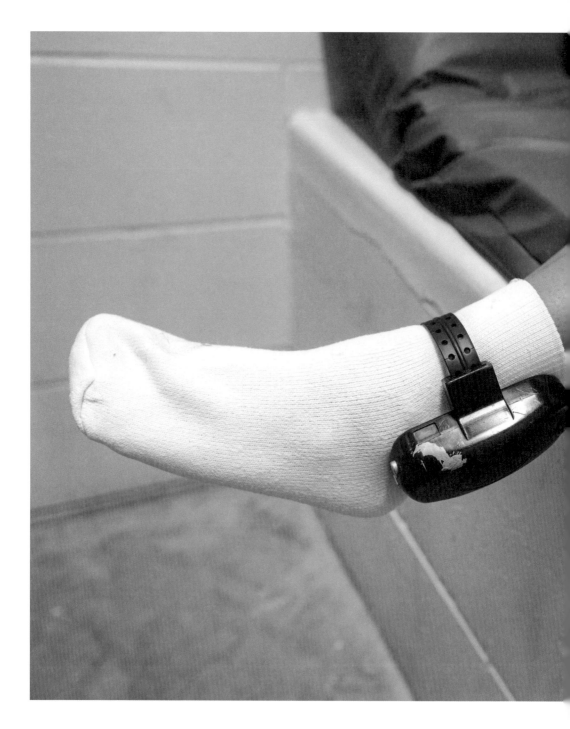

I've been here 15 or 16 times. Right now I'm here for **probation violation—possession of a firearm**. I have four brothers. All in different gangs. Only one of my brothers has the same mom. And I have a sister. She's not in a gang. I'm with the **Sureños**. My dad's in a gang also. A prison gang. I don't ask him what he is in for. I don't live with him. He has **warrants** so he can't visit. Food here is the bomb. There are a lot of gang members here... but you don't get in trouble as long as you don't **represent** or **throw up your hood** to your rivals. I was on **ISP**. Wore an **ankle bracelet** for two weeks, but then I cut it off. I won't be back because in

all my visits they never threatened me to be **committed**, but now they have brought that one up... and I don't want it. I get out Sunday and will be on ankle bracelet. I'll keep it on this time.

-J., Age 14

PROBATION VIOLATION- failure to obey the conditions of one's probation as set forth by the court, which may result in new charges and/or detention.

POSSESSION OF A FIREARM- refers to the crime of carrying a gun, either because the defendant is a minor, on probation, or fails to follow a state's laws regarding legal gun possession (e.g. obtaining permits).

SUREÑO- a Latino-American gang with origins in Southern California.

WARRANT- "a written order issued by a judicial officer or other authorized person commanding a law enforcement officer to perform some act incident to the administration of justice... most commonly, police use warrants as the basis to arrest a suspect and to conduct a search of property for evidence of a crime."

REPRESENT- to express loyalty to a place or group.

THROW UP THE HOOD- to show your gang sign, which is generally associated with a particular neighborhood or "hood".

ISP- short for Juvenile Intensive Supervision Program, assigned to juvenile offenders on conditional release or probation to provide structured and frequent contacts with an intensive supervision officer for youth who may otherwise be placed out of the home, as an alternative to incarceration.

BRACELET- refers to the electric monitoring device worn around the ankle, which is used to track the movement of individuals on house arrest, probation, or parole; see also Ankle Monitor.

COMMITTED- sentenced to time in a correctional facility, as opposed to detained, which is one's status prior to disposition or trial.

I was in **TGK** for a year and 10 days. Now here for nine days. **Home invasion**, **kidnapping**, **armed carjacking**, **aggravated assault**, **armed battery**. These were dropped to **juvenile charges**—if they were filed as an adult it could've been 10 years. I will probably get a level 10 program—juvenile prison. I will serve three years if I behave… it can be dropped to one-and-a-half years. Mom lost her job two years ago. She lives with my step dad, who is a factory worker. For a year in TGK I was never able to touch my mom. She hugged me for the first time in over a year and we both cried and cried. There is no **secure communication** here. All visitation is in the gym. It's set up for a hug with a parent for a greeting and then holding hands. After the hug a youth's hands has to be above the tables at all times. I am here for writing "Fuck Folk" on a notebook. Been here for 48 hours. Food in here is not bad. It is terrible at TGK.

-T.N., Age 15

TGK- stands for Turner Guilford Knight Correctional Center in Miami-Dade County, Florida. It is a correctional center that holds inmates in both detention and corrections.

HOME INVASION- the illegal, and often forceful, entry into a dwelling without the owner's permission; often charged as burglary.

KIDNAPPING- "the crime of unlawfully seizing and carrying away a person by force or fraud".

ARMED CARJACKING- "the criminal taking of a motor vehicle from its driver by force, violence, or intimidation" while possessing a firearm.

AGGRAVATED ASSAULT- "when a defendant intends to do more than merely frighten the victim" by "threat of bodily harm coupled with an apparent, present ability to cause harm," including "intent to kill, rob, or rape".

ARMED BATTERY- an intentional act causing harmful, offensive or sexual contact with the body of another person while possessing or intimidating with a firearm.

JUVENILE CHARGES- charges that are litigated in juvenile court as opposed to adult criminal court.
Had T.N. gone to trial in adult criminal court, he could have faced 10 years in correctional facilities for a crime committed at 14.

SECURE COMMUNICATION- communication, via face-to-face visits or letters, that has not been interfered with or detected by the staff of a facility.

At the time of T.N.'s interview with Ross, he had been in solitary confinement for two days for writing gang-related slurs on a notebook.

I'm here for **armed robbery**. Well, something like that kind of. Other guys influenced me a lot. There was a football game and I owed some money and I found a gun by a tree two weeks before. My mom and sister visit. This is my first **charge**. I have been here two months. I went to **JAC**. Was charged with **trespassing**, but that was dropped. I ended up in juvie for a month, then they **direct filed** me and I have been here for two months. I couldn't **put up bond** so I have to stay here. I went to court in November. That was six weeks ago. I was in **lockdown** for fighting. But I was hit. Everyone that was hit rather than the kids fighting got put in lockdown.

I have been in lockdown 18 days. You can sleep all day. No school but you can do work in the cell. You can shower everyday, but I don't.

-A.S., Age 15

ROBBERY- a crime of theft "by force or intimidation" with possession of a firearm.

CHARGE- to formally accuse/a formal accusation within the legal system; does not necessarily indicate guilt.

JAC- Juvenile Assessment Center, where youth in A.S.'s jurisdiction go when they are first processed and assessed after being taken in for an alleged crime.

TRESPASSING- "the intentional and wrongful invasion of another's property," regardless of whether harm was caused during the invasion.

DIRECT FILE- "A prosecutor's discretion to bring charges against youth directly in adult criminal court instead of in juvenile court, without a prior certification hearing. States that permit this practice vary in what circumstances warrant it."

PUT UP BOND- to guarantee, in the form of a bond (typically 10% of bail), that the full bail amount will be paid if the defendant in question fails to attend scheduled court appearances, which allows a detained person to stay outside of confinement until trial or disposition.

LOCKDOWN- the confining of prisoners to their cells after a disturbance such as a riot or escape; can refer to solitary confinement when used by an individual.

I can stay here until I'm 21. I'm 19 now. I came here when I was 17... well, I was in **county** for a while before that. 14 and a half months. They had to keep me on my own. I was **charged as an adult** with **aggravated battery** and **unlawful use of a weapon**. I got a five year **fixed sentence**. My mom comes to visit every week. My brother and sister can visit because I am on level reintegration. I can wear my own clothes and shoes, but it is just as easy for me to wear this stuff. I finished all my credits for high school in here, but I still go to school here and read or do math. They let me stay in class. It's so boring doing nothing.

-U., Age 19

COUNTY- short for county jail, adult detention facilities.

Because U. was a juvenile in an adult detention facility, he had to be kept separate from the adult population, essentially in isolation.

CHARGE AS AN ADULT- to charge a child as a criminal in adult court as opposed to a delinquent in juvenile court, typically justified by seriousness/circumstances of the offense and age at the time of the crime, which removes youth from the rehabilitation-focused juvenile system and places them in the punishment-focused adult system.

AGGRAVATED BATTERY- an intentional act causing harmful, offensive, or sexual contact with the body of another person, specifically with the intent to murder or cause serious harm.

UNLAWFUL USE OF A WEAPON- refers to any number of crimes involving the possession of a lethal weapon with intent to use it unlawfully or the discharging of a lethal weapon in public spaces.

FIXED SENTENCE- also known as a determinate sentence; a sentence of a specific length of time that is not subject to review, although it can be lengthened.

U. is allowed to wear his own clothes and have visits with his siblings because has reached a level of privilege in the facility that is focused on reintegrating youth back into society.

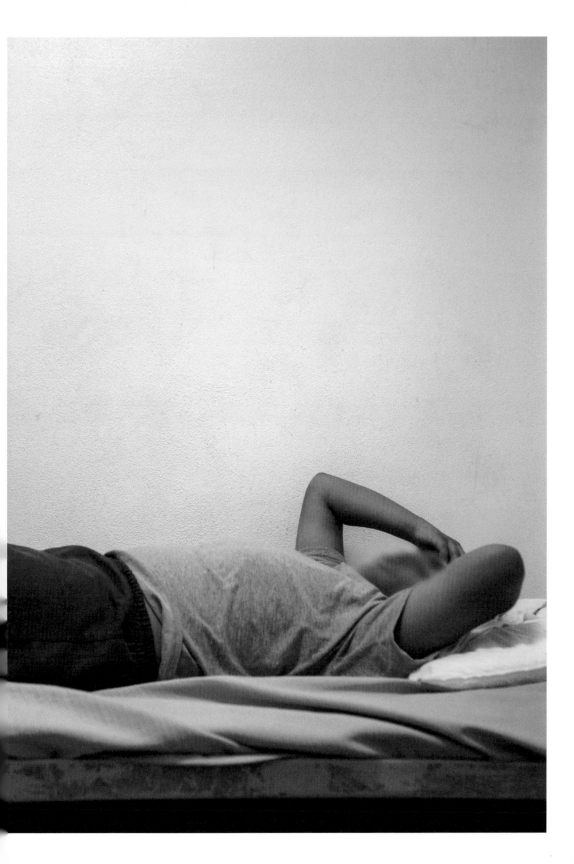

I shot my father. He abused me sexually and physically. He said he was going to do the same to my little brother and sister. When my dad said he was going to hurt the kids... I couldn't let that happen. He was asleep and I took his gun and shot him. I was in **detention** for over a year. The judge wanted to know everything. It took a long time. I pled guilty and took a **manslaughter plea**. I'm a sophomore. I do well in math; I'm in pre-calc right now. My brother and sister can't visit and I miss them a lot. I will be here at least a year with a **blended sentence**. My case is pretty **high profile**. The judge may not be able to release me early 'cause there's an election. I'd just turned 14 when this happened. **DJC** can say when I am ready to be released. Or if I screw up in here, I go to the adult prison. I am Christian and go to church every Saturday. No one ever knew about the sexual abuse; he told me I had to keep it secret. People on **the outs** don't really understand what it is to be in here. I don't like showing my emotions. I would rather keep things neutral. If I let my emotions get into it... control can all fall away. Being able to control them is my real strength.

-A., Age 16

DETENTION- "Usually refers to the placement of a youth in a secure facility under court authority at some point between the time of referral to court intake and case disposition." Post-dispositional detention is at times necessary for reasons including "awaiting placement, short-term sentencing to detention, or being a danger to self or others."

MANSLAUGHTER- "the unjustifiable, inexcusable, and intentional killing of a human being without deliberation, premeditation, and malice," distinct from murder in that the act must not have been premeditated.

PLEA- short for plea deal; "a plea agreement between prosecutor and defendant... the defendant agrees to plead guilty without a trial, and, in return, the prosecutor agrees to dismiss certain charges or make favorable sentence recommendations."

BLENDED SENTENCE- a sentence that is outside of the court's "normal realm of consideration," whether juvenile or criminal. "For example, in some states a criminal court may impose a juvenile disposition for certain youth tried as adults... or a combined juvenile-and-adult sentence against an offender. While a court will impose an age-appropriate placement followed by a term in adult prison, the adult sentence is on hold pending a review of the youth's progress in the juvenile system."

HIGH PROFILE CASE- a case that is well-known to the general public and/or has had a lot of media coverage. Because the judge wants to maintain a positive public image with the community, he may not release A. for fear of the negative repercussions in the next election. In some areas judges are appointed rather than elected, insulating them from the political repercussions of leniency.

DJC- stands for Department of Juvenile Corrections.

THE OUTS- short for "the outside," often used by people in locked institutions when referring to life outside of institutional settings.

AUTO BURGLARY- "the criminal offense of breaking and entering a [vehicle] illegally for the purpose of committing a crime."

HOUSE ARREST- "confinement to one's home or another specified location instead of incarceration in a jail or prison," most often enforced with an ankle monitor.

CAR HOP- to walk through an area of parked cars while checking if their doors are unlocked, and looting the car for valuables when unlocked cars are found.

TAKE THE RAP- to take the blame.

YCAT- a juvenile correctional facility.

COMMITMENT- "A court order giving guardianship of a juvenile to the state department of juvenile justice or corrections. The facility in which a juvenile may be placed... may range from a secure correctional placement to a nonsecure or staff-secure facility, group home, foster care, or day treatment setting."

UPPER- a drug that acts as a stimulant.

DOWNER- any of a number of drugs that act as depressants.

CORICIDIN- an over the counter cough/cold medication, sometimes referred to as "Triple C's," that is abused recreationally by ingesting quantities far above the directed dose.

PROBATION- the status of a delinquent youth under court ordered supervision within the community, with specific conditions such as school attendance, the wearing of an electronic ankle monitor, refraining from interaction with other youth on probation, drug testing, etc. Failure to obey the conditions of probation may result in new charges and/or detention.

I got charged with an **auto burglary**. I was already on **house arrest** for **car hopping**. I was brought in with two other kids, but I **took the rap**... let them skate. I think I am going to the **YCAT**. It's **commitment**. I get sentenced in about 10 days. I will probably be there for about three months. Mom is unemployed. Dad is a welder. Family is Mexican. Both are citizens. I have an older brother. He doesn't have any charges. I should be in 10th grade but I am actually in ninth. I think my score level is sixth grade. I went to a boys' home for nine months for drug and alcohol therapy... and then I caught these car hopping charges. Doing pills is my thing. **Uppers** or **downers**... **Coricidin**—if you drink a few bottles you get pretty high. I have been in the system or on **probation** since I was 12.

-D., Age 15

AID AND ABET- a crime of assistance in committing a crime or helping a guilty party avoid law enforcement.

BATTERY- an intentional act causing harmful, offensive or sexual contact with the body of another person.

GRAND THEFT AUTO- the crime of theft of an automobile, which is a felony in most states regardless of the car's value.

ISP- short for Juvenile Intensive Supervision Program; assigned to juvenile offenders on conditional release or probation to provide structured and frequent contacts with an intensive supervision officer for youth who may otherwise be placed out of the home, as an alternative to incarceration.

SHOPLIFTING- "theft of merchandise from a store or business establishment."

CRACK- "a form of cocaine that has been processed to make a rock crystal (also called 'freebase cocaine') that can be smoked."

FEDERAL- short for federal prison; federal prisons are run by the Federal Bureau of Prisons (BOP) as opposed to state courts.

OUTPATIENT- medical or rehabilitative treatment that does not require the patient to live on the premises of the care facility.

PROBATION- the status of a delinquent youth under court ordered supervision within the community, with specific conditions such as school attendance, the wearing of an electronic ankle monitor, refraining from interaction with other youth on probation, drug testing, etc. Failure to obey the conditions of probation may result in new charges and/or detention.

BATTERY- an intentional act causing harmful, offensive or sexual contact with the body of another person.

POSSESSION WITH INTENT TO DIS-TRIBUTE/SELL- the crime of not only being found in possession of a controlled substance, but intending to distribute the substance, which is determined by factors such as quantity of substance in question, presence of packaging materials, or large amounts of cash.

AGGRAVATED ROBBERY- a crime of theft "by force or intimidation," with the use of a deadly weapon, infliction of serious bodily injury, or the presence of accomplices.

.22- a term that technically refers to the width of ammunition required by certain guns, but is more often used to refer to the gun itself.

CLIP- a device that holds multiple rounds of ammunition in one unit for facilitated insertion into a magazine or firearm.

PLEA- short for plea deal; "a plea agreement between prosecutor and defendant... the defendant agrees to plead guilty without a trial, and, in return, the prosecutor agrees to dismiss certain charges or make favorable sentence recommendations". D.F. tries to convey himself as a threatening and dangerous individual, as made evident by his self-designation as a "level-one class offender"—a label that does not exist in his jurisdiction.

BOYS IN BLACK- correctional officers; a variation from the phrase "boys in blue," meaning law enforcement.

I've been here four months. I've been in seven times. First charge was **aiding and abeting** when I was 12 years old. My mom is unemployed. My dad works at a warehouse. I have two brothers. One is 15—in jail for **battery** and **grand theft auto**. The 13-year-old is on **ISP**. I have a 19-year-old sister who is finished with her term for **shoplifting**...and a 10-year-old sister. No trouble. My whole family is drug abusers and criminals. My mom is four years recovered—clean from **crack** and alcohol. My aunt did a year in **federal** in Texas...for driving with a child in a car while intoxicated. This is my first long stay. I was in **outpatient** rehab when I was 13. I was on **probation** for **battery**. I was in junior high and living with my dad because my mom was in rehab. Then I moved in with my mom. I went to another middle school, but got kicked out for **possession of narcotics with intent to distribute**... I was 14. I caught a new charge of **aggravated robbery**. I harmed them while doing a crime. Me and my friend decided to rob this kid of some headphones. We robbed him with a gun. How did I get a gun? You can get a gun, a **.22**, for $50 with a **clip**. I got it from a friend. It's a criminal world and I am a danger to society. They expect me to change over night but they don't realize progress takes time. I've changed in the last four months here by trying to control my anger, my mouth, my disrespect... they say I have grown a bit. My **plea** is two years. Society says I am a level one class offender—the most dangerous people walking around. That's my brother (points across room). Me and him strike fear in the hearts of the **boys in black**. We have been locked up so many times together. I am sort of a senior in high school and will get my diploma by the end of the year. I want to take some college classes and maybe get a trade... maybe work and get some money so I have some cash to spend when I get out.

-D.F., Age 17

Yea, D.F. right there's my brother. No, not from the same parents. We both been here for a while. We are probably going to the same place. We both going to **YCAT** for a couple of years. This is the 10th time I'm here. I started coming in when I was 11. First time? I don't really remember... I think it was a fight at school. A couple of times for fighting—aggression stuff. I have been in some **foster homes**. Had trouble at school. One time at school I almost fought a security guard. The state took me away from my mom when I was ten. She was smoking heavily. I was smoking with my mom when I was five. It was the first time she let me hit it. She was into a lot of stuff. She has done **PCP** and **heroin**. When she had me she was 15—my age probably. She was 14 when she got pregnant with me. They put me in a foster home with my two sisters. Then they put me in an adoptive home. They were a good family but I probably messed that up. My mom probably knew I was doing stuff. I took a switchblade to middle school to protect myself from other kids. I've been to Marillac, Crittenton, then TLC long term for four months. It was a residential care facility for behavior stuff. I caught a **felony** on a **JCO** Christmas 2012. I said I was going to fight some kid. Said I was going to kill myself. A JCO opened the door and tried to restrain me. I kicked him in the chest... intentionally. He tried to say that I broke some chick's wrist... but I didn't. I'm a sophomore. I like school. I get good grades when I'm paying attention. I didn't pay attention 'cause it's kind of boring. Police would describe me as "gang member." I'm back in foster care now. I've been in **placement** all around. I'll probably be at a foster home 'cause I got no place to go. My adopted mom and dad moved to Virginia. My adopted aunts and uncles and grandparents visit me. I got a visit today from my aunt and grandpa. I'm not destined for institutional life. If I was to get out of here, I have to think about what I think is right and what they thinks is right... If I am going to react to what I think is right I would probably be right back in here. Like if I'm on the outs and someone is talking trash or shit to me, I'll fight them. I don't think being in here is that bad... It's sort of like daycare. I don't have anywhere to go to call home... so no big deal. During the evening shift me and D.F. manipulate the JCOs. We decide what we are going to do if we get mad. We strike fear into the hearts of the **boys in blue—actually black**. I'm going to do 36 months at YCAT.

-N.C., Age 15

YCAT- a juvenile correctional facility.

FOSTER HOME- a single-family home placement in the child welfare system "in which a child is raised by someone other than their natural or adoptive parent" and lives with the caretaker's family.

PCP- Phencyclidine, also known as "angel dust;" a schedule II controlled substance that acts as a dissociative anesthetic and is known to cause many adverse psychological effects.

HEROIN- an extremely addictive opioid drug. Placements dealing specifically with mental health and behavioral issues.

FELONY- a serious crime, characterized under federal law and many state statutes as any offense punishable by imprisonment in excess of one year.

JCO- Juvenile Correctional Officer. Whether N.C. is actually a member of a gang, being labeled as a gang member or "gang affiliated" weighs heavy in the court system. Many youths employ phrasing such as N.C.'s to refer to their status in the eyes of the court due to the extreme consequences of gang affiliation in court proceedings (i.e. gang enhancement charges).

PLACEMENT- court ordered residential assignments in both the delinquency and dependency systems, which may "be secure and prison-like or have a more open setting, like group homes or foster care."

BOYS IN BLACK- correctional officers; a variation from the phrase "boys in blue," meaning law enforcement.

This is my first time here. I'm a straight A student. I am a senior and plan on going to college...once I get out of this mess. This is a bump in the road. A speed bump. I was in the **JDC** twice. I had trouble and was accused of a sexual crime. Later I was found to be not guilty. She was nine or 10—I was 11 or 12. 18 months ago this week I was convicted of **indecent liberties with a minor**. She was 15—I was 16. This time I broke **probation** and was fired from my job for **sexual harassment**. I asked the girl I work with on a date outside of work and I was caught looking at porn. Not sure how long I'm in here for now. They haven't given me a date. On the 12th I am either sentenced to **YCAT** or a **foster home**. I had counseling. I successfully finished my sexual counseling... but not quite. I had two more sessions but I blew it. The laws here say you can't have any relations if you are 16 and your girlfriend is 15—**"Romeo and Juliet" laws**. Her parents found out. At home I live with my dad and my step-mom and stepbrother. Dad is an ironworker. My stepmom stays home and does schoolwork for

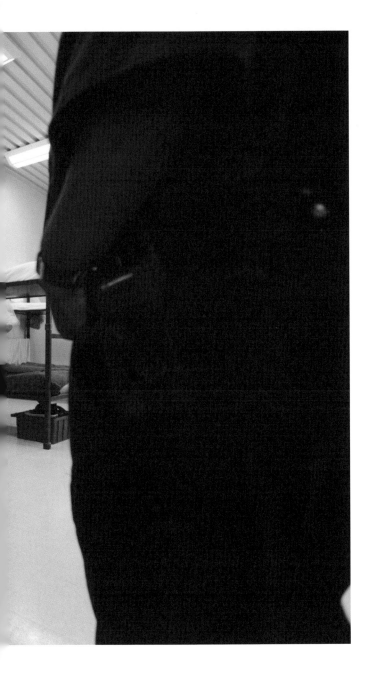

college. I hang out by myself or upstairs. My stepfather physically and sexually abused me. He started showing me porn when I was in fourth grade. My stepdad lives in Texas and was never charged. I reported it to my therapist, but my mom lied and told the therapist it never happened. There is a **court order** that I can't see her. Here I've been going to church. I read my bible daily. I'm going to lead a clean life and stop messing up.

-D.D., Age 17

POSSESSION OF MARIJUANA- the crime of carrying marijuana on one's person or property.

GANG BANGER- active gang member.

AFFILIATED- to be part of a gang, friends or family with someone in a gang, or to act for the benefit of a gang; to be declared gang affiliated by law enforcement can result in increased supervision in the streets or gang enhancement charges added onto other criminal charges.
Sureños, Folks and Crips are names of gangs active where F.I. lives.

YCAT- a juvenile correctional facility.

ISP- short for Juvenile Intensive Supervision Program, assigned to juvenile offenders on conditional release or probation to provide structured and frequent contacts with an intensive supervision officer for youth who may otherwise be placed out of the home, as an alternative to incarceration.

PV- Probation Violation.

CONDITIONAL RELEASE- when used pre-adjudication in juvenile justice, refers to release of a child to a specific place (e.g. family home or group home) until their court date; when used post-adjudication in juvenile justice, refers to re-entry and aftercare programs for youth being release from commitment to assist in a successful reintegration to society.

CHOICE POINT- a cognitive behavioral therapy program for youth in the juvenile justice system which combines 12 weeks of residential treatment with 12 weeks of aftercare.

HOUSE ARREST- "confinement to one's home or another specified location instead of incarceration in a jail or prison," most often enforced with an ankle monitor.

I have a little sister, seven, and an older sister, 28. My half brother was in juvie for running, fleeing, invading. Mom and dad are from Mexico. They are separated. I've been here two weeks. This is my sixth time. I was 13 when I first was brought in for **possession of marijuana**. Mom is a housewife and works at the mall. Mom visits every week. Law enforcement would describe me as a **gangbanger** but I'm not **affiliated**. The majority of kids are Sureños but there are also Folks, Crips, stuff like that. Dad and mom are not affiliated. I became a senior this semester. I have 17 credits. Recently I was at **YCAT**. I was in there seven months, and then out on probation on **ISP**. I was picked up for a **PV** and picked up a new charge. I was out for two and a half months. I was going to school but hanging out with the same kids. I have been in and out of jail a couple of times but I am going to do it differently. None of those friends come to visit me here, and when I need them, they disappear. I ask, "Where was you at when I was in there?" I will be better for my family. Monday I see the judge and I could get **conditional release**. I'm looking at **Choice Point** for 12 weeks or **house arrest**. I wrote a letter to the judge. It is three pages long, front and back. I have to explain to her how I blew it so many times before but this time, I am ready to do it right. I have to make her believe me; that I want to make these changes. "Your honor, I hereby stand in front of you once again. I have had bad influences." I will explain how my mom is sick and I am ready to make these changes.

-F.I., Age 17

I got in trouble here. Criminal damage, destruction of property. I kicked down a door in my mom's house. She took all my electronics. I wanted to be on Facebook. I broke into my room to get my laptop. They originally took it away from me because I was suspended from school. I got in a fight with a girl at school. I've known her since kindergarten. She was talking a lot of **smack**. Calling me a bitch, a whore. She told me my boyfriend was cheating on me with her. My boyfriend is 17. We are having sex, but nobody is going to find out. I was out on a **probation violation** and I failed a **UA**. I ran again to be with my **homeboys**. Doing some weed and pills. I would be labeled as **gang affiliated** with Southside. I get A's and B's in school. I live with my mom and stepdad. My stepdad works at a factory making trashcans with lids on them. I don't know my real dad. Mom is a RN at a hospital. I don't know my dad's real name. He lied to my mom about everything including his name and left. My stepdad visited me once. My grandparents, uncles, aunt, and mom visit. I was placed in **JJA custody**. I am leaving Sunday to go to a **group home**. I've never been to a group home, but I hear stuff goes on there. Too many fights. I don't want to get any more charges. I had a **PV**, flunked a **UA**, and they put out a **warrant** for **running** and not going home. I ran to Missouri to hang with some **homies** I know. I was always treated good... but I have anger in me. My friends have dads and I am always asking: "Where is my dad?"

-S.Q., Age 14

SMACK- disrespectful comments or gossip. S.Q. is referencing the Romeo and Juliet laws; see Romeo and Juliet Laws.

PROBATION VIOLATION- failure to obey the conditions of one's probation as set forth by the court, which may result in new charges and/or detention.

UA- short for urine analysis test, the most prevalent form of drug testing.

HOMEBOYS- Close male friends.

GANG AFFILIATED- to be part of a gang, friends or family with someone in a gang, or to act for the benefit of a gang; to be declared gang affiliated by law enforcement can result in increased supervision in the streets or gang enhancement charges added onto other criminal charges.

JJA CUSTODY- to be under the supervision and care of the Juvenile Justice Authority.

GROUP HOME- an out-of-home placement for kids who have been removed from their home "which provides 24-hour non-medical care and supervision to children, provides services to a specific client group and maintains a structured environment, with such services provided at least in part by staff employed by the licensee."

PV- Probation/Parole Violation.

UA- short for urine analysis test, the most prevalent form of drug testing.

WARRANT- "a written order issued by a judicial officer or other authorized person commanding a law enforcement officer to perform some act incident to the administration of justice... most commonly, police use warrants as the basis to arrest a suspect and to conduct a search of property for evidence of a crime."

RUNNING- a status offense that can bring a child into conflict with law enforcement, juvenile court, detention, or dependency court, depending on the runaway's circumstances; running away often leads children to commit more serious crimes in order to survive.

HOMIES- close friends who have your back and are there for you in times of need.

Nobody comes to visit me here. Nobody. I have been here for eight months. My mom is being charged with **aggravated prostitution**. She had me have sex for money and give her the money. The money was for drugs and men. I was always trying to prove something to her… prove that I was worth something. Mom left me when I was four weeks old—abandoned me. There are no charges against me. I'm here because I am a **material witness** and I **ran away** a lot. There is a case against my pimp. He was my **care worker** when I was in a **group home**. They are scared I am going to run away and they need me for court. I love my mom more than anybody in the world. I was raised to believe you don't walk away from a person so I try to fix her. When I was 12 my mom was charged with **child endangerment**. I've been in and out of **foster**

DRUG DOG
ON DUTY

NO
WEAPONS.
NO
DRUGS.
NO
ALCOHOL.
NO
CONTRABAND.

homes. They put me in there when they went to my house and found no running water, no electricity. I ran away so much that they moved me from temporary to permanent **JJA custody**. I'm refusing all my visits because I am tired of being lied to.

-B.B., Age 17

PROMOTION OF PROSTITUTION- the charge for a wide variety of acts related to the facilitation of prostitution, including managing a house of prostitution, soliciting patrons, and recruiting prostitutes.

AGGRAVATED HUMAN TRAFFICKING- "recruiting, harboring, transporting, providing, or obtaining, by any means, a person under 18... to engage in forced labor, involuntary servitude or sexual gratification."

MATERIAL WITNESS- a witness who is believed to have information significant enough to affect the outcome of the case.

RUNNING AWAY- a status offense that can bring a child into conflict with law enforcement, juvenile court, detention, or dependency court, depending on the runaway's circumstances; running away often leads children to commit more serious crimes in order to survive.

CARE WORKER- person who is employed to directly care for youth in a group home or emergency shelter.

GROUP HOME- an out-of-home placement for kids who have been removed from their home "which provides 24-hour non-medical care and supervision to children, provides services to a specific client group and maintains a structured environment, with such services provided at least in part by staff employed by the licensee."

CHILD ENDANGERMENT- "an act or omission that renders a child to psychological, emotional, or physical abuse."

FOSTER HOME- a single-family home placement in the child welfare system "in which a child is raised by someone other than their natural or adoptive parent" and lives with the caretaker's family.

B.B.'s pattern of running away is not unusual for girls who have been sex trafficked. Possibly out of fear or loyalty, they are rarely willing to testify against their pimps and often return to them despite the system's efforts to rehabilitate them from a life of prostitution. B.B. has been moved to permanent juvenile justice custody so the court can ensure that she does not run away again.

JJA CUSTODY- to be under the supervision and care of the Juvenile Justice Authority.

POSSESSION OF A FIREARM- refers to the crime of carrying a gun, either because the defendant is a minor, on probation, or fails to follow a state's laws regarding legal gun possession (e.g. obtaining permits).

BRACELET- refers to the electric monitoring device worn around the ankle, which is used to track the movement of individuals on house arrest, probation, or parole; see also Ankle Monitor.

PROBATION VIOLATION- failure to obey the conditions of one's probation as set forth by the court, which may result in new charges and/or detention.

ON THE RUN- avoiding contact with authorities; a term generally used for fugitives; synonymous with "on the lam."

TAMPERING WITH ELECTRONIC MONITORING EQUIPMENT- *charge given when an individual damages, removes, or otherwise alters the electronic monitoring bracelet they are required by parole or probation to wear.*

TRAVIESOS/TVS- The name of the gang S.W. is a member of.

HOMIES- close friends who have your back and are there for you in times of need.

DRIVE-BY- to shoot at someone from a passing vehicle.

CUSTODY- refers to the responsibility to care, control, and make decisions for a child.

HOUSE ARREST- "confinement to one's home or another specified location instead of incarceration in a jail or prison," most often enforced with an ankle monitor.

Someone was shooting at me 10 days ago. They got me in the hand. Bullet went from my thumb out through my pinky. They had to take a piece of my hip to replace the bone in the hand. It's my right hand. My first time I was here was when I was 14 for **firearm possession**. Been here five times since. Now I'm here for cutting my **bracelet**... a **PV**. I also violated because I ran and got a new tattoo. I was **on the run** from the law and charged with something like tampering with technology. I guess I would be described as affiliated with a gang... because I am a gang member. The **Traviesos** or **TVs**. That's what my tattoo says. In English

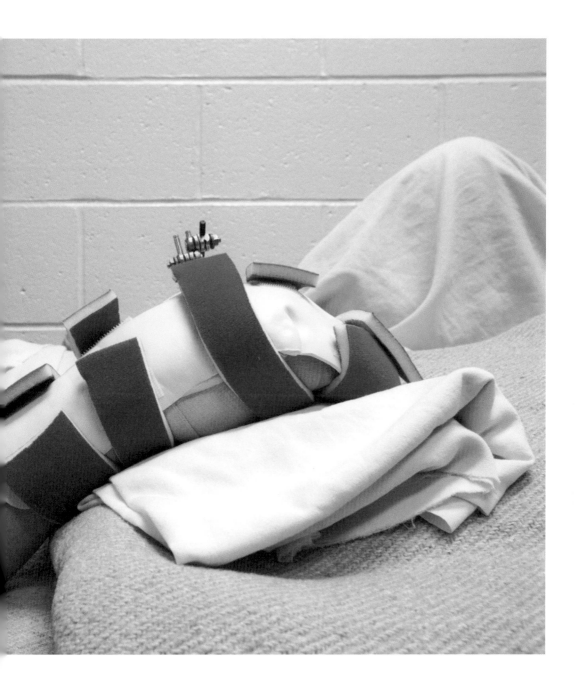

it's rascals. This is the first time I got shot. I'm alive though; it's all good. Why did they shoot me? I don't have a clue. It was four in the afternoon on the 22ⁿᵈ of April and I was with two other of my **homies**. One kid was shot in the leg, the other in the leg and the arm. It wasn't really a **drive-by**. Yeah, they were in a car, but they were sort of behind us. My dad visits. My mom doesn't visit me. She doesn't have **custody**. My dad started taking care of me since I was little. I have one brother who is 14. He is under **house arrest**. I don't go to school. I was going until I was 14 then it was stop and go. Nothing there interested me except the girls. There were lots of fights at school.

-S.W., Age 17

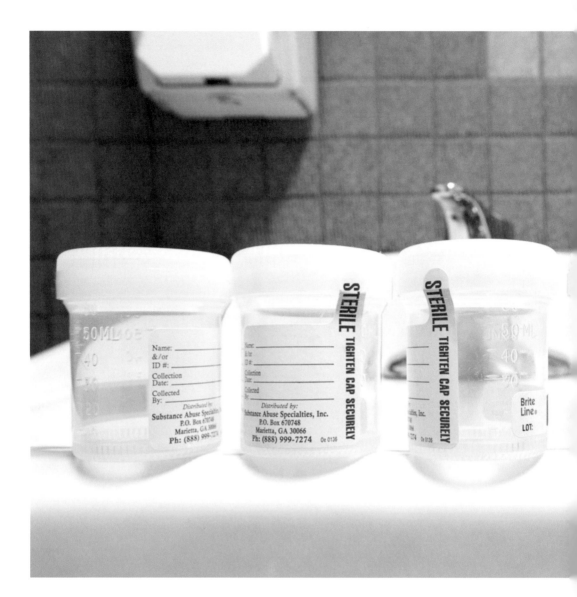

I first came here at 13. My first charge was having a knife and drugs. Weed. I was here for a week—was the last place I'd ever want to be... locked up. I came back a couple of months later. More weed charges. They put me on adult **probation** at 13. This went on and on. They call this **sanction house**, where a judge outs you if you keep on misbehaving. But whatever they call it, a jail is a jail. Same thing. I came back for a **bad UA**. Dad asked if they could put me on **house arrest**. He came from Laos. He came by plane when he was about 19. He welds and works side jobs at car lots. I don't know much about my stepmom. My real mom lives in California. My brother lives with her. He gets in trouble on and off. I was going to school until about seventh grade. Then I started bringing weed around and by eighth grade I was **gang-banging**. I'm a member of the **Piru Bloods**. There are about 15 of us. The other gangs are just fake. I met different people and they disliked me for **the colors I was showing**. I guess I got in trouble when I started looking for respect. It was eighth grade when I got a gun. A shotgun costs $50. A handgun, about $150. You have to be careful and make sure a **gun isn't dirty or has a body on it**. I'm charged with **murder**. I was with a friend who did it. The older guy started to come at me. He had a knife. He dropped the knife when he was coming at us and my friend picked it up and stabbed him. He is in **county**, charged with overkill. When you keep on shooting somebody after they are dead... or in this case he was coming at me with a knife

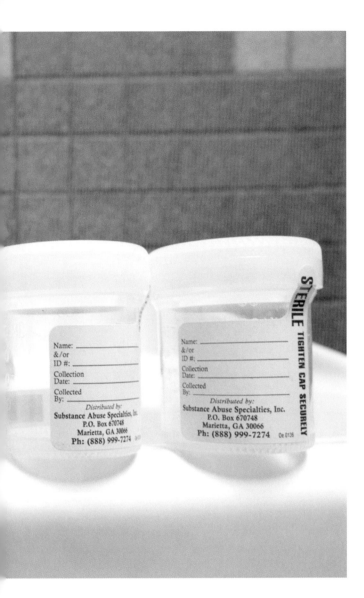

PROBATION- the status of a delinquent youth under court ordered supervision within the community, with specific conditions such as school attendance, the wearing of an electronic ankle monitor, refraining from interaction with other youth on probation, drug testing, etc. Failure to obey the conditions of probation may result in new charges and/or detention.

SANCTIONS HOUSE- in Kansas, a locked facility—most often a juvenile detention facility—where the judge might place a youth for a number of days (called a "sanction") "in addition to a sentence like probation, or as a consequence of violating probation."
The judge will send a youth to sanctions house as a kind of "last straw" before detention and commitment.

BAD UA- a bad urine analysis test, meaning one tested positive for illicit substances.

HOUSE ARREST- "confinement to one's home or another specified location instead of incarceration in a jail or prison," most often enforced with an ankle monitor.

GANG BANG- to participate in activities (often illegal) on behalf of a gang.

PIRU BLOODS- gang that originated in Los Angeles.

SHOWING COLORS- to represent a gang; gangs are often associated with a specific color that indicate one's loyalty when worn.

DIRTY GUN- "Gun with a body on it" a gun that has previously been used in a murder or other serious crimes, lowering its value.

MURDER- "the unlawful killing of another human being without justification or excuse."

COUNTY- short for county jail, adult detention facility.

XANAX- a prescription drug in the benzodiazepine family used to treat anxiety and panic disorders; one of the most abused prescription drugs with potential for addiction.

WAIVER HEARING- a hearing to determine whether or not a youth's case should be tried in adult criminal court, taking into consideration the youth's age and seriousness of the offense.

PAROLE- a period of supervision and monitoring by a parole officer in the community following a juvenile's release from commitment.

25-TO-LIFE- a life sentence with possibility of parole at 25 years.

BACK UP- refers to the sentence one will have to serve if caught violating parole.

so I threw a rock. Then we started beating him and I tried to get him to drop the knife. I was on drugs and blacked out. I started drinking alcohol and was taking **Xanax**. I've been in here a year. I went to a **waiver hearing** and they are talking about me pleading guilty and getting three to seven years in juvie, then **parole** for five years, with **25-to-life back up**. I go to court in 16 days to plead guilty so I be gone. I'll be there 'til I am 23. I heard it was better than this. Better food, better programs, and people don't act like little kids. I never visited Laos. One day I would like to.

-T.Q., Age 17

I'm a member of the 38th Street Gang. I have a high school diploma. I have an older brother in college. Dad is a mechanic; my mom does housekeeping at a hotel. They're together. I'm in for **VOP**. I was originally charged with **burglary**, even though I walked through an open door. They caught me smoking weed in this abandoned house. I violated 'cause my **PO** came and searched my room and found a gun. Now I'm ready to change my ways. My best friend passed away. He was shot. Yea, he was a gang member, but it wasn't a gang thing. His neighbor and him were fighting and the neighbor shot him six times. That's when I lost it and got my own gun.

-E.B., Age 17

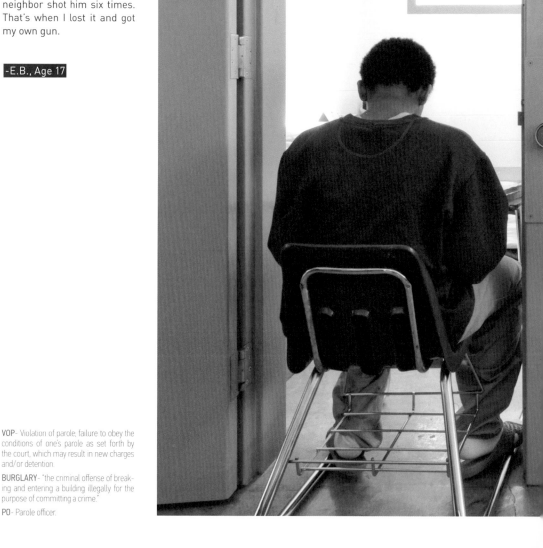

VOP- Violation of parole; failure to obey the conditions of one's parole as set forth by the court, which may result in new charges and/or detention.

BURGLARY- "the criminal offense of breaking and entering a building illegally for the purpose of committing a crime."

PO- Parole officer.

No one visits me. **Social Services** brings my baby. The baby is four months old. I have been here a month. I was in **foster care** for a year but I **ran away**... so I got placed here. I don't get along with my parents or my siblings. There is a lot of fighting because I get a lot of attention. I do horrible in school. I am sort of in the 11th grade. The father of my baby left the scene when I got pregnant. I am here because I cut off my **ankle monitor**. It is called **failure of placement**. Originally there were some **battery** charges. My dad is a welder; mom works for a heating and air-conditioning company. Haven't seen them in over a year. I have been in and out of **detention** since I was 14. Hopefully, this time it will work. I have been at Willow three times. Last time there was seven months. Arroyo Pines, one week; ATC, two weeks; Actions, three or four weeks. I do better in school here. I fought this girl here for telling on me. I am here for five days as a **LUT**. I am in the room for 23 hours, with 30 minutes for walking in the morning and 30 minutes in the evening. I can

SOCIAL SERVICES- refers to the department of state/local government that exists to serve vulnerable children, adults, and families.

FOSTER CARE- "the informal and formal custodial care of children outside of their own biological family home when their parents are unable, unwilling, or prohibited from caring for them."

RUNNING AWAY- a status offense that can bring a child into conflict with law enforcement, juvenile court, detention, or dependency court, depending on the runaway's circumstances; running away often leads children to commit more serious crimes in order to survive.

ANKLE MONITOR- refers to the electric monitoring device worn around the ankle, which is used to track the movement of individuals on house arrest, probation, or parole for the sake of supervision.

FAILURE OF PLACEMENT- in the context of juvenile justice, refers to a violation of probation or a court order.

BATTERY- an intentional act causing harmful, offensive or sexual contact with the body of another person.

DETENTION- "Usually refers to the placement of a youth in a secure facility under court authority at some point between the time of referral to court intake and case disposition." Post-dispositional detention is at times necessary for reasons including "awaiting placement, short-term sentencing to detention, or being a danger to self or others."

R. has been moved from mental health treatment centers to group homes and back again.

LUT- stands for lock-up threat; term for the status of youth who have been determined to be a danger to others and are for all intents and purposes placed in solitary confinement.

SHACKLES- a device with two cuffs connected by a chain, used on the ankles, wrists, and occasionally connecting the ankles to the stomach, used to severely limit the movement of prisoners.

NEGLECT- "the failure of a parent/guardian or caretaker to provide the care and protection necessary for a child's healthy growth and development. Neglect occurs when children are physically or psychologically endangered."

STRAIGHT- clean cut, rule-abiding; conventional; sober.

come out only in **shackles**. My baby boy was taken away. I had him for a month. Then the foster parents said I was **neglecting** him. They are pretty **straight**. I took parenting classes before he was born. I am hoping to get him back when I am out. If I do good, I can get out in 4 months. I go some time next week. I did the artwork on the wall with toilet paper.

-R., Age 17

71

CATCH A CASE- to be charged with a crime

ROBBERY- a crime of theft "by force or intimidation."

KNOWN GANG MEMBER- a person who is known to be a gang member by law enforcement and, as a result, can be subject to increased observation on the streets and gang enhancement charges if convicted of a crime.

THROW THE BOOK AT- to impose the most severe punishment, with the word "book" referring to mean the collection of laws and penalties of a jurisdiction.

AFFILIATED- to be part of a gang, friends or family with someone in a gang, or to act for the benefit of a gang; to be declared gang affiliated by law enforcement can result in increased supervision in the streets or gang enhancement charges added onto other criminal charges.

ITP- stands for intensive treatment program; the maximum security area/program of the facility.

B. was placed in the ITP as a punishment because he picked up some charges while in the facility, such as fighting.

The laws in B.'s jurisdiction have changed regarding the maximum age a youth can be held in juvenile correctional facilities. Age limits range from 18 to 26 depending on jurisdiction.

RECORD SEALING- the practice of making one's delinquent/criminal record inaccessible to the public and eliminates the need for one's criminal history to be reported, e.g. to potential employers or landlords.

FELONY- a serious crime, characterized under federal law and many state statutes as any offense punishable by imprisonment in excess of one year.

CRACK- "a form of cocaine that has been processed to make a rock crystal (also called 'freebase cocaine') that can be smoked."

THROW THE BOOK AT- to impose the most severe punishment, with the word "book" referring to mean the collection of laws and penalties of a jurisdiction.

PRISON- adult commitment facilities, correctional facilities that generally house individuals with sentences longer than one year.

BURGLARY- "the criminal offense of breaking and entering a building illegally for the purpose of committing a crime."

PACK- to carry.

MURDER- "the unlawful killing of another human being without justification or excuse."

I've been here for two and a half years. I was 16 when I **caught my first case—robbery**. It was the first time I was in trouble. I was a **known gang member**. They wanted to **throw the book** at me, but this was my first charge. I am not **affiliated** anymore. I have a three-year-old daughter at home. I can't do that anymore. Mother has two jobs and goes to school. I was 16 when my girlfriend was pregnant. She was six months pregnant when I caught these charges. There is at least one other kid here who's a father. I used to be in **ITP**. Had a little stuff while in here, a few majors. Now I'm in medium security. There are four kids in there with me. I got my GED. I'm fixin' to get my high school diploma. I am here

under the old law. I age out of here at 20. I have my **record sealed** unless I get a **felony**. I was smoking a little weed and sold **crack**. They knew what I was doing, so they **threw the book** at me. My mom visits me. I have two sisters and two little brothers. My girlfriend can't visit. My dad just got out of **prison**. Now he is in the ministry. He is a Blood and been a member of a gang his whole life. Now he is born again. Me, I'm not too religious. Gangs here are territorial. I am a member of the Bloods, but I am a member of the 52nd Street Gang. Most of the time there are about 20 or more people spread out. They do **burglary**, selling crack, we **pack** pistols, sometimes there was **murder** involved. That was before. You do good here, you get more privileges. You can be outside more, more time in the game room, you can move around more, you're not so isolated.

-B., Age 19

In prison for 30 months so far; I got five years and 10 months total. It was for a **rob II**. I never had a way out. My whole family was **gang affiliated**. At age nine I was in the gang. My mother was a gang member. At age 12 I was formally inducted in the gang. My earliest memories are of my mother doing drugs. I was in and out as a youth from 12 to 17: 30 days, six months... casual sentences that I never really thought about. I went from **OYA** to **DOC** and did eight months. I didn't know how to be a human being. When I was about 16-17 I was put in a **CIU**. I remember thinking: I am tired of this, but I don't know how to not be involved. Two weeks ago after I was locked up **Measure 11** my cousin was shot in front of my house. I got the opportunity to look at who I am. I was 17, my girlfriend was pregnant, I had a car, I sold meth, and I had set up something where I was going to have a treaty with another drug dealer, but I knew I was going to rob him. And I robbed him, stabbed him—didn't just stab but pulled the blade up. That was my

Measure 11 crime, which led to me being here. Unfortunately, I have to go back to the city where the crime was committed when released. If I'm in college, they might allow a **transfer of jurisdiction**. For OYA that's not where the **parole officer** is. So they make it where the parole officer is located, close to the crime scene. Not where the family or support is. Going back to the same place that started this is like going back into a burning building.

-H., Age 20

I was here six times. The first time I was 13. I live with my mom, step dad, sister and two brothers. My mom visits me once or twice a week. I had a lot of **VP**. I broke an iPhone so they called it **criminal damage**. My mom called the police. They had me in programs for drug and alcohol rehabilitation. I did the program. 14 Weeks. I was on pills like **Xanax** and **Molly**. I experimented with anything and everything. I used the program to learn how to cope with my life. There are better things to do than drugs. It was a mandatory program where I was a resident. It was **lockdown treatment**. I violated probation by having arguments with my mom. I violated the rules of **house arrest**. At age 14 I picked up an **MIP** for alcohol and weed. My mom sent me to Alabama to live with my dad. He was a drill sergeant in the army. He would wake me up at 4:30 AM and beat me if I didn't wake up. He would give me $20 at the

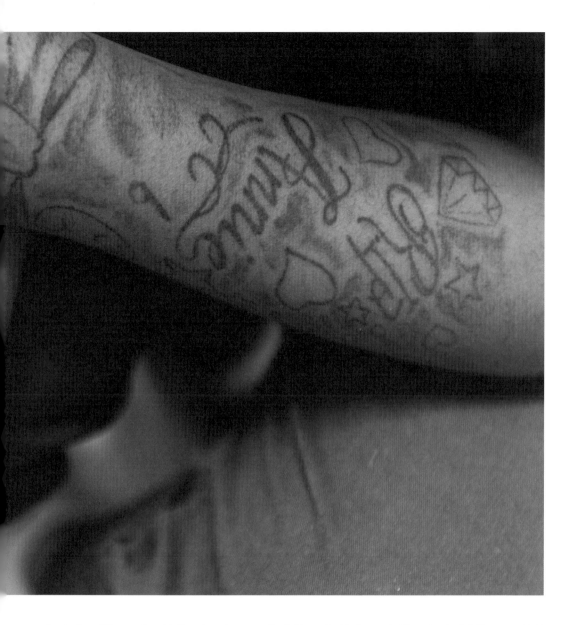

beginning of the week and tell me to get my own food. He worked in the post office after he left the army. I told my mom how bad it was for me, but she thought I was just saying that. I got myself kicked out of his house so I went to live with a friend. My father came and kicked the door down. He pretty much beat me. I had a black eye and bruises. He put me on a bus back from Alabama by myself. I have been here a month now. The judge knows I keep on getting into arguments with my mom. I am going to go to community college and then to Kent State and do a degree in psychology... if I ever get on track. **CPS** was never involved. My parents always wanted all the issues to stay in the house. After the fight in Alabama, I had so much resentment. My sister is a 4.0 student. My grandma is not my actual grandma. She went through a lot of physical and sexual abuse when she was little. My mom went through the same. I think my mom sees a lot of myself in her. She treats me badly. She sent my little sister to my dad's house as well. Ever since I left Alabama, I never spoke to my dad. He does things like calls on his birthday, not mine. He only thinks of himself.

-F.E., Age 17

WHAT GOD KNOWS ABOUT ME IS MORE **IMPORTANT** THAN WHAT OTHERS *THINK* ABOUT ME.

GOD'S AVAILABLE NOW

I've been here twice. I live with my great grandmother. She's 85. I don't know where my mother is. I know my dad is incarcerated. He has been there about eight months now for drug trafficking. My mom went to jail numerous times for selling drugs. She was incarcerated when I was born—so was my dad. My great grandma adopted me. She was given **full custody** when I was born. I'm in 10th grade. I have one younger brother and a younger sister. I see them twice a year if I am lucky. I think my mother takes care of them. I don't even know where she is or even her phone number. I saw them at a family gathering once. We don't have a good relationship. I feel she abandoned me and I never had a chance to really be. She put so much pressure on my great grandmother to take care of me without giving no help, no support. I am here for **aggravated robbery**. Wrong place, wrong time. I was with two guys when they snatched a phone. I was guilty 'cause I was with them. I have been here a month now. This is my first time in. I think I get out tomorrow. I was in for a **PV** for cutting off my **ankle bracelet**. I had an aunt and cousin both dying of cancer. My aunt and my cousin both passed. I went to their funeral. I don't look at this as punishment but as a learning experience. Monday I go talk to a judge and either I go home or they make me stay. But I know this is not the place for me.

-N.I., Age 16

FULL CUSTODY- also known as sole custody, gives one parent or guardian the full responsibility of caring for a child, including making decisions about the child's welfare, education, medical care, and moral/religious development.

AGGRAVATED ROBBERY- a crime of theft "by force or intimidation," with the use of a deadly weapon, infliction of serious bodily injury, or the presence of accomplices.

PV- Probation Violation.

ANKLE BRACELET- refers to the electric monitoring device worn around the ankle, which is used to track the movement of individuals on house arrest, probation, or parole for the sake of supervision.

I've been here two months now. The first time I was here was on a **burglary** charge. I was 14. Two other times I was here for cutting off my **bracelet**. Old charges that popped up and they sent me back downstairs from the courtroom down to detention. My **PO** is having a placement meeting for me. My dad and mom don't live together. My mom lost custody a couple of years ago. I was about nine years old. My mom and dad have both been involved with me. I was never in a **foster home**. My grandmother has been raising me for more than six years. I'm in regular high school classes, but we have about 12 to 13 kids in each class. We do a lot of work on computers there. I have always been falling into a bad crowd. Only a few of my family members share the same behavior—my uncle and my god brother. They're not in any gangs—they just like to be out on the streets. Having fun, getting money—the easy way of doing what they enjoy doing. They hustle and look for easy money. It's hard and very, very tempting, but best to stay away from it. My mom is at home with my sister. She straightened up her life after she got out of jail. She completed **probation**. She drinks here and there but she doesn't smoke anymore so I'm proud of her for that. A drink here and there or a smoke here and there is normal. It's not like kids don't know what they are doing is wrong. They are just not thinking of the consequences. When we do things like **hitting licks**—robbing someone or breaking into a house—it's a way to make money. People use that phrase everywhere. "Me and my friend just hit a lick on a house down the street for $500." I always stuck with school. I always had good grades. No one ever checked on my homework. My grandmother is responsible for me.

-N.K., Age 15

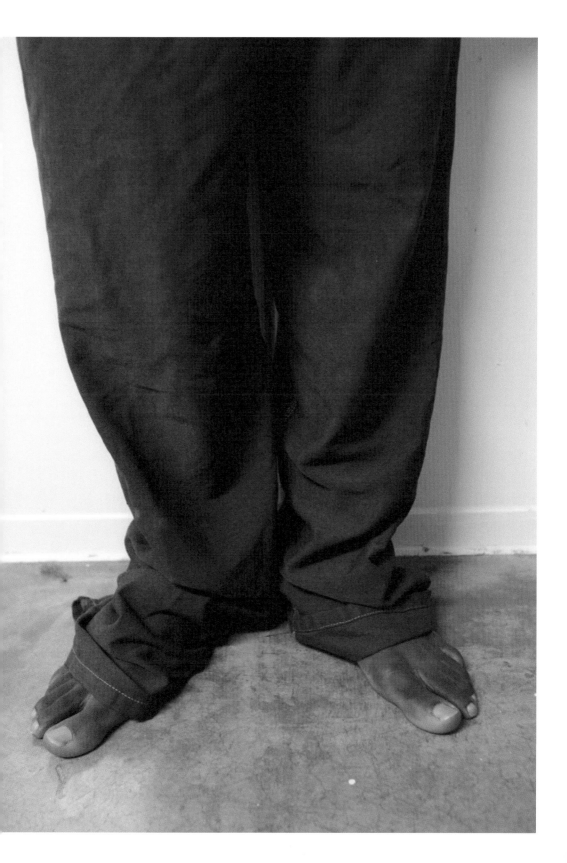

I've been here seven months. I ain't glad. The first time I was 12 years old and brought in for fighting in school. I was hanging with the wrong friends. I've been here four times before. I'm in the ninth grade. Not in any special ed. I'm doing great. I learned that, y'know—going through this—you got to go with the hand that you're dealt. School is the only option that I have to be successful in life. Being myself, believing in myself, because I realized you have to believe in yourself first, before anyone else can believe in you. Because when other people try to believe in you, it's not much unless you believe in yourself. My dad lives with my mother and three little brothers. They are five, 11, and 12 years old. Best way for kids to succeed is to have them do a lot of sports. And not have a lot of the wrong people around them. A lot of kids are not the right kids. Only the ones that have positive minds for their futures. I wanted that for me. I used to be bullied on. And I wasn't going to get bullied, so it lead to a lot of **aggravated assaults**. I have to believe in myself before others will believe in me. I don't do alcohol or drugs. I smoked a couple of times, but was

never a drug person. I'll be serving my time here and then go to a **residential treatment center**—or **youth prison**. I caught some **major charges**. A weapon was involved. I had a hard time being myself. Life is all about decisions. What you say, what you think, what you do. Might have to spend a year or two in youth prison at the most from the earlier charges. I learned and am maturing a lot. I can do a lot of things like write, sing, track, and draw.

-L.K., Age 15

AGGRAVATED ASSAULT- "when a defendant intends to do more than merely frighten the victim" by "threat of bodily harm coupled with an apparent, present ability to cause harm," including "intent to kill, rob, or rape."

RESIDENTIAL TREATMENT CENTER- refers to any number of residential facilities for youth in both the juvenile justice and child welfare systems, including juvenile halls, detention centers, camps, emergency shelters, and group homes.

YOUTH PRISON- juvenile correctional facility.

MAJOR CHARGE- the term could be generally used to refer to more serious crimes, although seven specific major crimes have been designated by the FBI Uniform Crime Reporting System: homicide, rape, robbery, aggravated assault, burglary, larceny/theft, and vehicle theft.

I've been here 245 days. I caught a gang case—**robbery**. I was 12 when I first came here. They have me as a member of the **Heartless Felons**. Mom works at the clinic. My dad doesn't have a job. My mom and dad live together. I have four brothers and two sisters. I'm the oldest. My dad went on trial when I was nine. I tried to find a way to get it going on my own. He went down for six years on drug charges. I have been here eight times. I hope they send me home on **house arrest**. Sometimes when you are on house arrest it is a set up because **the box** don't work—then the police come and get you. I was **on the run** for a month—then I turned myself in. I just want to be free. They used to have programs for kids when I was younger but they stopped. They gave me on **RICO charges** as a gang member. They had me for **assault, vandalism, menacing, participating in a criminal gang, engaging in corrupt activity**, and two **conspiracy** counts. I fought somebody. Then they dropped all the charges except the menacing, vandalism, and attempt to participate

ROBBERY- a crime of theft "by force or intimidation."

HEARTLESS FELONS- a gang originating in Ohio.

HOUSE ARREST- "confinement to one's home or another specified location instead of incarceration in a jail or prison," most often enforced with an ankle monitor.

THE BOX- in this instance, refers to an electronic ankle monitor.

ON THE RUN- avoiding contact with authorities; a term generally used for fugitives, synonymous with "on the lam."

RICO CHARGES- refers to the Racketeer Influenced and Corrupt Organization Act (RICO) and the severe consequences that can be brought upon an individual who has engaged in a pattern of criminal activity as a member of a criminal enterprise.

ASSAULT- though what exactly constitutes an assault varies by jurisdiction, it generally refers to the crime of causing another fear that "he/she is about to suffer physical harm," with the degree of the assault depending on how much harm was caused.

VANDALISM- "willful or malicious destruction or defacement of public or private property."

MENACING- in Ohio, the crime of making someone believe that one will cause physical harm to a person, the person's property, or the person's immediate family.

Participating in a Criminal Gang- the crime of participating in any criminal street gang with knowledge that its members have a pattern of engaging in criminal activity.

ENGAGING IN CORRUPT ACTIVITY- in Ohio, a charge that can be brought onto someone who shows a pattern of engaging in crime, and has done so with more than one person.

CONSPIRACY- "the agreement between two or more persons to engage jointly in an unlawful or criminal act."

CHARGE AS AN ADULT- to charge a child as a criminal in adult court as opposed to a delinquent in juvenile court, typically justified by seriousness/circumstances of the offense and age at the time of the crime, which removes youth from the rehabilitation-focused juvenile system and places them in the punishment-focused adult system.

SNITCH- to tell on someone, specifically giving law enforcement or some other authority incriminating information.

PLEA DEAL- "a plea agreement between prosecutor and defendant... the defendant agrees to plead guilty without a trial, and, in return, the prosecutor agrees to dismiss certain charges or make favorable sentence recommendations."

in a criminal gang. I have a private lawyer. My parents hired him. It's all a lot of gang stuff... so the RICO. But I ain't in no gang. I'm in 10th grade. Not in special ed. They **charged me as an adult.** The kid I was charged with ain't going to **snitch** so they dropped the assault. They gave me a **plea deal,** so the most time they can give me is 18 months.

-E.X., Age 17

I go to education alternatives. I'm in 10th grade. I have been here a month now. The people I see are my mother, grandmother and **probation officer**. Since treatment, I have been in a **Christian home** and **residential treatment center** and **shelter care** for about a year. I was in YFCP—Youth Family Community Partnership—with my grandmother who was taking care of me. My mom lost **custody** when I was nine months old. I was being neglected. My mom used to smoke weed and cigarettes. She's doing good right now. Mom is going to **AA** meetings. I used to smoke weed and drink and hang out with the wrong peer group. Sad as that. They say I have the social age of a 17 or 18 year old and the mental age of a five or six year old. I am here for **grand theft auto** and **misuse of a credit card**... and I had a firearm. I got picked up with my friends, and with a quarter ounce of weed and a gun. They were all trying to blame it on me. They have it as a **conspiracy** case. The police charged us all with the same thing. I am not **gang affiliated**. My dad is deceased. came to see me when I was born. He was stabbed... involved with cocaine and other stuff. I just go with the flow. I didn't use my head before I acted. The first time I was here I was 13 or 14. I had a **home detention violation**. I was 13 when I had a **theft**. Some kids at that time would steal stuff at home depot and they would blame it on me because I was the youngest. My mom works as a maid. I did have a job as a busboy, but I guess I don't have a job no more. I usually do better when I am working. I am a hands-on type of person. They have me on drugs here. Vyvanse 70s and 30s, Fluoxetine, and Hydroxyzine for anxiety; the others are for ADHD. Oh, and Intuniv.

-D.T., Age 16

PROBATION OFFICER- the public official supervising youth on probation, with whom youth have regular meetings.

CHRISTIAN HOME- a group home run by a Christian organization or a Christian family.

RESIDENTIAL TREATMENT CENTER- refers to any number of residential facilities for youth in both the juvenile justice and child welfare systems, including juvenile halls, detention centers, camps, emergency shelters, and group homes.

SHELTER CARE- refers to emergency shelter care in the child welfare system, temporary placements or drop-in facilities for youth who must be immediately removed from their home or current placement; these facilities generally have a 30-day maximum stay by law.

CUSTODY- refers to the responsibility to care, control, and make decisions for a child; can also refer to being held by law enforcement (i.e. "in police custody").

AA- stands for Alcoholics Anonymous; a 12-step program that exists as an international mutual aid fellowship in which men and women meet regularly to share their experiences, help one another remain sober, and help other alcoholics achieve sobriety.

GRAND THEFT AUTO- the crime of theft of an automobile, which is a felony in most states regardless of the car's value.

MISUSE OF A CREDIT CARD- the charge given for a number credit card related crimes, such as using false information to obtain a credit card or intending to defraud a credit card to obtain property or services knowing that it was expired.

CONSPIRACY- "the agreement between two or more persons to engage jointly in an unlawful or criminal act."

GANG AFFILIATED- to be part of a gang, friends or family with someone in a gang, or to act for the benefit of a gang; to be declared gang affiliated by law enforcement can result in increased supervision in the streets or gang enhancement charges added onto other criminal charges.

HOME DETENTION VIOLATION- to violate the terms of one's home detention, most likely resulting in the youth being placed in a confinement facility; see also Home Detention.

THEFT- includes a number of crimes involving the intentional taking of personal property of another without permission.

It is not uncommon for detention facilities to have kids on several of psychotropic medications.

My first time here. I have been here seven months. I came in August for **armed robbery**. My mom and grandma visit me. Sometimes my uncle and my little sister come too. I got braces a year ago. I'm in 10th grade. I am in special ed. My mom is a manager at Wendy's. She's 35. She had me at 19. My dad is deceased. He had cancer. He died when I was 12-years-old. I was cleaning up the **pod**. Someone asked me if I could get the **72 hours** in **lock-up** pod. They take my mattress every morning. They want us to be cold while we are in the room. The **CO**'s call it "the cold room." I'm hungry here too. I'm in room nine.

-E.J., Age 16

ARMED ROBBERY- the crime of theft "by force or intimidation" with a deadly weapon; depending on jurisdiction may be charged as aggravated robbery.

POD- term for a group of cells, similar to wing, unit, etc.

72 HOURS- the standard minimum period of time for a youth to be in solitary confinement for many facilities.

LOCK-UP- in most cases refers to disciplinary detention in a segregated unit or wing of the facility, i.e. solitary confinement.

CO- stands for correctional officer.

I'm from Salem. I've been here for four years. I've been locked up for five years. I've got 15 more to go. My sentence is 20 years and seven months. I'm here for three counts of **Measure 11**. **Manslaughter**, **robbery**, and **unauthorized use of weapon** against another. It was dropped down from two counts of **aggravated murder**. I was 15. I was doing **meth** since I was seven. My mom gave it to me... but that doesn't really matter now. My dad is a **SO**. He never did anything to us but he can't visit. He's been in and out of jail. I have 13 brothers and sisters. I'm not really mean, I'm **DOC**. I wanna go upstate. I got my diploma, so I have nothing to do here. I'm here because of my age, and because I'm 36 when I get out—they capped it at that because the guy I killed was 36. Or maybe I just made that up in my head. I wouldn't give my kid meth. I took the **deal** because I didn't have many options. I was 15 and they were trying for a **death penalty**. This was my first time getting locked up with the law. I wanted to go back to school but my mom wouldn't let me. I was finally in **DHS custody**. They put me in a **foster care** family where my foster mother saw I had lice in my hair so she sprayed us all with Raid, so they took us out of foster care and put us back with our mom. My mom kept saying things would be different, and why would you want to be at foster care? I left between 10 and 13 foster homes.

-K.Q., Age 19

MEASURE 11- refers to Oregon Ballot Measure 11, passed in 1994, which applies mandatory minimum sentences for serious or violent crimes (e.g. a conviction of robbery in the first degree will result in a minimum sentence of seven years and six months, with the judge having no discretion to hand down a shorter sentence).

MANSLAUGHTER- "the unjustifiable, inexcusable, and intentional killing of a human being without deliberation, premeditation, and malice," distinct from murder in that the act must not have been premeditated.

ROBBERY- a crime of theft "by force or intimidation."

UNLAWFUL USE OF A WEAPON- refers to any number of crimes involving the possession of a lethal weapon with intent to use it unlawfully or the discharging of a lethal weapon in public spaces.

AGGRAVATED MURDER- the intentional killing of another human being under a number of aggravating circumstances that vary by jurisdiction, such as receiving payment for committing the murder, murder of an on-duty police officer, or killing someone under a specific age.

METH- short for methamphetamine, also known as crystal meth, crystal, ice; an extremely addictive stimulant drug.

SO- stands for sex offender.

DOC- stands for Department of Corrections; the branch of government dealing with adult offenders.

DEAL- short for plea deal; "a plea agreement between prosecutor and defendant... the defendant agrees to plead guilty without a trial, and, in return, the prosecutor agrees to dismiss certain charges or make favorable sentence recommendations."

DEATH PENALTY- "the lawful infliction of death as punishment." Not allowed to be used against minors.

DHS- stands for the Department of Human Services; the department of state/local government that exists to serve vulnerable children, adults, and families.

FOSTER CARE- "the informal and formal custodial care of children outside of their own biological family home when their parents are unable, unwilling, or prohibited from caring for them."

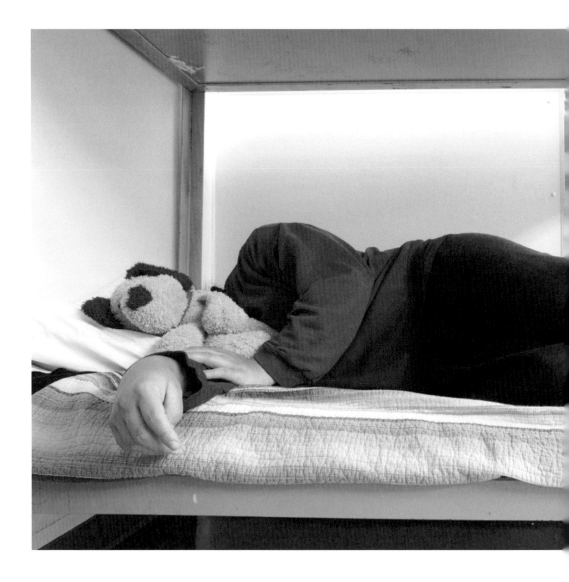

My mom visits me once a month. This is my fifth time here. I've been in and out. I was **off paper** for two years. I was twelve when this first started. I was charged with **assault** for defending myself against my step mom. I'm a drug addict with a **run record**. I have a hard time staying in one place. Normal is not normal to me. When I take responsibility I get overwhelmed. I've been to drug and alcohol detox twice as an **inpatient**, once as an **outpatient**. They're all great but I was not in the right mind to take it. I was 10 when I started with marijuana. I don't think it's bad, but I personally can't handle it. I've been doing **heroin** and alcohol. I do lots of thefts for my expenses... bikes, cars, houses. For a long time I took pride in not prostituting. My last relapse, I started prostituting on my own. This **commitment** is for selling. This arrest is for **PV** and **using** and **running**. I been here over three months. I'm going into a transition program. I hope I can step up to the **YWTP**. My mom and dad were both alcoholics. They owned a bar. I was left alone a lot. When I got a taste of a social life, I was resentful that I couldn't join. My mom was drunk when she found me on the street. I had run away. She attacked me and wouldn't let go. I punched her in the face. It wasn't that hard, but when she appeared in court a month later, she still had an ugly bruise. I think she did it to herself. When I was taken into **custody** for 28 days, I was in shock. I didn't consider the crime, I was uneducated and had poor **representation**. My stepmom and dad divorced. I've seen my dad twice in the past six or seven years. I haven't lived with my mom for a long time. My mom rents a room at a home, so it's not comfortable for me to stay with her. Mom's a recovering alcoholic who's three years sober. First time I was here for a year. Second time seven months, third time

three months, fourth time nine months. Now I've been here three and a half months. I dropped out of school almost right away, like sixth grade. I've been doing school since I was locked up. I have my GED and I am working towards my diploma. I got third prize in a poetry competition; my poem was called "Split Personality." It's about my addiction and me as an addict versus the polar opposite, me sober. I got it published in the paper. Me and my fiancé both write poems. He's in prison. He's 37. I was on the street and coming down off **LSD**, he rode up on his bike and came back later with blankets and food. We camped together; we were both in active addiction. We stole for support. He encouraged me to get my shit together. We've been together four years. I was 14 when I met him. He was 33.

-B.X., Age 18

SUICIDE BED- a bed engineered to prevent the possibility of its occupant committing suicide, which is not bunked and built with as few pieces as possible, if not a single plastic piece.

GANG AFFILIATED- to be part of a gang, friends or family with someone in a gang, or to act for the benefit of a gang; to be declared gang affiliated by law enforcement can result in increased supervision in the streets or gang enhancement charges added onto other criminal charges

PAROLE VIOLATION- failure to obey the conditions of one's parole as set forth by the court, which may result in new charges and/or detention.

ABSCOND- "to hide, conceal, or absent oneself" from the jurisdiction or supervision of the court to avoid prosecution or supervision, e.g. failure to report to one's probation officer as assigned.

INDEPENDENT LIVING PROGRAM/ILP- a program providing "training, services, and programs to assist current and former foster youth achieve self-sufficiency prior to and after leaving the foster care system."

CASE MANAGER- "social worker whose role is to oversee and coordinate a client's (child/family) services in keeping with the client's goals and needs," such as identifying the most appropriate placement option for an abused child, or connecting a youth to mental health services.

SPONSOR- in the context of addicts and addiction recovery, refers to a recovering addict who shares their knowledge of fighting addiction with a less experienced addict and provides one-on-one support in times of weakness.

MAJOR- short for major charge, the term could be generally used to refer to more serious crimes, although seven specific major crimes have been designated by the FBI Uniform Crime Reporting System: homicide, rape, robbery, aggravated assault, burglary, larceny/theft, and vehicle theft.

ASSAULT- though what exactly constitutes an assault varies by jurisdiction, it generally refers to the crime of causing another fear that "he/she is about to suffer physical harm," with the degree of the assault depending on how much harm was caused.

METH- short for methamphetamine, also known as crystal meth, crystal, ice; an extremely addictive stimulant drug.

FOSTER HOME- a single-family home placement in the child welfare system "in which a child is raised by someone other than their natural or adoptive parent" and lives with the caretaker's family.

DSD1- stands for "down since day one," refers to a person who has been willing to be involved from the beginning.

GAY FOR THE STAY- a term for someone who is not homosexual outside of confinement, but during their time in confinement engages in homosexual relationships.

GROUP- short for group therapy, "a form of psychosocial treatment where small groups of people meet regularly to talk, interact, and discuss problems with each other and the group leader."

I have a **suicide bed**. I've been here three times. The top bunks are the safest, because if the other girls are attacking you they can't get to you as fast. There's not a lot of gang activity but I would be called **gang affiliated**. I've been in programs since I was 12. Nobody visits me. I've been here two weeks on this trip for **parole violation, absconding**. I fled an **independent living program**. I didn't steal, but somebody said I was stealing. I was skipping school, being rude, and had a bad attitude. My **case manager** was saying all these bad things about me but it wasn't true. I didn't like the **ILP**; I fled to go where my sponsor was and people I knew respected me. My mom couldn't call me because it's long distance. When I was about 12 years old I started smoking weed. When I was 14 I picked up my first **major**. I **assaulted** four cops; they put their hands on me. No one's going to take care of you. You have to take care of yourself. There was a lot of **meth** involved.

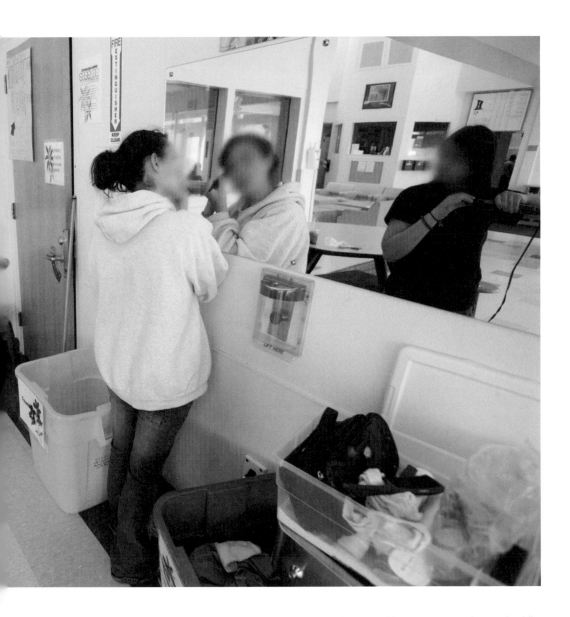

I have two autistic little brothers, and a little cousin my mother takes care of because my aunt is a meth addict and couldn't take care of my cousin, and my uncle beat a guy with a hammer, so he's doing time—mom's a little busy. She doesn't work. My dad is an alcoholic. I haven't seen him in a long time. I go to rehab, I work at it, and then something happens and I give up. I've been in **foster homes** that were pretty abusive. My mom doesn't have any time for me. I never missed school a lot. When I was in a program for homeless youth they wanted me to do a GED. I wanted to do a diploma, but they forgot to switch me on the roster. I don't mind this place... they don't bug me here. I'm a **DSD1** girl. I'm gay. I don't think being gay is bad at all, but everyone has their own beliefs. Not a lot of gay girls here. Some are bi-sexual—of convenience—or gay for the stay. I don't keep track of the time in here. There's no point. Oh yeah, I was raped when I was 15. People cry here all the time in **group** and everyone is all supportive. Then they walk away and people talk shit about it. Sometimes I help the other girls put on make up 'cause it helps them like how they look and they feel better about themselves.

-I.T., Age17

They had me in a **takedown** a week or two ago. I got in a fight with a girl so they split us up and I spit on one of them. I have six sisters, one stepsister, two stepbrothers, and one real brother. Nobody visits me. I've been here three months. My mom does a lot of **meth**. My dad lives in Arizona and works for Babies 'R' Us. The first time I was here was for three months. I was in juvie for three weeks after being on the street. My mom started doing meth when her dad died. I'm here for **disorderly conduct, false information**— giving a fake name to a cop. I was in a car where the driver was driving crappy. We were driving in snow and he couldn't see the white lines. Yeah, he was on meth. I've been using since I was 15. I wasn't in any drug program on the outside. My dad moved out of the house. I **ran away** from my stepdad and my mom to some friends' houses. They were like 15, 16, 17. They were drug dealers. They gave me a place to stay and all the meth and weed I wanted. I didn't go to school and I was on probation, so I had a **bad UA**. My two older sisters were in here as well. When they took me down I got tackled because I wasn't looking at the wall when I was supposed to be looking at the wall. The **COs** pick you up and put you in handcuffs. I was in isolation for five days. I was released two days ago. They only let you out to shower. I got to have a book

TAKEDOWN- a restraint technique for aggressive or unruly youth in a crisis situation that "redirects a youth to the ground in a controlled manner in order to limit the youth's physical resistance and to facilitate the application of a restraint device."

METH- short for methamphetamine, also known as crystal meth, crystal, ice; an extremely addictive stimulant drug.

DISORDERLY CONDUCT- "a crime that is charged when a person is being disruptive and disturbing the peace in which the public has gathered. Often, these types of crimes include the usage of alcohol."

FALSE INFORMATION- the criminal offense of knowingly giving law enforcement false information concerning the commission of a crime.

RUNNING AWAY- a status offense that can bring a child into conflict with law enforcement, juvenile court, detention, or dependency court, depending on the runaway's circumstances; running away often leads children to commit more serious crimes in order to survive.

BAD UA- a bad urine analysis test, meaning one tested positive for illicit substances.

CO- stands for correctional officer.

Birch is the name of the solitary confinement unit at L.N.'s facility.

AA- stands for Alcoholics Anonymous; a 12-step program that exists as an international mutual aid fellowship in which men and women meet regularly to share their experiences, help one another remain sober, and help other alcoholics achieve sobriety.

NA- stands for Narcotics Anonymous, a program following the 12-step tradition developed by Alcoholics Anonymous that exists as an international mutual aid fellowship in which men and women meet regularly to share their experiences, help one another remain sober, and help other narcotics addicts achieve sobriety.

GANG AFFILIATED- to be part of a gang, friends or family with someone in a gang, or to act for the benefit of a gang; to be declared gang affiliated by law enforcement can result in increased supervision in the streets or gang enhancement charges added onto other criminal charges.

BANG- to participate in activities (often violent and criminal) on behalf of a gang.

REP- short for "represent."

CLAIM- to assert one's association to a location or membership in a group, such as a gang.

Gangs are often associated with a specific color that indicate one's loyalty when worn. L.N. is most likely referring to loyalty to her gang when saying she's "all red."

EXTRADITE- to "transfer an accused from one state or country to another state or country that seeks to place the accused on trial."

there. I read Twilight. The girls in there were talking crap. I'm here, and I can go to the **AA** program and the **NA** program. You can stay in this program until you're 25. I'm tough no matter what. If I wasn't, these girls would walk all over me. I'm **gang affiliated**, but I don't **bang**. I **rep** and I **claim**. I'm all red. I have a boyfriend, I have girlfriends. I'm a very hungry person. I love to eat. I don't like the rain or the clouds. I'm scared to die. I like the color purple. The rain makes me sad or hungry. I'd like to go to Arizona, they can't **extradite** me there.

-L.N., Age 17

MEASURE 11- refers to Oregon Ballot Measure 11, passed in 1994, which applies mandatory minimum sentences for serious or violent crimes (e.g. a conviction of robbery in the first degree will result in a minimum sentence of seven years and six months, with the judge having no discretion to hand down a shorter sentence).

All Measure 11 crimes have a mandatory minimum sentence of at least five years. This mean the judge cannot hand down a sentence of less than five years for these crimes, regardless of the circumstances.

PROBATION- the status of a delinquent youth under court ordered supervision within the community, with specific conditions such as school attendance, the wearing of an electronic ankle monitor, refraining from interaction with other youth on probation, drug testing, etc. Failure to obey the conditions of probation may result in new charges and/or detention.

ASSAULT- though what exactly constitutes an assault varies by jurisdiction, it generally refers to the crime of causing another fear that "he/she is about to suffer physical harm," with the degree of the assault depending on how much harm was caused

GANG ENHANCEMENT- refers to a set of laws allowing courts to increase the severity of a sentence due to a crime's perceived commission for the benefit of a gang. Gang enhancement charges can result in a youth's case being transferred to adult criminal court or time added to one's sentence.

Pow wows, sweats, and sundances are important ceremonial events in many of the indigenous communities of North America.

MIP- stands for minor in possession, the crime of having alcohol or a controlled substance on one's person or property while under the age of 21; see also Status Offense.

My dad is Klamath-Modoc. Mom lives in Oregon. My sister and mom and dad live together. Mom stays at home. Dad is a drug and alcohol counselor with Native Americans in Portland, with the Siltez tribe. I'm here 10 years. I'm a **measure 11** kid. Measure 11, that's mandatory 60 months. I got into a fight while under the influence of drugs and alcohol. I was on **probation**. I saw a person from a different gang. I just attacked her. I was still drinking. I broke her arm, wrist, eye bones. She pressed charges. I was told to plead guilty rather than face charges of **assault** with a **gang enhancement**. I've been in here since I was 15. I grew up in the native ways, going to sundances, sweats, pow wows. Then out of nowhere I was hanging out with the wrong crowd, the wrong people. I was on probation from a **MIP**, then I was drinking, smoking weed, and I picked up the assault. I was 14 when it started. I was straight A's in school, but I was pretty bored. So I started drinking and partying. My mom and my grandma both have diabetes. My mom was a user and both of them were alcoholics. My aunt uses and drinks all the time. From the start I knew I could have done better. When I was using or drinking, I wouldn't care about the sacred ceremonies. They have sweats here once a week, in the yard. They have powwow too. Now I am back to my culture.

-D.O., Age 16

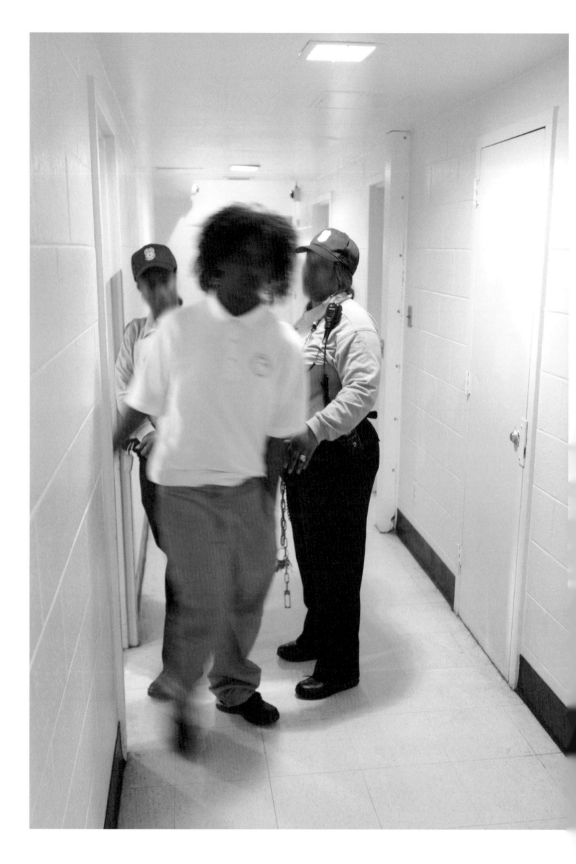

I've just been here two days. Came from **detention**. Was there a year and a half. It was so long because I was awaiting trial in three cases. **Assault II, assault III, rob II,** and **murder**, with a gun. I'm **DOC**. I have a 15 year sentence. I can be here till I'm 25, eight years. I served a year and a half in detention, so I got **time served**. So I'm looking at 30 or 31 when I get out. My brother is 23; I aided him in a robbery. He turned me in, so he's out already. I lived with my mom, my brother and my sister. My two little brothers both have rare bone diseases, where their hands twist back. My grandma helped raised them. My dad was murdered before I was born. Gang and drug related. There's no man in the house. My mom used to work in a nursing home but she's stopped working. I was 13 when I got involved in the system. I was **tagging** and I got caught. I run with the 13th Street Sureños. Most girls carry knives rather than guns. You can get a gun for 50 or 70 dollars. A small handgun, probably a **.22**. I was caught with two **codefendants**. They killed him. I didn't know they were going to kill him, but I set it up for them to meet. I never really went to school. Dropped out in seventh grade... I used to go to middle school. My older brother was a gang member and my dad was a gang member before he was killed and I felt that's what I should be doing. My dad was in **drug trafficking** in the Cartel. He would traffic drugs and send back money to his mom and dad. He didn't really think about us kids. How do you stay out of this place? You get different friends. You stay out of drama with activities, like volunteering or afterschool programs. If you're hanging out with your friends you have to do positive things, like going to carnivals or festivals. Or sports. I was never into sports. I'm going to educate myself. Stay off the drama and gang stuff.

-K.S., Age 17

DHS- stands for the Department of Human Services; the department of state/local government that exists to serve vulnerable children, adults, and families.

FOSTER CARE- "the informal and formal custodial care of children outside of their own biological family home when their parents are unable, unwilling, or prohibited from caring for them."

TRIBAL COUNCIL- the legislative body of a tribe.

DOMESTIC VIOLENCE- "any abusive, violent, coercive, forceful, or threatening act or word inflicted by one member of a family or household on another can constitute domestic violence."

YWTP- stands for Young Women's Transition Program, a program for girls transitioning out of Oregon juvenile correction facilities that teaches independent living and social skills and prepares them for a successful reintegration to society.

CRIMINAL MISCHIEF II- in Oregon, the crime in which "having no right to do so nor reasonable ground to believe the person has such right, the person intentionally damages the property of another; or, the person recklessly damages the property of another in an amount exceeding $500."

CRIMINAL MISCHIEF I- in Oregon, the crime of intentionally damaging the property of another person under a variety of aggravating circumstances, including: causing damage in excess of $1,000; using an explosive or starting a fire; damaging a public utility or medical facility; etc.

MIP- stands for minor in possession, the crime of having alcohol or a controlled substance on one's person or property while under the age of 21; see also Status Offense.

TRIBAL COURT- "a Court of Indian Offenses, a court established and operated under the code or custom of an Indian tribe, or any other administrative body of a tribe which is vested with authority."

Though Native American tribes in the U.S. function under their own governments with their own justice systems, lack of funding and resources often leaves the tribes no choice but to rely on the federal justice system to handle repeat offenders.

YIR- stands for Youth Incident Report, a reporting mechanism for youth who commit offenses within a facility.

BURGLARY II- in Oregon, refers to the charge for the crime of burglary; see also Burglary.

ON THE RUN- avoiding contact with authorities; a term generally used for fugitives, synonymous with "on the lam."

METH- short for methamphetamine, also known as crystal meth, crystal, ice; an extremely addictive stimulant drug.

Both my mom and dad's parents are Klamath. I grew up on the Chiloquin reservation. I lived with my mom until I was nine. Then I was taken away by **DHS** and put in non-tribal **foster care**. My grandma fought to get me back through **tribal council**. She adopted me when I was nine... me and my two sisters and my brother. My mom passed away at 41 from alcoholism. My dad's in prison. Drug charges and **domestic violence** against my mom. Mom would start fights with him; she tried to kill him. I witnessed all of it. She would hit him in the head with a hammer. He stayed with her because of the four kids. Normally it's the other way around, but I think my mother was the one guilty of domestic violence. I think I understand my father more now. I've been here seven months. I was 15 when I first came here. I'm in **YWTP**. I'm trying to get out in time for my senior year of high school. I would live with family friends when released, on the reservation. They live outside of town and have five horses. I have my GED, but I want my diploma. They committed me when I was 13. When I got charged with **criminal mischief II** and **I**. And an **MIP**. If you get into much trouble, you get off the **tribal court** and into the state. I was written up as a **YIR**. Tribal court didn't want to deal with me anymore. I was charged with **burglary II**. I broke into a store, we pulled off the swamp cooler and I slid down into the store and passed alcohol to my friends. All the programs I've been in, I've run from. I was **on the run** for four months. I started weed at nine, alcohol at 12, meth at 14. There's free healthcare from the tribe; mostly it deals with alcoholism. A lot of grandparents are raising kids. On the res we had two food stores. One of them was actually a liquor store. There's not much there. My grandma took care of eight kids. She was in recovery from breast cancer but now she's not doing well. School starts September ninth; I hope I'm out before then. I've been to programs like Healing Lodge of Seven Nations in Spokane. They're made for native kids. But I ran. Lithia springs, but I ran. When I got into the system I spoke one way, like an Indian. Everybody around me was judging me, making me feel uncomfortable as an outsider. I have 12 siblings, three full siblings. This is my destiny—to be an alcoholic and a **meth** addict. But I was also selling. My mom had mental personality issues. I'm not sure why she hated my dad so much. We lived off of commodity food: bread cheese, powdered milk, Saltine crackers. We were always poor or hungry. When my mom drank, she would be happy or mean drunk. Sometimes she would lock us in a room. Indians would have parties and bring their kids. We were used to being around our parents when they were drunk.

-U.X., Age 17

I was the valedictorian of my class. I graduated from school in Louisiana. Then my mom and I were in a shelter, so I **ran away**. That was nine months ago. My mom was on drugs and drinking heavily. I was hospitalized with a concussion, and got charged with **assault** on a family member. My mom has visited me three times, but I haven't seen my dad since I was six. There was a lot of physical and mental abuse. My brother goes to school and works two jobs. My mother lives with him now. I also have a 13-year-old sister who is living with a family friend. I stopped going to school for a while because I felt beneath everybody because I lived in a shelter, but then the lady at the YMCA helped me. Now I'm taking my SATs next month.

-K.O., Age 17

RUNNING AWAY- a status offense that can bring a child into conflict with law enforcement, juvenile court, detention, or dependency court, depending on the runaway's circumstances; running away often leads children to commit more serious crimes in order to survive.

ASSAULT- though what exactly constitutes an assault varies by jurisdiction, it generally refers to the crime of causing another fear that "he/she is about to suffer physical harm," with the degree of the assault depending on how much harm was caused.

This is my first time here. I was 13 when I first came in. I had three **priors**. I'm in for **burglary**. Nobody visits me. I sleep on the streets. The only way I know how to eat is burglary, small crimes. That's the position I'm in. I'm about to be sent up to Green Hills—**JRA**. I'll be there until I'm 21. Me on the outs? No I don't see it. No, not really. I went to high school until 10th grade. I was expelled a lot for fighting. I don't use drugs. My mom does. My dad's incarcerated. I live with grandma and ma who takes care of the kids.

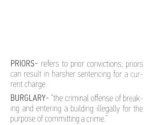
-D.T., Age 17

PRIORS- refers to prior convictions; priors can result in harsher sentencing for a current charge.

BURGLARY- "the criminal offense of breaking and entering a building illegally for the purpose of committing a crime."

JRA- in Washington, stands for Juvenile Rehabilitation Administration, the arm of the Washington State Department of Social and Health Services dealing with the highest-risk youth offenders.

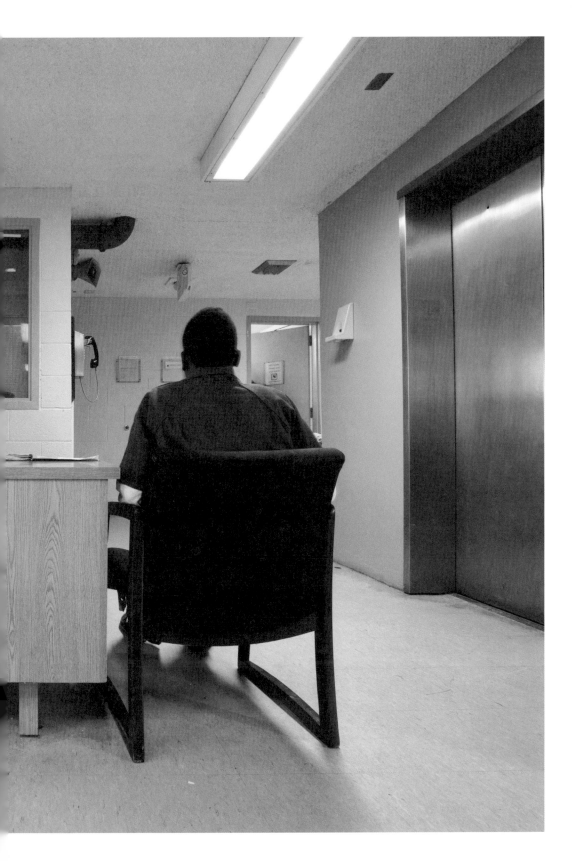

I'm a **Becca** kid. I was brought in for **truancy**. I was truant for three weeks. Went to court first. I had **run away** from home because my uncle was threatening to rape me. My father has just gotten back to being involved in my life. My mom and auntie live there with my little cousins. I didn't want to report my uncle's threats to **CPS** because I didn't want to hurt my mom. I ran away with my friend. My mom didn't like my friend. He is older. He plays basketball a lot and takes classes online. I was sort of in 10th grade. My mom had to take me to court every Friday. I think I'll get my GED. My dad is not really around. I only see him on holidays. This is the second time I was brought in as a **ARY**. My mom says I'm at-risk. She decided this.

-J.C., Age 16

BECCA LAWS- refers to Washington State laws on truancy, at-risk youth (ARY), and children in need of services (CHINS), which are intended to ensure all youth receive education and protect children who are in danger or a danger to themselves.

TRUANCY- the status offense of repeated absence from school, which breaks compulsory education laws in the U.S.

RUNNING AWAY- a status offense that can bring a child into conflict with law enforcement, juvenile court, detention, or dependency court, depending on the runaway's circumstances; running away often leads children to commit more serious crimes in order to survive.

CPS- Child Protective Services, the agency that in many states provides services in cases of child abuse or neglect.

ARY- stands for at-risk youth, the status of a child after a request for services by the child's parent or guardian because the child has: been absent from the home for more than 72 consecutive hours without consent; is beyond parental control to the point that the behavior threatens health and safety; or has drug or alcohol abuse problems for which there are no pending criminal charges.

I'm 13 years old. I've been here 20 times...committed some crimes. Mostly **PV**. I been here a couple of months. I've done some stupid shit—**arson, reckless burning, burglary**. I live with my mom. My dad lives all the way in Oregon. I go to school. This year I am going to start high school. I do weed, but nothing of the shit some other kids do. Other kids do heroin at 16. Not me. No one visits me. Only attorneys. My mom doesn't come here. When I was five my dad chained me to the toilet and raped my mom. I haven't even seen my dad in six years. I have four sisters and two brothers. Being here doesn't even help. You just want to come back after a bit. They should help us more. They don't really teach us anything like real school, but it's school to them. I have a radio because I am on honors. There is base level...that's three days when you come in. Then level two for seven days, level three for 15 days. If you behave you get honors. Honorable means you can play video games, movies, candy. Every Sunday you get **commissary**. You can get

deodorant, cheerios, other stuff. I've been here 60 days now and haven't been sentenced. I caught a new charge. I beat an older guy's ass. Not in school, on the street. He was 35 years old. He was a mental but I didn't know it. So I got **assault** and **harassment**. I'm a member of the **Sureños**. Was I **jumped in**? Yes and no. I got beat up. Then I had to **put work in**.

-K.Q., Age 13

From age one to seven I lived on the reservation; age ten to fifteen lived in Tacoma. I went to school until sixth grade. Started going back a little bit, but I got locked up at 15 and a half. Mostly for **assaults** and **running away**. I was on **probation** till 16 then locked up. Charges? Running away from **foster homes, group homes**. Nobody's visited me for over two years. Just my **social workers**. My mom and dad both live in Tacoma about an hour away. I was in a foster home from age seven. My parents lost **custody** at a year and a half. They left me for drugs. I was placed with my step dad on the reservation with my baby sister. She was an infant. My mom and I are in contact. She's sober but we still argue. My dad's in Tacoma, I've talked to him but he has three others to look after—they're my brothers and sisters. I went to **tribal court** and I came in with up to four years. I got two years in juvie and then I had four **custodial assaults**. Actually two **assault I's**, that's the highest level of assault. They were against kids, no staff. I was in lots of treatments. I succeeded in one, the other I got arrested out of. It was for threatening another youth.

-E.T., Age 17

ASSAULT- though what exactly constitutes an assault varies by jurisdiction, it generally refers to the crime of causing another fear that "he/she is about to suffer physical harm," with the degree of the assault depending on how much harm was caused.

RUNNING AWAY- a status offense that can bring a child into conflict with law enforcement, juvenile court, detention, or dependency court, depending on the runaway's circumstances; running away often leads children to commit more serious crimes in order to survive.

PROBATION- the status of a delinquent youth under court ordered supervision within the community, with specific conditions such as school attendance, the wearing of an electronic ankle monitor, refraining from interaction with other youth on probation, drug testing, etc. Failure to obey the conditions of probation may result in new charges and/or detention.

FOSTER HOME- a single-family home placement in the child welfare system "in which a child is raised by someone other than their natural or adoptive parent" and lives with the caretaker's family.

GROUP HOME- an out-of-home placement for kids who have been removed from their home "which provides 24-hour non-medical care and supervision to children, provides services to a specific client group and maintains a structured environment, with such services provided at least in part by staff employed by the licensee."

SOCIAL WORKER- in the context of youth in the delinquency and dependency systems, most often refers to a case manager in investigations of child abuse and neglect; see also Case Manager.

CUSTODY- refers to the responsibility to care, control, and make decisions for a child.

TRIBAL COURT- "a Court of Indian Offenses, a court established and operated under the code or custom of an Indian tribe, or any other administrative body of a tribe which is vested with authority."

CUSTODIAL ASSAULT- in Washington, refers to the charge of assault in the first or second degree when the victim is a staff member, volunteer, service provider, or community correction officer at a corrections or detention facility.

ASSAULT I- in Washington, the crime of assault performed with a deadly weapon or force likely to produce great bodily harm, causes great bodily harm, or exposes the victim to the human immunodeficiency virus.

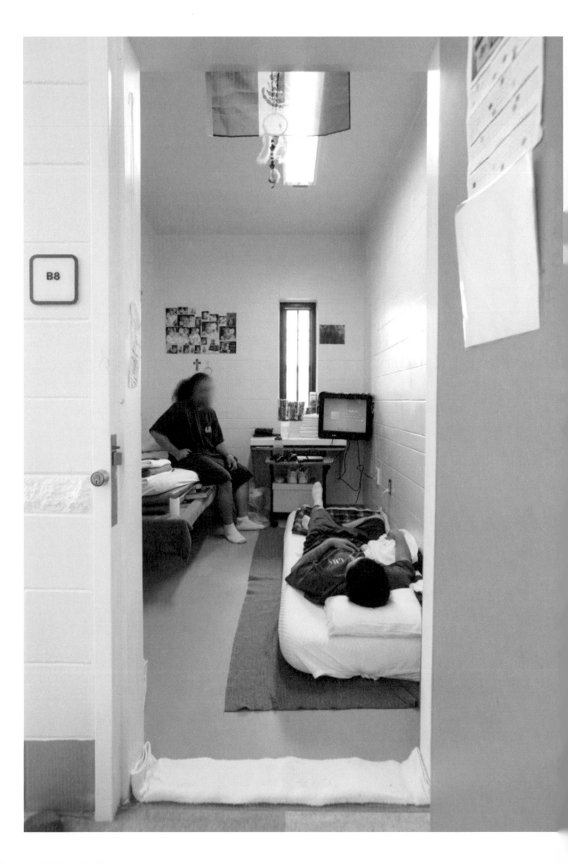

I was born in Samoa. We pronounce it "shamore." I'm 100% Pacific Islander. My family moved to Long Beach, then Washington. My dad was transferred to Fort Lewis. He was deployed to Iraq three times. Then he came home and spent a tour at Fort Drum in New Jersey. My mom is a stay at home mom. She takes care of my four brothers and four sisters. My oldest brother went to the **penitentiary** but he's out now. A bunch of people visit me: my mom, my dad, brothers and sisters. I caught a 10 year sentence for **robbery**. I been here three years. I hope I get out in 2016—that will be six years. That's the minimum sentence. The maximum is ten and then there's a medium. If I get released after six, I still would have to do one year where I can't stay here, 'cause I **age out**. So I hope I get **work release** from 21 to 22. I came in when I was 16. I had another offense when I was 14 and 15. **Assault** and robbery. It's all physical stuff. That was my second offense. So they have a point system, where class B felonies all add up a half point and I added up to 8 points. So I got ten years. Sometimes they take into account the number of **ACEs** you've had. I was with two **codefendants**. They got out. It was their first offense. I was **charged as an adult** although I was 16. It was a class A felony. Kids get **declined**; they declined me my second day. Of course of I was under the influence of alcohol. I have a high school diploma. I want to get into a college program. Then I want to open a Samoan restaurant.

-T.N., Age 19

PENITENTIARY- prison; when used by youth, often refers to adult correctional facilities.

ROBBERY- a crime of theft "by force or intimidation."

AGE OUT- refers to the point when a youth reaches an age where they are no longer eligible to receive services such as in the foster care or juvenile court system.

WORK RELEASE- "a program in which certain prisoners are permitted to leave a penal institution for a specified time in order to hold jobs, prior to their full release."

ASSAULT- though what exactly constitutes an assault varies by jurisdiction, it generally refers to the crime of causing another fear that "he/she is about to suffer physical harm," with the degree of the assault depending on how much harm was caused.

Washington State uses an offender scoring system as a sentencing guide, which takes into account prior convictions, relationship of prior offenses to current convictions, number of current convictions, length of time crime-free between offenses, etc.

ACE- acronym standing for "adverse childhood experiences," originating from the Adverse Childhood Experiences Study's screening, designed to gather information on a youth's history of childhood maltreatment, trauma, and family dysfunction.

CODEFENDANT- "one of multiple defendants sued in the same civil action or formally accused of committing together the same crime."

CHARGE AS AN ADULT- to charge a child as a criminal in adult court as opposed to a delinquent in juvenile court, typically justified by seriousness/circumstances of the offense and age at the time of the crime, which removes youth from the rehabilitation-focused juvenile system and places them in the punishment-focused adult system.

DECLINE- in Washington state, to transfer a juvenile offender's case from juvenile court to the adult court system, i.e. a youth is "declined jurisdiction in the juvenile court."

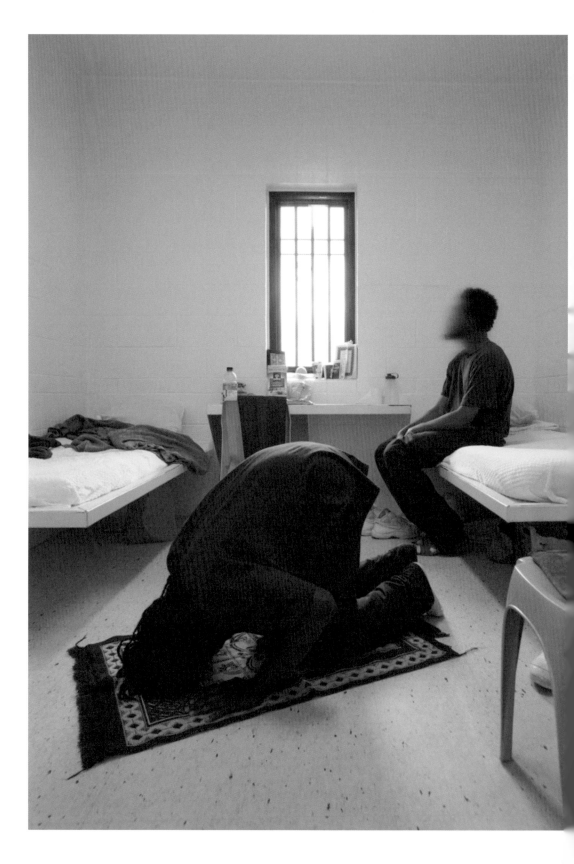

I was 16 when I was first incarcerated. I was **declined** 'cause it was **armed robbery**. Yeah, there were victims. I'm not **gang affiliated**. My dad was a longshoreman. My mom passed away at 10, she was over-medicated. I think that was the root of all my problems. I was the youngest of ten kids. I've got a brother in the system but my other siblings are clear. My dad visits as much as possible and he calls me every day. I'm close to graduating high school. I am a Muslim. I've been a Muslim for two and a half years and my dad's a Muslim. My favorite passage from the Quran is Al-Fatiha (the opening). I don't get any special meals, but I'm on the no pork list. I pray five times a day; I have a real prayer rug. The Imam comes in every two months. There are 20 kids that identify as Muslim. They're sorta 50/50. Muslim out of convenience, but 50 percent are sort of true believers. The first time I was taken in I was 11— an **assault** charge. I got in a fight with another kid right in front of the police. I get out in three more years. I'm doing five and a half. I was declined but I have to stay six months after my 21st birthday. They're talking about if I stay here or go to the **penitentiary**. Depends on the rules, but things are changing. For the most part I'm clean. The bad part of my life I was a gang member. I was very into the street life. I was angry, mad at the world for the death of my mother. Every time I went to jail I came out angrier. I was in with the adults at age 16. I was trying to figure it out, but I ended up getting seven years. But everything is getting better. I came in contact with an older fellow when I was in **RJC**. We became friends. He became my mentor.

-K.S., Age 18

DECLINE- in Washington state, to transfer a juvenile offender's case from juvenile court to the adult court system; i.e. a youth is "declined jurisdiction in the juvenile court."

ARMED ROBBERY- the crime of theft "by force or intimidation" with a deadly weapon; depending on jurisdiction may be charged as aggravated robbery.

GANG AFFILIATED- to be part of a gang, friends or family with someone in a gang, or to act for the benefit of a gang; to be declared gang affiliated by law enforcement can result in increased supervision in the streets or gang enhancement charges added onto other criminal charges.

ASSAULT- though what exactly constitutes an assault varies by jurisdiction, it generally refers to the crime of causing another fear that "he/she is about to suffer physical harm," with the degree of the assault depending on how much harm was caused.

PENITENTIARY- prison; when used by youth, often refers to adult correctional facilities.

RJC- Regional Justice Center in Washington, a detention facility for adults and juveniles.

I was 15 my first time here. I did three and a half months. Now I have been in and out six times. I had an **escape** charge for leaving a **residential treatment center**. There were 24 other kids in the cottage. They tried to charge me with stuff. They identified me as a **Heartless Felon**, but I'm not. When I was in here I had to keep fighting. People in here want you to argue with them and want you to fight them. My mother comes to visit me. It's been over a month since she has come. I've been in **AS** for three days now. It is boring. You can't do anything. I be hungry in here all the time. You have to go to sleep when the sun is still up—eight or seven o'clock. They didn't give me a book. I get out on second shift today. I do push-ups and take naps to pass the time. When they move me around here they put handcuffs on my hands and sometimes on my feet. It depends on where staff is taking me. In here I watch TV through the door. I used to go to my grandma's everyday to see how she is. My dad is in college I think. I have an 18-year-old brother in jail for robbery. He is in the **penitentiary** for two years. I'm not in a gang. And I didn't do none of what they said I did. I smoke weed... but I don't smoke when I am on **probation**. I drank liquor twice but I don't like it. I can do 200 pushups.

-T.D., Age 16

ESCAPE- "the criminal offense of fleeing legal custody without authority or consent."

RESIDENTIAL TREATMENT CENTER- refers to any number of residential facilities for youth in both the juvenile justice and child welfare systems, including juvenile halls, detention centers, camps, emergency shelters, and group homes.

HEARTLESS FELONS- a gang.

AS- stands for administrative segregation, which is the practice of confining inmates to their cells for 23 hours a day as a response to disruptive behavior; see also Solitary Confinement.

T.D. will be released for her hour or thirty minutes of recreation time with the second group of youth held in administrative segregation.

PENITENTIARY- prison; when used by youth, often refers to adult correctional facilities.

PROBATION- the status of a delinquent youth under court ordered supervision within the community, with specific conditions such as school attendance, the wearing of an electronic ankle monitor, refraining from interaction with other youth on probation, drug testing, etc. Failure to obey the conditions of probation may result in new charges and/or detention.

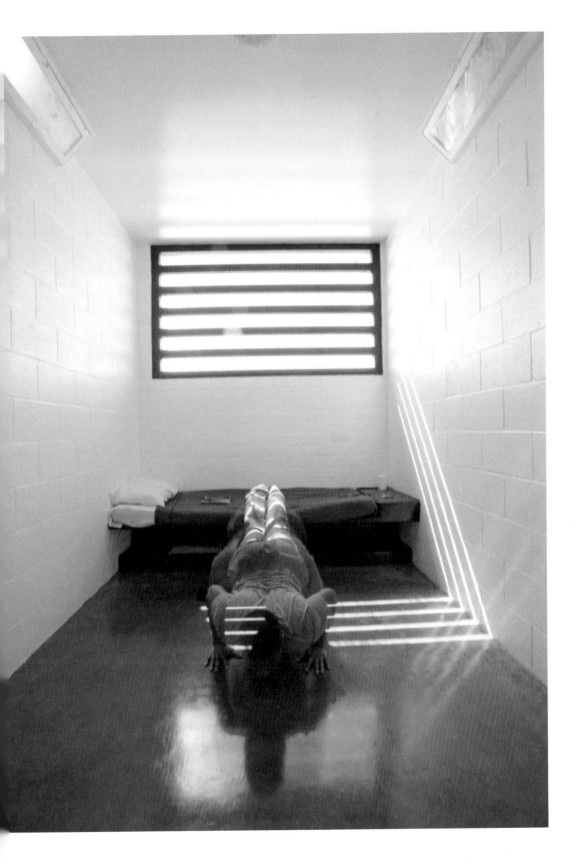

ADULT TRIAL- the practice of trying children in the adult criminal court, typically justified by seriousness/circumstances of the offense and age at the time of the crime, which removes youth from the rehabilitation-focused juvenile system and places them in the punishment-focused adult system.

AGGRAVATED ASSAULT- "when a defendant intends to do more than merely frighten the victim" by "threat of bodily harm coupled with an apparent, present ability to cause harm," including "intent to kill, rob, or rape."

KIDNAPPING- "the crime of unlawfully seizing and carrying away a person by force or fraud."

ROBBERY- a crime of theft "by force or intimidation."

ATTEMPTED MURDER- the crime of attempting to kill another person without cause or justification, proven by substantial steps being taken towards committing the crime.

PAROLE VIOLATION- failure to obey the conditions of one's parole as set forth by the court, which may result in new charges and/or detention.

BOUND OVER- in Ohio, transfer of a youth's case to adult criminal court.

ADA- stands for Assistant District Attorney.

PLEA BARGAIN/PLEA DEAL- "a plea agreement between prosecutor and defendant... the defendant agrees to plead guilty without a trial, and, in return, the prosecutor agrees to dismiss certain charges or make favorable sentence recommendations."

MANDATORY BIND OVER- in Ohio, refers to the mandatory (i.e. the judge has no discretion) transfer of a youth's case to adult criminal court for trial of certain offenses, and offenses committed by kids over a certain age.

JUVIE LIFE- refers to a sentence lasting until the youth has reached the age limit for juvenile custody in a given jurisdiction (in some jurisdictions, youth can stay in a juvenile corrections facility until age 25); the maximum possible sentence in juvenile court.

I've been here 10 months. I am waiting for trial. I get **tried as an adult**. They have me for two **aggravated assaults, kidnapping, robbery**, and **attempted murder**. This is my first time here. I was with the wrong kids. They didn't catch anyone else, but they caught me and charged me. I have three brothers and a sister. One of my brothers is in jail for **parole violation**. My dad is travelling. I don't talk to him a lot. He is a music producer. He came to visit me about three weeks ago with my mom. He lives with his wife. I just got moved to 11th grade. I think I am in special ed, but I'm not sure. My mom transports people places like the grocery store or home. The minimum I can get is six (years), the maximum 25. They **bound over** my

case to the justice center. The **ADA** tried to get me to **plea**. I told them I would take it to trial, so there was a **mandatory bind over**. They wanted to give me **juvie life**, or 'til I am 21. I didn't want to take that. I have a private attorney. My mother hired him. After school I would usually go have fun with my girlfriend or go to a rec center. This place made me think a lot. Made me change. They have a lot of speakers that come in that relate to me. They talk about smoking and drinking and how they have changed and I know I can do it too. Especially when I'm in the cell I think about what I can do. I figure everything happens for a reason.

-P.X., Age 16

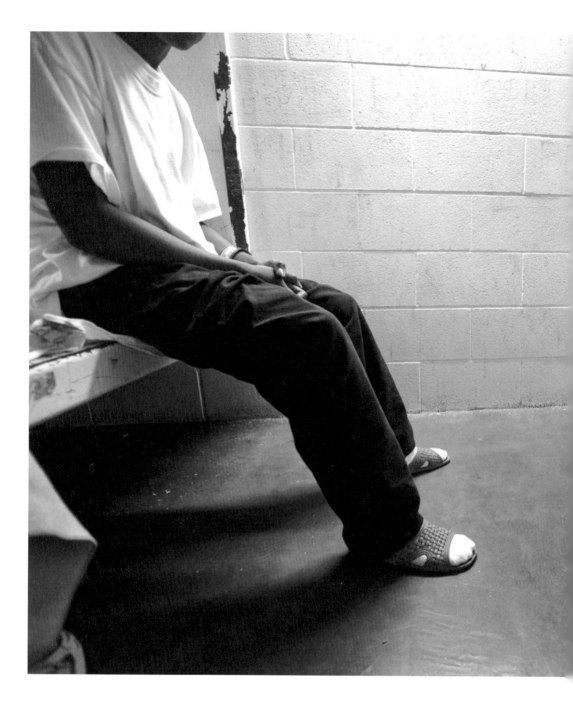

My mom is a nurse's assistant. I have two sisters. I am the oldest kid. I've been here three months. I think I'll be sentenced next month. I have **juvenile charges**. I have a meeting to see what is best for me. I don't think I am going home though. My case ain't very violent. My first time here I was 15. It was for a **burglary**. I have been here three times. I am in special ed in ninth grade. I was just being a follower. Now I have to think for myself. I have a summer job of landscaping but no after school job... I guess I may not have that job anymore. I can get an education in here same as on **the outs**. This is my first time coming for a case. I was 15 and coming in for **house arrest**... for a **violation**. I went to sentencing for house arrest and then went AWOL between June and December. I caught another case—a house **burglary** with my friend. My

tattoo says "family first." My grandma is 59. My mom is 32. Grandpa wasn't around. Dad was in and out. My "grandfather" was my uncle's dad.

-X.E., Age 16

I have been here six months, my second time. First time I was 14. I was charged for **robbery** over a hat. I ended up doing four months. I was suspended from school for arguing with teachers. I was **catching little cases**. It was a couple of robberies they were trying to pin on me. I didn't kill nobody, but I did hit them. My **codefendant** is in **county**. I hoping he ain't **snitching** on me. He be solid. He be a real nigga. I be praying. I am **bound over** as an adult and facing 27 years. They can send me to county any time they want. In June I have to be bound, but I could stay in House Three until I am 21. They usually send people out at 18 but it is all about behavior and I have been getting into a lot of fights. My temper is bad and I have a big mouth. I did a week straight in the **timeout room**. No eating the regular food in there. You eat a regular three meals but it is crap. I can only use the bathroom in there every three or four hours. Sometimes they don't let you out of the room. I be trying to stay on the staff's good side, but they treat me **grimey**. They enforce all the rules on you. If you are on their good side they might give you an extra tray of a little extra juice and other little things. I was in House Three—that's for over 18. They treat you like county there. I live with my mom, mom's boyfriend, my sister, and her boyfriend. I have four sisters; one's married and one's suicidal. My dad is around somewhere. I just talked to him two days ago. He's unemployed, but he has excuses. He's drinking more than he's working. Thursday was when my mom could have come but she worked all night so she slept all day and didn't come. She drinking beer at 6AM and listening to angry music. Only so much I could do. I tried to kill myself. I wrapped my neck with the cable cord of a TV. I was depressed. I robbed a store with no mask. I was just trying to kill myself. Now I am reading a bible. One day I will get somewhere. But here I got in two fights in one hour. I was at a breaking point. Why did I have to be locked up to realize what is right and what is wrong? It can't be no coincidence. My mom started drinking all day, everyday since I was 13 or 14. There were **DV** calls. She would get drunk and swing on me. She used to beat me up when I got into trouble. She put rings on and punched me in the face. My mom was into punishing me a lot.

-L.W., Age 17

ROBBERY- a crime of theft "by force or intimidation."

CATCH A CASE- to be charged with a crime.

CODEFENDANT- "one of multiple defendants sued in the same civil action or formally accused of committing together the same crime."

COUNTY- short for county jail, adult detention facilities.

SNITCH- to tell on someone, specifically giving law enforcement or some other authority incriminating information; one who tells on others or gives authorities incriminating information.

BOUND OVER- in Ohio, transfer of a youth's case to adult criminal court.

House Three is a wing or unit of the juvenile facility L.W. has been placed in where youth who are over 18 are held. L.W. uses the word "bound" to refer to getting transferred to an adult facility.

TIME-OUT ROOM- refers to solitary confinement.

GRIMEY- slang for wrong or unjust.

DV- stands for domestic violence, "any abusive, violent, coercive, forceful, or threatening act or word inflicted by one member of a family or household on another can constitute domestic violence."

BOUND OVER- in Ohio, transfer of a youth's case to adult criminal court.

ODYS- Ohio Department of Youth Services; refers to Ohio's juvenile corrections facilities.

HEARTLESS FELONS- a gang.

AGGRAVATED ROBBERY- a crime of theft "by force or intimidation," with the use of a deadly weapon, infliction of serious bodily injury, or the presence of accomplices.

GUN SPECIFICATION- the mandatory imposition of an additional year to an offender's sentence because the offender possessed a firearm during the commission of a crime.

ATTEMPTED MURDER- the crime of attempting to kill another person without cause or justification, proven by substantial steps being taken towards committing the crime.

PLEA BARGAIN/PLEA DEAL- "a plea agreement between prosecutor and defendant... the defendant agrees to plead guilty without a trial, and, in return, the prosecutor agrees to dismiss certain charges or make favorable sentence recommendations."

EXPUNGE- to remove or seal someone's arrest and conviction records, a practice that varies by age, type of crime, and jurisdiction; expungement is important because a criminal record can pose difficulties for ex-offenders seeking employment, residence, etc.

I did the artwork (in the cell). I'm here eight months. I am waiting for trial. The case was **bound over** to the adult system. My mom and stepfather would visit. My dad is deceased. I was shot when I was six or seven. I was 14 when I was in **ODYS**. They tried to say I was in the **Heartless Felons**—it is a prison thing. It started in youth detention system. No one ever sent me to treatment. There was never any of that, just punishment. My mom tried to get me counseling once. They prescribed meds like Adderall for ADHD and Ritalin at night. When I was 14 I got an **aggravated robbery** with a one-year **gun specification**. That's an extra one to three (years) on

the sentence. They never charged me with gang stuff. I didn't really need counseling. I have a good relationship with my mother, but not with strangers. She is unemployed and doing hair in the house. She is a respiratory therapist looking for work. She is also going to school. I live with her and three sisters. Here there are other kids that are older, but many of them are in ODYS and some younger ones like 11 or 12. The staff here are bullies. They abuse their power. I think I am on **attempted murder**. I can get 12 to 15 if I lose. They offered a **plea** of six to eight. I have a paid lawyer. I hope they will expunge my record when I am older and I can go in the military. My dead friends are written on the wall here. They all died last year—all gunshots.

-O.S., Age 18

I've been here three weeks. I'm on **one-on-one**. My mom is 28.
At home there is me a 15 year old, me, a 12, 10, 8, 6, 5, 4, and 1
year old. We have the same mom, different dads. We are all in the
same **foster home** now. I've been here seven times. I was 12 the
first time. I don't even remember the first time I went to a foster
home. Since May I have been with this foster home. I've been with
a different foster family for about two years now. I was with my
mom until I was 11. My mom lived with my stepdad. He doesn't
live with her anymore. We are on **Section 8**. My dad died when I
was little. I never found out why. I've been in **placement**—a foster
home. Then I went back and forth to the hospital for **cutting**. I talk
to my mental health counselor here once a day for 30 minutes.
She helps to tell me to use my coping skills. I'm learning how
to cope with my anger. I'm here because I **violated probation**.
I was charged with **battery against a police officer**. My friends got
caught up. They stole something... headphones and some phones
at Best Buy. They tried to put it on me. The cops came and I spit
on one of them. I was twelve. Nobody has visited me here. I go to
placement from here I think after I see the judge.

-F.N., Age 14

ONE-ON-ONE- 24-hour observation where a guard is appointed to constantly watch an inmate, typically assigned for youth who are perceived to be a liability to themselves.

FOSTER HOME- a single-family home placement in the child welfare system "in which a child is raised by someone other than their natural or adoptive parent" and lives with the caretaker's family.

SECTION 8- refers to the Housing Choice Vouchers Program, which "provides qualifying families with assistance in paying the monthly rental fee for homes and apartments that are located anywhere, not just in subsidized housing projects."

PLACEMENT- court ordered residential assignments in both the delinquency and dependency systems, which may "be secure and prison-like or have a more open setting, like group homes or foster care."

CUTTING- a type of self-injury that is often the result of attempting to cope with intense emotions and problems for which the cutter doesn't have the skills to overcome alone.

PROBATION VIOLATION- failure to obey the conditions of one's probation as set forth by the court, which may result in new charges and/or detention.

BATTERY AGAINST A POLICE OFFICER- the crime of causing injury to a law enforcement officer, considered a much more serious crime than standard battery; if the battery results in serious injury, the sentence can be between five and 25 years depending on jurisdiction.

CAUGHT UP- refers to getting caught by law enforcement, most often when the interaction results in charges.

I've been here two and half months. I was 12 the first time I was in the system. I've been here five times. Aggressive behavior I guess. I live with my mom and my sister. Me and my mom get into it a lot. It sometimes is verbal but then it gets physical. My sister is 12 and my brother is six. My mother is thirty-three. My dad lives in Vegas. I saw him last when I was two. My mom treats me bad; she made me sleep outside with the dogs. I was with **DCFS** but the case got closed. There were charges but my brother and sister and mom said there was no abuse. So it was three against one. If I don't live with my grandma they will send me to **camp**. My grandma wants me with her. My mom smokes weed all the time. I mean all the time. And she'll whoop me with anything around. The last time she had a bat, one of those little bats. I backed up and picked up a knife to defend myself. My brother called the police and my brother and sister backed up my mom. I just held the knife and we were fist fighting. When the police came to my house because I was fighting with my mom they arrested me, not her, and then they charged me with battery for kicking the police. They called it **battery with serious injury against a police officer**.

-E.E., Age 13

DCFS- stands for Department of Child and Family Services, the governmental agency serving vulnerable children and families in some states.

CAMP- refers to juvenile boot camps, a type of juvenile corrections facility.

In many jurisdictions throughout the U.S., an arrest is mandatory when dealing with domestic violence calls. The child is most often arrested in situations such as E.E.'s, when a single mother has other children to care for, because the alternative is removing all children from the home and arresting the mother, which is much more disruptive.

BATTERY AGAINST A POLICE OFFICER- the crime of causing injury to a law enforcement officer, considered a much more serious crime than standard battery; if the battery results in serious injury, the sentence can be between five and 25 years depending on jurisdiction.

This is my third week here. I have a court date next week. No one's visited me here. I'm here for a **VP**. I was on **house arrest** but I left to go to church. They won't even let you go to church if you are on house arrest. I live with my mom, grandma, great-grandma, two siblings, mom's husband. I'm a senior. I have been to nine different schools. I was pushed around from one house to another... **group homes**. I went **AWOL** a lot, then to a **foster home**. I lived with my grandma for five years. I don't have anywhere to go right now. I'd probably go back to a group home. I'm half DCFS, half probation. Mom and dad were never actually together. I was a **meth baby** when I was born. I used meth before but I have been clean for a year. I was six years old when my dad left. He had beaten me. He ended up going to prison for child abuse and drug abuse. When I was seven years old I was abused by a guy that worked with kids at the Boys and Girls Club. I was in an **IOP** program for six months but then got kicked out. I'm planning on getting my GED next week. I'm here for **misdemeanor theft**. The only one I really trust is myself. I don't want to go back to my house. Everyone that's there is stuck there. They never move on to anywhere else. It was my great grandmother's house and she's 92 and she's still there. My grandmother never left. And my mom never left either until she was arrested for production and distribution and use of meth, and a stolen vehicle. She got five years for that. I did a drug program for a year, so I'm clean. They tested you every month so you had to be clean.

-U.G., Ag 17

VP - Violation of Probation.

HOUSE ARREST- "confinement to one's home or another specified location instead of incarceration in a jail or prison," most often enforced with an ankle monitor.

GROUP HOME- an out-of-home placement for kids who have been removed from their home "which provides 24-hour non-medical care and supervision to children, provides services to a specific client group and maintains a structured environment, with such services provided at least in part by staff employed by the licensee."

AWOL- an acronym originating from the military meaning Absent Without Leave; in the context of dependency refers to a minor leaving their assigned placement without permission.

FOSTER HOME- a single-family home placement in the child welfare system "in which a child is raised by someone other than their natural or adoptive parent" and lives with the caretaker's family.

DUAL CUSTODY- the status of youth involved in both the dependency and delinquency systems (e.g. went from foster care to detention).

METH BABY- a child who was exposed to methamphetamines in the womb, which is linked to behavioral complications such as difficulty sustaining attention, anxiety, and a greater likelihood of aggressive behavior.

IOP- stands for intensive outpatient program, a program most often used for drug dependency treatment for those who do not need medically-supervised detox, which allows patients to stay in their own homes while participating in a highly structured treatment program.

MISDEMEANOR THEFT- the crime of intentionally taking of personal property of another without permission, charged as a misdemeanor due to value of the property stolen; similar to petty theft. Production and/or distribution of a controlled substance is a much more serious offense than possession.

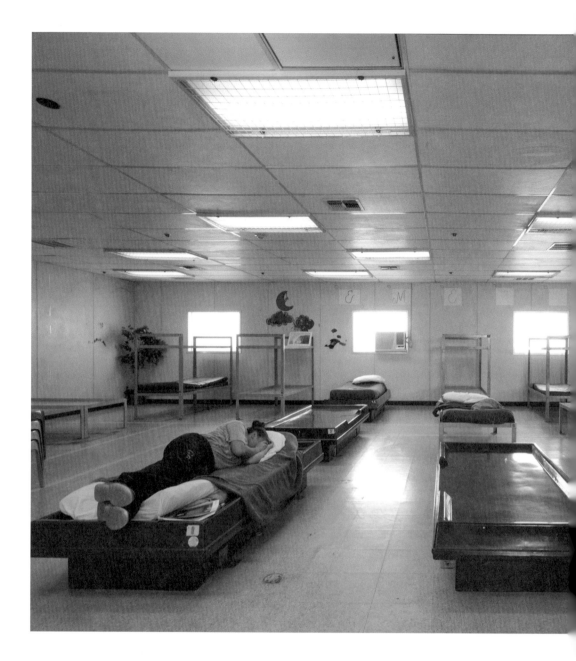

I was adopted when I was five. People that end up here aren't all dumb. Some are smart. You are here not because it is something you choose. It's something you were given. You followed the last generation. I went to **foster care** when I was born. My sister is 20 and she has been in and out of the foster care system. My mom was doing **meth** when I was born and I started doing it when I was 15. It gives you the illusion of a different world where everyone is always accepted. You don't have to impress anybody. I can stop caring or trying to be the best. I could be the best at being the worst, and that was something. I was taken away from my mother when I was three and my sister was eight. Then we were adopted when I was five. My mom beat us all the time. I was taken away by **CPS**. When my sister was taken away from me and put in **detention**, it was the worst day of my life. I was alone. When I was three, I was sexually abused by my cousin. But that never affected me as much as my mom's emotional abuse. Words hurt more than physical abuse. They cut deep. She would put us down. She put our dreams and our hopes down. At 14, I started

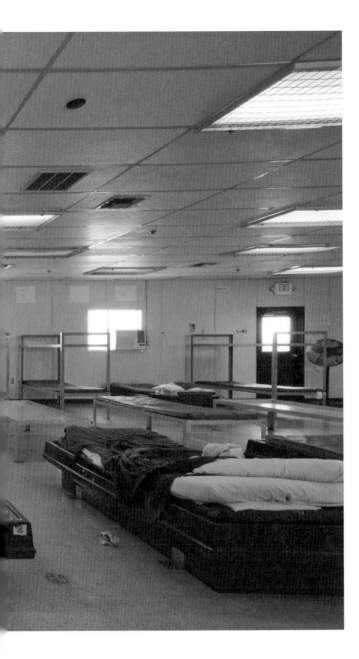

rebelling. I wouldn't let her get into my brain no more. So I started smoking, drinking, doing **triple Cs**. It's when you take twenty pills, like little red pills. I was doing it everyday and started overdosing. Then I started doing meth. That brought me here. I was **AWOLing**. Running from a **group home**. Ever since I was little for 10 years since I was adopted I ran. I would rather be in a house with people I know and love rather than six people I never met before. So I ran and ran.

-T.B., Age 17

DCFS- stands for Department of Child and Family Services, the governmental agency serving vulnerable children and families in some states.

In Z.B.'s current jurisdiction, the "level" of a facility indicates how secure the facility is and the intensiveness of services provided there.

METH- short for methamphetamine, also known as crystal meth, crystal, ice; an extremely addictive stimulant drug.

DUAL- the status of youth involved in both the dependency and delinquency systems (e.g. went from foster care to detention).

While Z.B. is currently under the custody of both the delinquency and dependency systems, her dependency case may be closed, meaning she will be under the custody of family upon release from the detention center.

MIP- stands for minor in possession, the crime of having alcohol or a controlled substance on one's person or property while under the age of 21; see also Status Offense.

RESISTING ARREST- the crime of obstructing a law enforcement officer's attempt to perform an arrest, which can range from running and hiding from officers to striking or pushing an officer during an arrest, unintentional or otherwise.

FOSTER HOME- a single-family home placement in the child welfare system "in which a child is raised by someone other than their natural or adoptive parent" and lives with the caretaker's family.

CUTTING- a type of self-injury that is often the result of attempting to cope with intense emotions and problems for which the cutter doesn't have the skills to overcome alone.

AWOL- an acronym originating from the military meaning Absent Without Leave; in the context of dependency refers to a minor leaving their assigned placement without permission.

GROUP HOME- an out-of-home placement for kids who have been removed from their home "which provides 24-hour non-medical care and supervision to children, provides services to a specific client group and maintains a structured environment, with such services provided at least in part by staff employed by the licensee."

PROBATION- the status of a delinquent youth under court ordered supervision within the community, with specific conditions such as school attendance, the wearing of an electronic ankle monitor, refraining from interaction with other youth on probation, drug testing, etc. Failure to obey the conditions of probation may result in new charges and/or detention.

PLACEMENT- court ordered residential assignments in both the delinquency and dependency systems, which may "be secure and prison-like or have a more open setting, like group homes or foster care."

CAMP- refers to juvenile boot camps, a type of juvenile corrections facility.

I live wherever **DCFS** puts me. Last time I was in a group home with 60 girls; there were nine or ten girls in a unit. It was a level 12 facility. I'm the oldest. I lived with my mom until I was 13. My mom was using **meth** and was neglective. She would leave us at grandpa's with nothing to wear or eat and go off with her boyfriends for days or weeks. I'm **dual**. They might be terminating my dependency case. I was arrested on drinking charges—**MIP**— and **resisting arrest**. I was living with my mom for while and her boyfriend. I have two younger siblings from a different dad. I went to my grandma and my younger siblings went to their grandma. I went to a **foster home** with two kids of her own and two other foster kids. I stayed there for two months. Then I was hospitalized for **cutting**. I don't remember how long... months. I haven't cut since I was 13. Then I went to another foster home for two

months, then the hospital, and then my mom's friend took me in when she married my uncle. Then I went **AWOL** from a group home where I was staying for seven months. Then went back, then I went to a foster home for three months, and then went AWOL but turned myself in again. Then it was another foster home—AWOLed, returned, and then another group home. It was messed. Another group home for eight months then on **probation** last year. In January, I was locked up here and then went to a rehab **placement** for three months. It's a nine-month program, but I went AWOL after three. They caught me and I went to another group home... somewhere... nowhere. When I go AWOL I go to my boyfriend's house or friend's or people's houses. I always had a friend to sleep with or I would stay in a park or an abandoned house. I hit rock bottom when I was using meth. I was given it by this guy, a friend who I was hanging out with. I've actually done meth with my mother, but she's clean now. They wanted to send me to **camp** for nine months. But I get the time I spent here and this counts as probation time. So I might only spend six months.

-Z.B., Age 17

I have been here for 12 days. This is my second time here. I've been to LP over 10 times and Sylmar once. I am here mostly for **violations of probation**. Now I am here for **running away** from **placement**. I got a warning first. I've been in a lot of placements. Never been in **foster homes**, just placements. The placements are pretty bad. Some have six beds, some 32. I was 11 or 12 the first time I went to one. I live with my grandma, my second oldest brother and my grandma's boyfriend. My grandma is about to give up **custody** of me and give it to my dad. He lives in Lancaster. He just got out of prison for two **attempted murders**. He came to visit me in placement and said he wants me. My original charge was **petty theft** then just violations of probation, **truancy**, **AWOL**. I had a **bad UA**—I was using **crystal**. The first time I was raped by my brother was when I was seven. I only started prostituting recently, when I was **on the run**. I ran into this pimp. He beat me. He told me I was going to be with him. I was there for three weeks. They are going to transfer me from Long Beach to Compton, for **STAR court**. It is a court for kids that are **sex trafficked**.

-U., Age 15

VIOLATION OF PROBATION- failure to obey the conditions of one's probation as set forth by the court, which may result in new charges and/or confinement.

RUNNING AWAY- a status offense that can bring a child into conflict with law enforcement, juvenile court, detention, or dependency court, depending on the runaway's circumstances; running away often leads children to commit more serious crimes in order to survive.

PLACEMENT- court ordered residential assignments in both the delinquency and dependency systems, which may "be secure and prison-like or have a more open setting, like group homes or foster care."

FOSTER HOME- a single-family home placement in the child welfare system "in which a child is raised by someone other than their natural or adoptive parent" and lives with the caretaker's family.

CUSTODY- refers to the responsibility to care, control, and make decisions for a child.

ATTEMPTED MURDER- the crime of attempting to kill another person without cause or justification, proven by substantial steps being taken towards committing the crime.

PETTY THEFT- theft of goods or money valued at less than a specific amount designated by the jurisdiction (e.g. less than $500).

TRUANCY- the status offense of repeated absence from school, which breaks compulsory education laws in the U.S.

AWOL- an acronym originating from the military meaning Absent Without Leave; in the context of dependency refers to a minor leaving their assigned placement without permission.

BAD UA- a bad urine analysis test, meaning one tested positive for illicit substances.

CRYSTAL- slang for methamphetamine.

ON THE RUN- avoiding contact with authorities; a term generally used for fugitives, synonymous with "on the lam."

STAR COURT- in Los Angeles County, stands for Succeeding Through Achievement and Resilience Court, a specialized court that provides multidimensional intervention services for underage victims of sex trafficking.

SEX TRAFFICKING- "recruitment, harboring, transportation, provision, or obtaining of a person for the purpose of a commercial sex act."

The three main detention facilities in B.U.'s jurisdiction.

CRYSTAL- slang for methamphetamine.

METH- short for methamphetamine, an extremely addictive stimulant drug.

ARYAN BROTHERHOOD- a white supremacist gang.

GANG AFFILIATED- to be part of a gang, friends or family with someone in a gang, or to act for the benefit of a gang; to be declared gang affiliated by law enforcement can result in increased supervision in the streets or gang enhancement charges added onto other criminal charges.

PLACEMENT- court ordered residential assignments in both the delinquency and dependency systems, which may "be secure and prison-like or have a more open setting, like group homes or foster care."

DETENTION- "Usually refers to the placement of a youth in a secure facility under court authority at some point between the time of referral to court intake and case disposition." Post-dispositional detention is at times necessary for reasons including "awaiting placement, short-term sentencing to detention, or being a danger to self or others."

DRUG RECORD- one's history of drug use and drug offenses.

RUNNING AWAY- a status offense that can bring a child into conflict with law enforcement, juvenile court, detention, or dependency court, depending on the runaway's circumstances; running away often leads children to commit more serious crimes in order to survive.

LOCKDOWN TREATMENT- a secure residential placement for mental health or drug rehabilitation, in which youth are confined for the duration of their treatment.

SHOPLIFTING- "theft of merchandise from a store or business establishment."

STAR COURT- in Los Angeles County, stands for Succeeding Through Achievement and Resilience Court, a specialized court that provides multidimensional intervention services for underage victims of sex trafficking.

THE LIFE- can refer generally to life outside of the law, hustling, or can be used more specifically to refer to selling drugs, prostituting, participating in gangs.

I've been here three times. I've been in all three: Central, Sylmar and LP. I was 13 when I was charged with **crystal**. 14 when I went into the system. My mom... I don't live with her anymore. She's on drugs—I don't know what. I was given **meth** by a guy who was in his 30's. He was my boyfriend. He gave me some weed and then meth. He started abusing me physically, emotionally and sexually. He made me prostitute. I've been in and out of prison. My dad is in prison in Pelican Bay. In 2000 he shot at some cops. I don't have any **gang affiliation**. I ran away from my first **placement** at age 14. I was in the **detention** before that for seven months. I been to Kirby Center—a mental health facility. They put me there

for my **drug record** and for **running away**. They wanted me in **lockdown**. I used to take anti-depressants, but not in here yet. I just came in last night. I was with my pimp. I had $100 cash on me and they caught me for **shoplifting** a $20 pair of shorts. I was 12 years old when this older guy manipulated me. Lot of bad things happened that year. I was bullied at school. I snuck out of the house. On my way home, I got raped by five guys at about 2 a.m. I shouldn't have been out at that hour and I shouldn't have been doing drugs, so I guess I am partially responsible. My mom is addicted to drugs. She recently relapsed. I don't have a grandma. My grandpa put his hands on me the wrong way so I don't talk to him anymore. I think I will go to **STAR court**. It's for girls involved in **the life**. If I can stay in placement and not run away, maybe I can make it.

-B.U., Age 15

HOUSE ARREST- "confinement to one's home or another specified location instead of incarceration in a jail or prison," most often enforced with an ankle monitor.

CUTTING- a type of self-injury that is often the result of attempting to cope with intense emotions and problems for which the cutter doesn't have the skills to overcome alone.

PROBATION VIOLATION- failure to obey the conditions of one's probation as set forth by the court, which may result in new charges and/or confinement.

PLACEMENT- court ordered residential assignments in both the delinquency and dependency systems, which may "be secure and prison-like or have a more open setting, like group homes or foster care."

FELONY- a serious crime, characterized under federal law and many state statutes as any offense punishable by imprisonment in excess of one year.

BATTERY- an intentional act causing harmful, offensive or sexual contact with the body of another person.

ASSAULT- though what exactly constitutes an assault varies by jurisdiction, it generally refers to the crime of causing another fear that "he/she is about to suffer physical harm," with the degree of the assault depending on how much harm was caused.

CRIMINAL INTENT- a factor in establishing that an action was criminal that "involves a conscious decision on the part of one party to injure or deprive another."

I was born in Chicago. I moved here when I was 11 or 12. I went into foster family when I was three. I live with my mom, my biological sister, foster sister and foster brother. First my mom was living with her boyfriend and then she met another man. They got married when I was six or seven. I didn't like him. I just got a negative vibe from him. I was abused by my foster mom and him. Physical abuse from my mom and sexual abuse from him. That's why I had the negative vibe. I told her but she didn't believe me. I didn't tell anyone else. When we were moving he didn't want to come out here so he stayed in Chicago. My mom had some family out here. I was bullied in school so I took a butcher knife to school

with me and they freaked. I'm in here waiting for a court date. First time they put me on **house arrest**. I heard my mom talking shit about me on the phone so I started **cutting** myself. Then she told the **probation officer** I was cutting myself. She told them to bring me here. Ever since then I have been in the system, moving from **placement** to placement. I didn't do any drugs. Only weed and alcohol. The problem I got is the knife was a **felony charge**. They have me at **battery, assault, criminal intent** now. My mother doesn't want me anymore so she signed the papers to give me up. I was in a situation before I took the weapon to school. I was picked up and put into placement. I was stressed out. People kept bothering me. I just electrified. I've been here since the day after Christmas. I talked to different therapists and tell them what happened. They say they know and they understand what it feels like. But they don't know what it feels like to be me. They just don't know at all.

-B.F., Age 15

I am half Yankton Sioux and half Japanese. I'm cute; it lets me get away with a lot. I think they're going to put me in **DCFS**, because there is abuse in my house from my brothers. A lot of physical abuse, not sexual. They hit me whenever they feel mad. I have nine brothers and two sisters, all from the same mom, some different dads. The boys that hit me are 16, 17, 18, 20, 22, and 24. I really wasn't going to school. My mom didn't have time to take me to school and would say, "Wait until next week." A year ago, I went regularly to seventh grade. I've been here four months. I was brought in for **burglary** and some gang activity... So it's also **receiving stolen property**, **distribution**, and **felony** for a gun. My **homeboy** is 17. He had a gun, but they were searching him, so he gave it to me. So they put a felony of a gun on me. I plan to change when I get out. My mom has me do a lot of Native American practices. We go to sundances and powwows. I haven't heard from my biological dad. My mom was supposed to visit me today, but I don't know if they will keep their word. I've been to **camp** in Florida and in North Dakota. I was with my tía, hanging with my cousins when we got in trouble—a kind of felony. I've been through so much, I don't bother to remember it 'cause it's all so bad. I think it was **identity theft**. I stole some people's credit cards. Sometimes they would leave that stuff in their cars. I'm here now for school **vandalism, battery**, and charges from teachers that I was threatening them and hitting other kids. I was 14. Last year they sent me to boarding school for Native American kids in North Dakota—a school called Circle of Nations. Then I was locked up for two months. I got a dirty drug test for **meth** and they brought me here ever since. I'm on level three, **one-on-one**. I have hallucinations. I have a psychotic disorder and I'm schizophrenic. They have me talking to a mental health counselor.

`-O., Age 15`

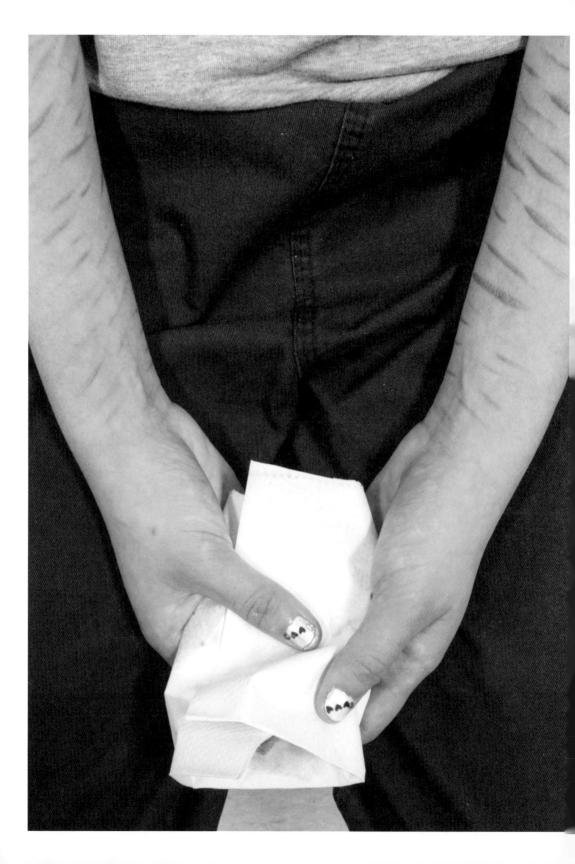

This is my third time here. I started coming here when I was 16. I'm here now waiting for **placement**. I have some addiction problems. And I am also a **cutter**. I was abused when I was a little kid. My mom would make me eat soap or beat me with a spatula or a metal soup thing. I was born drug addicted. I was positive on drugs when I came out. I went into **foster care**. Then I was adopted at age three. My mom died of cancer and my dad is in Mexico. I was abused when I was in my adopted home by my mom; she was the one that made me eat soap. I **ran away** when I was 13 and that's when I started being sexually abused. I was adopted with my two brothers and two sisters. All five of us biological siblings were adopted together. They already had two adopted kids. I'm the black sheep. I would always get beaten when something was not right or I wouldn't clean my room. My mother would just beat us. My sister, who is a year older, decided to call the child abuse hotline. They had somebody from **DCFS** come out and investigate, but they didn't see anything wrong. My brothers lied and the beating continued. Then we ran to my sister's boyfriend's house. I was 13 when everything happened. My mother believed in discipline; we called it torture. My dad would leave the house so he wouldn't hear us screaming. When I was 13, I would smoke weed and drink. When I got to 14 I started taking pills. At 15 or 16 I started doing **coke** and **meth**... then **PCP**. I would get it from my **homies**. It was just there. I'm here at 18 because I still have a **juvenile record** to finish. A **second-degree commercial burglary**. I'm supposed to do nine months to three years, but I've already completed most of my second year. I don't remember when I started cutting. I've basically been in **lock up** for three years. No one has ever visited me. I have been locked up and my family has forgotten. My older sister is locked up too. She's in for drugs, **public intoxication**, **robbery**, and I think a gun. I kick it with gang members, but they don't have it on my chart. My DCFS case was terminated when I was 16 and I went back with my mom. I just have to do a nine-month program then I'm on my own. I was going to live with my girlfriend. They have my chart **G-coded**; it means gay. So I can't have a roommate or the roommate also has to be gay. Everybody is pretty tolerant of gay people here, 'cause most of them are.

-B.H., Age 18

PLACEMENT- court ordered residential assignments in both the delinquency and dependency systems, which may "be secure and prison-like or have a more open setting, like group homes or foster care."

CUTTER- a person who self-mutilates, which is often the result of attempting to cope with intense emotions and problems for which the cutter doesn't have the skills to overcome alone.

FOSTER CARE- "the informal and formal custodial care of children outside of their own biological family home when their parents are unable, unwilling, or prohibited from caring for them."

RUNNING AWAY- a status offense that can bring a child into conflict with law enforcement, juvenile court, detention, or dependency court, depending on the runaway's circumstances; running away often leads children to commit more serious crimes in order to survive.

DCFS- stands for Department of Child and Family Services, the governmental agency serving vulnerable children and families in some states.

COKE- slang for cocaine, a highly addictive stimulant drug.

METH- short for methamphetamine, also known as crystal meth, crystal, ice; an extremely addictive stimulant drug.

PCP- Phencyclidine, also known as "angel dust;" a schedule II controlled substance that acts as a dissociative anesthetic and is known to cause many adverse psychological effects.

HOMIES- close friends who have your back and are there for you in times of need.

JUVENILE RECORD- "records kept by the juvenile court with information and documents relevant to a youth's delinquency charges."

SECOND DEGREE Commercial Burglary- in California, burglary of commercial spaces, i.e. not residential spaces, is charged as second degree burglary; see also Burglary.

LOCK UP- refers to incarceration.

PUBLIC INTOXICATION- also called drunk and disorderly or drunk in public, a charge alleging a person is drunk or intoxicated to the point of causing some disruption of public space.

ROBBERY- a crime of theft "by force or intimidation."

G-CODED- refers to an inmate's file having a flag because he or she is homosexual, and therefore cannot have a cellmate.

PROBATION OFFICER- the public official supervising youth on probation, with whom youth have regular meetings.

CUSTODY- refers to the responsibility to care, control, and make decisions for a child; can also refer to being held by law enforcement (i.e. "in police custody").

WARRANT- "a written order issued by a judicial officer or other authorized person commanding a law enforcement officer to perform some act incident to the administration of justice... most commonly, police use warrants as the basis to arrest a suspect and to conduct a search of property for evidence of a crime."

DCFS- stands for Department of Child and Family Services, the governmental agency serving vulnerable children and families in some states.

VOLUNTARY PLACEMENT- "an out-of-home placement of a minor by or with participation of a State agency, after the parents or guardians of the minor have requested the assistance of the agency and signed a voluntary placement agreement."

FOSTER HOME- a single-family home placement in the child welfare system "in which a child is raised by someone other than their natural or adoptive parent" and lives with the caretaker's family.

GROUP HOME- an out-of-home placement for kids who have been removed from their home "which provides 24-hour non-medical care and supervision to children, provides services to a specific client group and maintains a structured environment, with such services provided at least in part by staff employed by the licensee."

RUNNING AWAY- a status offense that can bring a child into conflict with law enforcement, juvenile court, detention, or dependency court, depending on the runaway's circumstances; running away often leads children to commit more serious crimes in order to survive.

WEIGHT- slang for a high volume of drugs.

HIT HOUSES- to rob a house.

CRIMINAL THREATS- in California, the willful threatening to commit a crime which could cause great bodily injury or death.

ASSAULT- though what exactly constitutes an assault varies by jurisdiction, it generally refers to the crime of causing another fear that "he/she is about to suffer physical harm," with the degree of the assault depending on how much harm was caused.

GREAT BODILY INJURY- a charge of causing significant physical injury or injury that causes permanent damage, usually accompanied with another more general charge (i.e. assault with great bodily injury), and significantly increases the length of the sentence if convicted.

POSSESSION OF A FIREARM/DEADLY WEAPON- refers to the crime of carrying a gun or other object designed to inflict death, either because the defendant is a minor, on probation, or fails to follow a state's laws regarding legal gun possession (e.g. obtaining permits).

JUVIE CHARGES- charges that are litigated in juvenile court as opposed to adult criminal court.

EXPUNGE- to remove or seal someone's arrest and conviction records, a practice that varies by age, type of crime, and jurisdiction; expungement is important because a criminal record can pose difficulties for ex-offenders seeking employment, residence, etc.

I'm in dependency and delinquency. Delinquency is in the lead right now. I have a **probation officer** and a **social worker**. They don't really talk to each other. You can see the hospital where I was born from here. I was born in the sheriff's part. My mother was in **custody**. She had **warrants** out for her arrest. She's in rehab now. I don't know my dad. I went with my grandma growing up. I went on and off with my mother who was a drug addict and with my grandmother who abused me physically. She threw knives at me. She locked me in my room for four or five days at a time. She gave me a bucket and I would have to shit in it. I pretty much raised myself. I like just being by myself. I have no self-pity. What happened, happened. I can't change it. The past is the past, but I can be successful in the future. Even **DCFS** left the problem. My aunt told them later what was happening, but when it was happening, nothing happened. Then my grandmother asked for **voluntary placement** for me. My mother is off in rehab as we speak. She continues to struggle. I pray for her every night. I was out of grandma's custody when I was six or seven. I went to **foster homes**. I think I was in 13 different foster homes and six different **group homes**. That was over seven years. There was never any man in my life, except the men that came back with my mom for an hour or a night or two. It's been a struggle. I **ran away** because I couldn't handle my mother. I knew it would fall apart. When I was 13, I started selling drugs—some real **weight**—and pimping. Then I started **hitting houses**. They charged me with **criminal threats**, **assault** with **great bodily injury**, and a **possession of a deadly weapon**. I've been here a year and a half. I just plead guilty last week. I think I'm gonna be sentenced in two days to **juvie charges**. I feel like doors have been opened. If I do good, things can be **expunged**, except for the assault with great bodily injury.

-B.D., Age 16

I came in yesterday. It was my first time. I was at Saturday school at middle school. You go there when you have low grades and they help you with math and reading and it raises your grade. There were a lot of kids there that were going to hurt me. So I brought a weapon on campus, a gun. I got it from my dad's cabinet. I just wanted to protect myself. I'd never been in trouble until yesterday. The gun dropped out of my pocket and the teacher called the police. My mom and dad came today. They're praying that I get out on Wednesday, which is my court day. I should have told my mom or dad about what was going on at school, but I was scared. My mom helps out kids at my school with special needs. I think they're gonna put me

in a different school. I hope they do and get me away from these kids who are in a gang. They are all eighth graders. They brought weapons to school on Saturday too.

-B.B., Age 12

I've been here three months this time. I'm from South Central. I've been here four times before. The first time I was 14. I was with my sister, her boyfriend and her best friend. She's 26; he's 31. This time I'm here for fighting which is a **violation of parole**. I live with my mom. My older sisters are out of the house. My dad lives in St. Louis. He came from St. Louis to visit me. Both my sisters, my grandma and my mom all visit me. My mom's ex-husband physically abused me. He would slap, punch and kick me. It was real complicated for her. She was in love with him but he was beating me. That's when I would start getting **PVs** for **running away** to friends' houses. All my charges are for running away. The first time I was here for a couple of weeks; the second time I was here for a year. That's how the system is. Then they put me on **house arrest** with an **ankle monitor**. I cut it off and ran away. They're trying to charge me now with **attempted murder**. They say I went at my ex-boyfriend with a knife. He's 36 and he called the police on me. He's on **parole**. The county provides counseling for people in abusive relationships, but my mom and I don't go to programs on **the outs**. As soon as I'm out, I'm not going down that same path. The system is bad, but that's how the system is.

-L.T., Age 17

VIOLATION OF PAROLE- failure to obey the conditions of one's parole as set forth by the court, which may result in new charges and/or detention.

PV- stands for Parole Violation.

RUNNING AWAY- a status offense that can bring a child into conflict with law enforcement, juvenile court, detention, or dependency court, depending on the runaway's circumstances; running away often leads children to commit more serious crimes in order to survive.

HOUSE ARREST- "confinement to one's home or another specified location instead of incarceration in a jail or prison," most often enforced with an ankle monitor.

ANKLE MONITOR- refers to the electric monitoring device worn around the ankle, which is used to track the movement of individuals on house arrest, probation, or parole for the sake of supervision.

ATTEMPTED MURDER- the crime of attempting to kill another person without cause or justification, proven by substantial steps being taken towards committing the crime.

PAROLE- though youth may use the terms "parole" and "probation" interchangeably, parole refers to the court-ordered community supervision of individuals who have been released from confinement prior to the end of their original sentence.

THE OUTS- short for "the outside," often used by people in locked institutions when referring to life outside of institutional settings.

Yeah, I'm an adult, but I got picked up on a few **warrants**. They were two warrants; one was a **bench warrant**. I've just been **on the run** basically. I did **meth** and **heroin**. I moved in with my boyfriend and the **feds** were watching him. We tried to escape. There was a high-speed chase. He gave me the drugs he had because he thought I was a minor. He ended up getting 25 years because he already had some **credit card frauds**. I took the dope for him. It wasn't even that much, only a **tenner**. That's less than a quarter ounce of meth. I was homeless living in Plaza Park. We would break into cars and sleep in them. He got me back onto heroin. I hope I get out next week. They're holding me longer than they should have because the judge wants me to have a better sober plan. I was in Van Nuys Live, Prime Time, Rodford Hall, Narcotics Anonymous—they're all programs with a lot of meetings. I live with my mom. I haven't lived with my dad since I was 16. There was a **restraining order** put on him. He was gone from when I was three to 15; then he came back and said he had been sober for five years, and he convinced my mom for her, me, and my sisters to move in with him. Then when I was 15 he introduced me to meth, and he started sexually abusing me. It was the same pattern—when I was a baby my mom said I would sit there all day in my crib when she went to work, and he wouldn't change me or feed me. He was a violent **tweaker** and **crackhead**. My mom said the last time she saw him she had to escape through a bathroom window. I studied at Paul Mitchell cosmetology school for about five months and then I dropped out. I don't get any **AA** or **NA** here. I wish they had something. Before I got in here, I was in the middle of psychosis from meth. I would hear stuff. Once I hid under a table for three days. Another time I nodded off in a gas station bathroom and they found a needle in my arm. They had me in a **holding cell** in Ventura for prostitution, and then they realized the warrants and they moved me. I was living with a crazy boyfriend who locked me in a hotel and starved me for four days. I was in a program for detoxing, then I ended up leaving, took the first bus to anywhere, went to the first person I saw who I thought would smoke shit. Next thing you know I'm homeless, shooting heroin and meth again, and then back in the system. I've been two months sober now here, but it's hard because they won't give me any Suboxone or Methadone.

-G.E., Age 18

WARRANT- "a written order issued by a judicial officer or other authorized person commanding a law enforcement officer to perform some act incident to the administration of justice... most commonly, police use warrants as the basis to arrest a suspect and to conduct a search of property for evidence of a crime."

BENCH WARRANT- a warrant issued by a judge when an individual fails to adhere to the rules of the court, e.g. not appearing to a court date or probation meeting, which enables an officer to immediately arrest an individual during a stop.

ON THE RUN- avoiding contact with authorities; a term generally used for fugitives, synonymous with "on the lam."

METH- short for methamphetamine, also known as crystal meth, crystal, ice; an extremely addictive stimulant drug.

HEROIN- an extremely addictive opioid drug .

FEDS- short for federal law enforcement.

In many cases where a group of people are caught committing crime(s), the blame will be put on the youngest of the group with the logic that the younger one is, the less harsh their punishment.

CREDIT CARD FRAUD- "a form of identity theft that involves the unauthorized taking of another's credit card information for the purpose of charging purchases to the account or removing funds from it.

TENNER- 10 dollars worth of something, most often some kind of drug.

Various addiction recovery and rehabilitation centers in G.E.'s area.

RESTRAINING ORDER- "a command of the court issued upon the filing of an application for an injunction," which prohibits individuals from performing certain acts, such as carrying out threats or coming within a specific distance of an individual who feels threatened.

TWEAKER- slang for a person who is heavily addicted to drugs.

CRACKHEAD- slang for a person who is heavily addicted to drugs, specifically crack.

AA- stands for Alcoholics Anonymous; a 12-step program that exists as an international mutual aid fellowship in which men and women meet regularly to share their experiences, help one another remain sober, and help other alcoholics achieve sobriety.

NA- stands for Narcotics Anonymous; a 12-step program in the tradition of AA for people who use narcotics.

HOLDING CELL- a courthouse cell where people awaiting to appear in court are held for short periods of time.

Suboxone and methadone are prescription medications used to treat opioid addiction and dependence.

BATTERY- an intentional act causing harmful, offensive or sexual contact with the body of another person.

ROBBERY- a crime of theft "by force or intimidation."

PLACEMENT- court ordered residential assignments in both the delinquency and dependency systems, which may "be secure and prison-like or have a more open setting, like group homes or foster care."

SHOPLIFTING- "theft of merchandise from a store or business establishment."

DCFS- stands for Department of Child and Family Services, the governmental agency serving vulnerable children and families in some states.

DETENTION- "Usually refers to the placement of a youth in a secure facility under court authority at some point between the time of referral to court intake and case disposition." Post-dispositional detention is at times necessary for reasons including "awaiting placement, short-term sentencing to detention, or being a danger to self or others."

CO- stands for correctional officer.

I'm reading *Forged by Fire*. I live with my mom and my sisters and my stepdad and my two dogs—Monday the girl and Tuesday the boy. I'm here for **battery** and **robbery**. I got in a fight with a kid on the block. I took his phone and his money. He had taken my little brother's PSP. The police came and took me. My mom looked pretty confused. I was in a **placement** with 55 kids. I was there for seven months. I was taken from my mom for fighting and they thought I was in a gang. I was there when I was eleven.

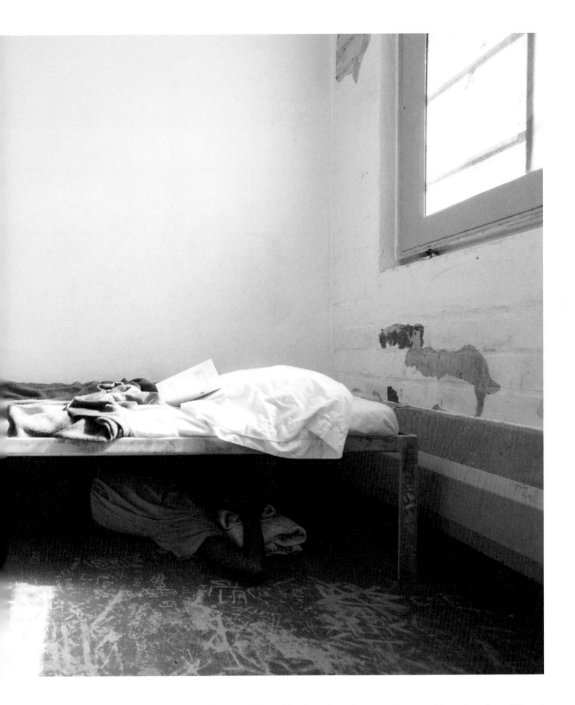

The second time I was in here was for **shoplifting.** Now I am here because they want to put me in a different placement and they can't find the right one. Now I have been here four months. I am here for **DCFS** as well as **detention**. I like to be under the bed. The **COs** are like hawks and I am the mouse or the rabbit. When they look down from the window, I don't want them to see me. I feel comfortable when I am by myself. I like sleeping under the bed so people don't look in the window at me all the time.

-N.K., Age 12

I'm in for a **PV**. I violated by not going to school for three days. The original charges were **armed robbery**. It was with another kid and a knife. I go to court tomorrow. I think they might put me in **placement**. My grandma visited yesterday. My mom came earlier for church. They're both sad 'n all when they see me. I'm in seventh grade. There are 33 kids in my class. I don't know my dad; I never met him. My mom works at a construction store. I was at Disneyland when I was two, but I never saw the Pacific Ocean. Yeah, I've been to the beach. Oh—I didn't know that was the Pacific Ocean. This is my fifth time here. I'm always here for PVs.

My first time here was three years ago, when I was nine. I was here for a week. That was the original charge. I took a scooter from a kid. They said it was worth $600. Then the other four times have been PVs.

-Y.C., Age 12

PV- Probation Violation; failure to obey the conditions of one's probation as set forth by the court, which may result in new charges and/or confinement.

ARMED ROBBERY- the crime of theft "by force or intimidation" with a deadly weapon; depending on jurisdiction may be charged as aggravated robbery.

PLACEMENT- court ordered residential assignments in both the delinquency and dependency systems, which may "be secure and prison-like or have a more open setting, like group homes or foster care."

I've been there 19 years. I normally do the night shift. Now I'm doing overtime on an ordinary shift. I've been working 16 hours straight. I get about $34 to $35 an hour when I'm doing overtime and staring salary is 20-something an hour. With these little kids, you have to be patient and repetitive. Older kids, you have to keep an eye on steadily; there can be a fight out in a matter of seconds. Most of these kids are **602s**, wards of the court. Not **300s**, they are dependency. With these kids it's repeat, repeat, repeat. The youngest one in here is 11 years old. Kids that young we deal with **one-on-one**. We keep a very watchful eye on them.

-K.S., Juvenile Correction Officer, Age 44

602- refers to section 602 of the California Welfare and Institutions Code, which states that kids who break the law, if found guilty, can become a ward of the court.

300- refers to section 300 of the California Welfare and Institutions Code which states that children who have been subject to abuse and neglect can be taken into the custody of the dependency court.

ONE-ON-ONE- 24-hour observation where a guard is appointed to constantly watch an inmate, typically assigned for youth who are perceived to be a liability to themselves.

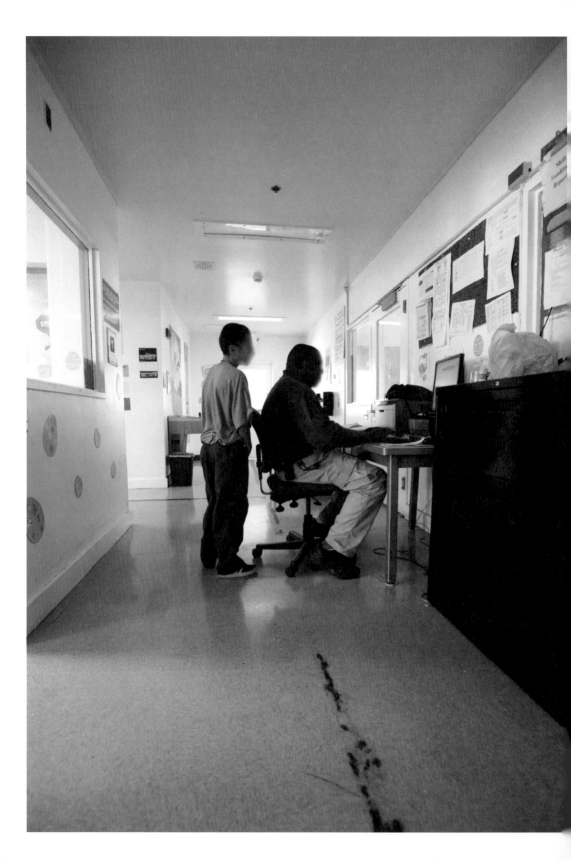

I've been doing this 26 years. Always juvie. I'm 58 years old.
The real rehab is done in here in bursts of two or three months.
Here might be the most intensive time they are going to school.
There are five kids in here today. This may be my last group that
I'll shepherd through here. Some of them just stop by, but others
I know I'll see again and again. It's about the economics and the
family structure. It's not the best for them. This is home for a lot
of them. Sure, there are success stories. There was one guy who
was here in '93, big Hispanic kid who ended up a realtor. There's
one who ended up playing for Washington State. But a lot of times
we're the safety net for them. The structure is just not out there
to hold them and help them. For some of these kids, I'm the first
time they've actually seen a black man working. After 26 years,
I make almost $6000 a month. I could make more in the field, but
I like it just fine in here with these kids.

- F.Z., Juvenile Correction Officer, Age 58

163

I've been here six weeks. No one visits me. The first time I was here I was 16. They charged me with **loitering with intent to prostitute**. I was 15 when I started. I met a guy on a train. He started telling me about **the life** and how I could make money for him. I didn't know he was a pimp. I was living at home and going to school. I was living with my mom and my grandma. I knew I was in **sex trafficking**; I was doing it for the guy. It was by choice, he didn't force me to do it. I was in love with him. He had one other girl working for him. Yeah, I was 15 and he was 25, but I knew what I was doing. The police came and talked to me here.

They said he's been putting girls in the hospital. I'm in the **STAR court**. I go home on Wednesdays to Las Vegas. **Probation** will drive me to Las Vegas. My grandmother has legal **custody** of me. My mother is on drugs. She left my little brothers and me on the street when I was eight. She lost her legs because she is diabetic. She's had a triple bypass. She's 35. My grandma is paralyzed on the left side from a stroke. She's been taking care of me since I was six months old. She gets an **SSI check** for my little brother and me. She's been doing really well. She's my guardian angel. I love her dearly. I've never known peace in my life and I've never known a mother's love. I haven't been to school since I was 15. I can't wait to go home and try to become a normal teenager.

-U.K., Age 17

I've been doing this for 17 years. I usually work Unit K. It's older kids 15 to 17. I work eight-hour shifts. I am a senior detention service officer. They call me "Mr. I;" I call them by their last name. They are raised by their grandparents, and the grandparents are tired. They have enough energy to tell the kids what not to do, but don't have the strength to do positive things with the kids. They don't listen to the grandparents. They go from here to smaller **placements** or **camps** for three or six or nine months. They have to have mental health services. They have **wraparound services** that help them when they get out, but kids have to have the parents help them get to these services. If the parents aren't engaged it's useless. Parents have to be stable enough to be able to help. They have to be there to allow services to help. You have to spend the time with these kids to give them structure. They love to know what is going on. They need to know they are going to be able to eat and they need to know it is expected to do their home-work. Anything that throws off their routine or their structure puts them at risk. They are never told they can be leaders. They are easily swayed to follow other negative paths. You need to create services that reunify and bring in the families. Families need medical services, food services. They have to have something for their kids and for themselves. Most of our kids are involved in gangs and **tagging** crews. Tagging crews focus on graffiti, but they quickly become territorial and become more aggressive when other crews tag over their tags. It is a slippery slope from tagging crews to gangs.

-U.I., Juvenile Correction Officer

PLACEMENT- court ordered residential assignments in both the delinquency and dependency systems, which may "be secure and prison-like or have a more open setting, like group homes or foster care."

CAMP- refers to juvenile boot camps, a type of juvenile corrections facility.

WRAPAROUND SERVICES- "a youth-guided, family-driven team planning process that provides coordinated and individualized community-based services for youths and their families to achieve positive outcomes."

TAGGING- the practice of quickly marking a signature, symbol, or sign in public spaces akin to graffiti, which can sometimes be used to mark territory.

This is my first time. I was just **AWOL** for a few days from a **foster home**. I'm there with my biological brother and my foster mom's daughter and another foster girl. I was with my aunt for two years. I was 11 when I was taken from my house. I didn't know what was going on. My mom didn't know what it meant for me to be **detained** either. The cops found a weed plant in my brother's room and then they started investigating my mom and my stepdad. They smoked **crack**. **DCFS** took me, my two brothers, and my little sister into custody. My mom was pregnant and when the baby was born they took the baby away. My dad lives in Mexico. I'm not sure if my mom has **papers**. My foster home is pretty good. There was really no reason for me to go AWOL. I was picked up for **truancy** but I had gotten into trouble for **vandalism**—graffiti. Putting white out on a bench in the park right next to school, during school. I lied to the police about what my name was. They handcuffed me. I went to court two months ago and they gave me **probation**. Then I **violated** by **running away**. I'm in ninth grade. My mom was in **AA** rehab. They want me to go to a **group home** when I'm doing well in the foster home. I stopped going to school in January. I tried going to **continuation school**. I missed a court date and they issued a **warrant**. I'm not even sure why. I didn't want to go to court. I was going through stuff with my mom— she talked to me about her drug abuse and how she couldn't stop.

-Z.O., Age 15

AWOL- an acronym originating from the military meaning Absent Without Leave; in the context of dependency refers to a minor leaving their assigned placement without permission.

FOSTER HOME- a single-family home placement in the child welfare system "in which a child is raised by someone other than their natural or adoptive parent" and lives with the caretaker's family.

DETAIN- "Usually refers to the placement of a youth in a secure facility under court authority at some point between the time of referral to court intake and case disposition." Post-dispositional detention is at times necessary for reasons including "awaiting placement, short-term sentencing to detention, or being a danger to self or others."

CRACK- "a form of cocaine that has been processed to make a rock crystal (also called 'freebase cocaine') that can be smoked.

DCFS- stands for Department of Child and Family Services, the governmental agency serving vulnerable children and families in some states.

PAPERS- refers to legal documentation that permits one to be in the country.

TRUANCY- the status offense of repeated absence from school, which breaks compulsory education laws in the U.S.

VANDALISM- "willful or malicious destruction or defacement of public or private property."

PROBATION- the status of a delinquent youth under court ordered supervision within the community, with specific conditions such as school attendance, the wearing of an electronic ankle monitor, refraining from interaction with other youth on probation, drug testing, etc. Failure to obey the conditions of probation may result in new charges and/or detention.

PROBATION VIOLATION- failure to obey the conditions of one's probation as set forth by the court, which may result in new charges and/or detention.

RUNNING AWAY- a status offense that can bring a child into conflict with law enforcement, juvenile court, detention, or dependency court, depending on the runaway's circumstances; running away often leads children to commit more serious crimes in order to survive.

AA- stands for Alcoholics Anonymous; a 12-step program that exists as an international mutual aid fellowship in which men and women meet regularly to share their experiences, help one another remain sober, and help other alcoholics achieve sobriety.

GROUP HOME- an out-of-home placement for kids who have been removed from their home "which provides 24-hour non-medical care and supervision to children, provides services to a specific client group and maintains a structured environment, with such services provided at least in part by staff employed by the licensee."

CONTINUATION SCHOOL- an alternative high school program "for students who are sixteen years of age or older, have not graduated from high school, are still required to attend school, and who are at risk of not graduating."

WARRANT- "a written order issued by a judicial officer or other authorized person commanding a law enforcement officer to perform some act incident to the administration of justice... most commonly, police use warrants as the basis to arrest a suspect and to conduct a search of property for evidence of a crime."

This is my first time here. I've been here for five days. I was in Sylmar for five days also. I'm going to placement. When you go to **placement** you don't want to go to **Five Acres**. You're in your room all day there. I've never been in placement before. My mom visits me. So does my grandma. My dad is back in prison on a charge of **domestic violence**. One of his girlfriends charged him. I'm in 7th grade. The kid in the next cell was yelling, "fuck Blacks," so I started yelling "fuck Mexicans." He was saying he was going to beat me and every Black person up. He's a racist. I do nothing but count bricks here. It's boring. I think I may be here six months, I don't know. When I was at Sylmar I was at level three. I told them I wanted to hurt myself. I saw other kids walking around with staff and asked them how come. They said, "You just have to say you're thinking about hurting yourself and you get privileges." So I did it. But I regret it. I told them I

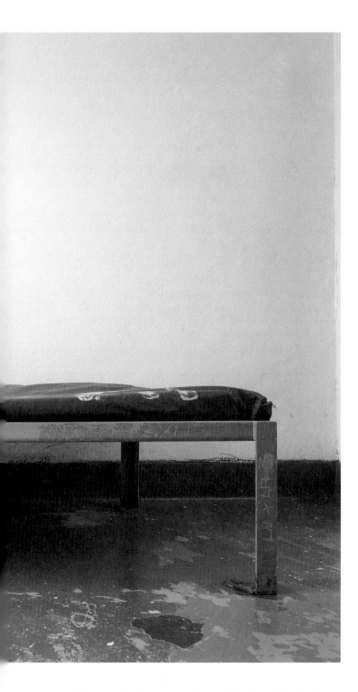

didn't mean it so they moved me to level two. But the kid in the next cell said the same thing and they took him off levels completely. After the stuff last night they shut off the water in the cells. So there is no water or toilet today. But they will turn it on again.

-U.Z., Age 12

PLACEMENT- court ordered residential assignments in both the delinquency and dependency systems, which may "be secure and prison-like or have a more open setting, like group homes or foster care."

5 ACRES- group home in Southern California.

DOMESTIC VIOLENCE- "any abusive, violent, coercive, forceful, or threatening act or word inflicted by one member of a family or household on another can constitute domestic violence."

In U.Z.'s county, levels at detention facilities refer to security level instead of privileges. Level three is constant observation, whereas inmates on level two are less closely monitored.

DUAL - the status of youth involved in both the dependency and delinquency systems (e.g. went from foster care to detention).

DAY ROOM - name for the common area of a wing or unit in a facility.

AWOL - an acronym originating from the military meaning Absent Without Leave; in the context of dependency refers to a minor leaving their assigned placement without permission.

TRUANCY - the status offense of repeated absence from school, which breaks compulsory education laws in the U.S.

FOSTER HOME - a single-family home placement in the child welfare system "in which a child is raised by someone other than their natural or adoptive parent" and lives with the caretaker's family.

DCFS - stands for Department of Child and Family Services, the governmental agency serving vulnerable children and families in some states.

COKE - slang for cocaine, a highly addictive stimulant drug.

RUNNING AWAY - a status offense that can bring a child into conflict with law enforcement, juvenile court, detention, or dependency court, depending on the runaway's circumstances; running away often leads children to commit more serious crimes in order to survive.

RESTRAINING ORDER - "a command of the court issued upon the filing of an application for an injunction," which prohibits individuals from performing certain acts, such as carrying out threats or coming within a specific distance of an individual who feels threatened.

GROUP HOME - an out-of-home placement for kids who have been removed from their home "which provides 24-hour non-medical care and supervision to children, provides services to a specific client group and maintains a structured environment, with such services provided at least in part by staff employed by the licensee."

SOCIAL WORKER - in the context of youth in the delinquency and dependency systems, most often refers to a case manager in investigations of child abuse and neglect; see also Case Manager.

ON THE RUN - avoiding contact with authorities; a term generally used for fugitives, synonymous with "on the lam."

SNITCH - to tell on someone; specifically giving law enforcement or some other authority incriminating information; one who tells on others or gives authorities incriminating information.

BATTERY - an intentional act causing harmful, offensive or sexual contact with the body of another person.

PCP - Phencyclidine, also known as "angel dust;" a schedule II controlled substance that acts as a dissociative anesthetic and is known to cause many adverse psychological effects.

B.E. refers to Alcoholics Anonymous (AA) and Narcotics Anonymous (NA) meetings. See AA and NA in Glossary.

RUNNING AWAY - a status offense that can bring a child into conflict with law enforcement, juvenile court, detention, or dependency court, depending on the runaway's circumstances; running away often leads children to commit more serious crimes in order to survive.

HEROIN - an extremely addictive opioid drug.

CRYSTAL - slang for methamphetamine; see Methamphetamine.

PROBATION - the status of a delinquent youth under court ordered supervision within the community, with specific conditions such as school attendance, the wearing of an electronic ankle monitor, refraining from interaction with other youth on probation, drug testing, etc. Failure to obey the conditions of probation may result in new charges and/or detention.

I'm **dual**. No one visits. I've been here five days. There is A/C in the day room but not in the cells. I live in Lancaster with my grandfather, mom, tío, and younger sister. My mom and me got into a physical altercation over me smoking some weed. She roughed me up so I went **AWOL** and stayed with my friend just around the block. My mom reported me missing. Then I went to school after being **truant** for three days with a busted lip, black eye, and a broken nose. When they saw how beat up I was they took my little sister and me away and put us in a **foster home** with this lady with two kids—a son and a granddaughter. My dad was incarcerated for 14 years. I was having attitude with my foster mom so **DCFS** put me living with my dad when he got out of prison. I was living with him and my half sister for four months. Then he raped me. My mom didn't believe me. He wasn't held behind bars; he was just walking around. Then when they found out, they re-incarcerated him for **coke** and being a pedophile. This was my biological dad. No one believed me and I **ran away** and had to find a police station by myself to report him. I was in junior high school. I went to a foster home. My little sister was able to go back home to my mom, but I have an **order** that I have to be separated from my mom for six months. They found me a place at a **group home**. I was there two months and I AWOLed. I made sure I had my plan straight and gave another kid $10 to help me. It took me a week to get where I was trying to go. My **social worker** knew I was **on the run** and she called my mom. My mom knew I was trying to get home and when I got there she **snitched** me out. I was standing on a corner in Lancaster at about 10 p.m. and a police officer asked what I was doing out after curfew. They took me to DCFS Headquarters and had me stay there overnight because they didn't have a place for me. Then they found me a group home and I was supposed to stay there for a month. I got in a fight with another girl and accidentally socked a security guard. I was at another place for nine months and then AWOLed—for a guy. Yeah, it's always for a guy. A guard told me I had to be in a different lunch period, and I pushed him, so that was a **battery**. I was on drugs a lot, doing weed, **PCP**, everything. There are no meetings here. In order to help me they told me I had to admit my addiction to myself and I wouldn't do that. At that point my mom didn't want me. I was living in an abandoned house for three weeks. I would go in an out of this boarded up house through a doggie door. Or I would sleep in a van. I'm here as a **runaway**. My first case is closed. I'm smart when I'm sober. I'm catching up on schoolwork a lot. I'm in 10th grade. I have two kids. The first I have from my dad when I was 14. The first thing he did when he got out of prison was rape me and get me pregnant. I didn't show until I was eight months. The baby was tiny, so I didn't know I was pregnant. I had irregular periods all the time anyway. I was still doing a lot of drugs, **heroin** and **crystal**. The baby was born three pounds eight ounces. I don't believe in setting goals, but I would like to stay sober. I'll get off **probation** as soon as possible. I want to build a relationship with my mother. I asked my mom for help, but she said I "should learn the hard way."

-B.E., Age 16

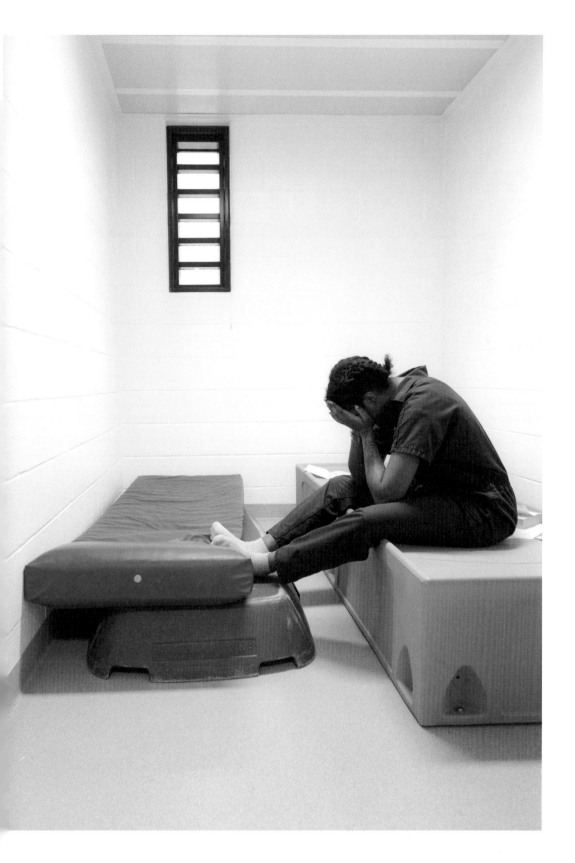

Nobody visits me. I've been in here four days. I am probably going home and will be on **probation**. I live with my great grandma who is my legal guardian. All my grandparents are dead and my mom is in and out of my life. I've seen my dad three times in my life. I've been with **DCFS** since day one. My great grandma took me. My mom was in a **foster home**. I was with her for about a year and then her foster mom told the police she was abusing me. My mom was 16 when I was born. I'm here because I **violated**. They say I was a **lookout** for something. But I have a clean record. But now I have to be in **placement** for six months and then on probation for a year. I can do it, especially if it is during school—it can go by really fast. I violated probation because I was **truant** from school for a day on my 16th birthday and drank with some friends. I'm just a normal teenager. I've never been to a rehab program and never needed one. I was going to school and doing well. I am **dual** but right now it's more probation because of the **VOP**. I got with the wrong crowd and I took responsibility for it. I need to be around the right people that help keep me up rather than drag me down. I understand that now. I've been going to school every day. My attitude toward my family has changed. I got distracted because of a boy. It happens. He was 18 and I was 14. We kept **running away** from my house. I was arrested a few times for **loitering**. He was protective of me. He ended up going to **county** for **burglary**. He must have really loved me because he got my name tattooed on his forearm really big. I'm not supposed to have any contact with him. His time is almost up. I need to put my life straight. Other girls here say, "If you love him, why don't you see him?"... but I'm not allowed and I don't want to violate for the next year and a half.

`-A.O., Age 16`

PROBATION- the status of a delinquent youth under court ordered supervision within the community, with specific conditions such as school attendance, the wearing of an electronic ankle monitor, refraining from interaction with other youth on probation, drug testing, etc. Failure to obey the conditions of probation may result in new charges and/or detention.

DCFS- stands for Department of Child and Family Services, the governmental agency serving vulnerable children and families in some states.

FOSTER HOME- a single-family home placement in the child welfare system "in which a child is raised by someone other than their natural or adoptive parent" and lives with the caretaker's family.

VIOLATION- generally refers to a probation or parole violation; see parole violation and probation violation.

LOOKOUT- a person who's job is to watch out for law enforcement or others while someone else or a group of people engage in some illicit activity, making them guilty by association.

PLACEMENT- court ordered residential assignments in both the delinquency and dependency systems, which may "be secure and prison-like or have a more open setting, like group homes or foster care."

TRUANCY- the status offense of repeated absence from school, which breaks compulsory education laws in the U.S.

DUAL- the status of youth involved in both the dependency and delinquency systems (e.g. went from foster care to detention).

VOP- Violation of Probation.

RUNNING AWAY- a status offense that can bring a child into conflict with law enforcement, juvenile court, detention, or dependency court, depending on the runaway's circumstances; running away often leads children to commit more serious crimes in order to survive.

LOITERING- the crime of lingering or hanging around with no particular or legal purpose.

COUNTY- short for county jail. adult detention facilities.

BURGLARY- "the criminal offense of breaking and entering a building illegally for the purpose of committing a crime."

SEX OFFENSE- refers to a number of crimes related to knowingly subjecting someone to unwanted or illegal sexual contact, including sexual assault, child pornography, and in some cases, sexting.

REGISTERED SEX OFFENDER- someone who has been convicted of a sexual offense that requires them to be placed on the Sexual Offender Registry due to federal, state, or local laws; being on the Sexual Offender Registry can create barriers for employment and residence.

Because K.M. has an indeterminate sentence (defined below), his progress in the program is evaluated at 24 months to determine whether or not he can be released back into the community.

INDETERMINATE SENTENCE- "sentences in which an administrative agency, generally a parole board, has the authority to release an offender and determine whether an offender's parole will be revoked for violations of the conditions of release."

TIME HANGING- when a youth's sentence involves time in an adult facility that may or may not need to be served depending on behavior during juvenile sentence, as in time hanging over one's head. See also Blended Sentence.

PROBATION- the status of a delinquent youth under court ordered supervision within the community, with specific conditions such as school attendance, the wearing of an electronic ankle monitor, refraining from interaction with other youth on probation, drug testing, etc. Failure to obey the conditions of probation may result in new charges and/or detention.

RELAPSE PREVENTION- a plan of action for addicts trying to prevent a drug relapse, including going to meetings, having a support network, and knowing what factors trigger one's addictive habits.

REOFFEND- to commit another crime.

I spent two years here. Today I was accepted to go to take my SAT. In July I'm going to North Carolina. They have a program in motorsports technology. It's a whole range from NASCAR to motocross to IndyCar to Formula One. I'm in here for a **sexual offense**. When I finish my treatment groups, I won't need to be a **registered sex offender**. I been here two years but I have a two-year review in July. I got my high school diploma. My mom and my three brothers and every once in a while my aunt comes to visit me here. And my birth mother too. My mom is my adopted mother. I was adopted at birth. My mom was 15 years old when she had me and she wanted me to have the best life I could possibly have to be successful in life. She lives in Florida; I write her letters sometimes. I haven't met my father. I appreciate my birth mother for being in contact with me later in my life. She supports me and everything. I'm working on a quilt for a fraternity. We get paid for some of the quilts that people order. It depends on the size of the quilt and the details. I also do embroidery so that adds value to it. The person that has the order

has done most of the work, so money goes into their account. This place is alright. I prefer to be at home. I've never been to any other institution. I was 18 when I came here—it was my first offense. I got an **indeterminate sentence**. 32 months. I may be released after 24 months. I don't have any **time hanging** and am free and clear when I'm out of here. I have to do **probation** and I have to have a mentor when I get out. I have to continue to do **relapse prevention** to keep me healthy and readjust and make sure I don't **reoffend**. I really like quilting as a way for me to enjoy myself, but also it's a huge coping skill that helps me to deal with anger and frustration, and it helps me release all the anger and frustration and stress that builds up. The stress is more about my family, not being able to help them out and having three younger brothers and worrying about them. Me being the oldest boy I always feel like it's my part to be at home and be the man of the house. I'm not from a rough neighborhood. The high school I went to was one of the top high schools in the country.

-K.M., Age 20

Been here since 2012. Two and a half years, going on three. I go to court in six months. Then I probably leave next year. I don't know my mother or father. I was held in the **detention center** for nine months. I got into the system when I was 11 or 12. This is my second time upstate. I just grew up in the system. I was doing what I had to do when I went home the last time, but I took charges for my brother. I have eight brothers that I know of and four sisters. I don't know where my mom is; she was never a part of my life. I never met my dad, never had the chance to. I really don't have a role model to look at. Everything I know I learned on my own. I take life as it goes. My charges are on my **adult record**, but I can get the charges **expunged**. I get out then I gotta go apply to a school and get on the right track. I graduate this June. If I go to **work release**, I can get an Associate of Arts. All my brothers and sisters are grown. When I leave I can think about independent living, but right now my home is living with my aunt. Nobody visits me here. That's three years. I was a football and basketball

player. I have a child. The mother of my child and me, we have a strong connection. My child is five. I was 15 when she was born. The mother of my baby came twice since I been up here, but I haven't seen 'em in a while now.

-U.K., Age 20

DETENTION CENTER- a secure residential facility that holds youth accused of delinquent or criminal activity while awaiting legal action, for the purpose of protecting both the detained youth and the community.

ADULT RECORD- the court's history of an individual's charges and convictions in adult criminal court.

EXPUNGE- to remove or seal someone's arrest and conviction records, a practice that varies by age, type of crime, and jurisdiction; expungement is important because a criminal record can pose difficulties for ex-offenders seeking employment, residence, etc.

WORK RELEASE- "a program in which certain prisoners are permitted to leave a penal institution for a specified time in order to hold jobs, prior to their full release."

I'm here in isolation. It's a lock unit. Isolation Behavior something...rehabilitation unit... I don't know. I been here two months. You get an hour out a day, but say you got seven residents, you might get out the end of the day for a little bit. Sometimes I play checkers during that time. I been in **isolation** for a month and a half. I used to be in my groups, but I started **wildin' out**. I used to take too many trays, like three breakfast trays, four lunch trays and three dinner trays. I didn't care. I took them because I was hungry. You gotta behave to get out of here. I was supposed to leave today. I'm waiting for a superintendent to sign for my release. If I'm here or in **open pop**, either way I'm still locked up. I was 11 or 12 when I was locked up. There are a lot of **MS 13** where I used to live. I hang with other people that don't like them. One day I was out there and there was this guy that had a knife, and on the handle there was blue tape that had MS written on it. He was drunk and stuff so I called my people. They started fighting and I was **bracking** a dude over a shoulder with a bat and he was backing up into the street and a white Escalade hit him. I got a **malicious wounding** charge. I got 15-21 months. My **early release date** is Nov 11th. I can't name my late release date, because I am not even looking to that date. My mother and my brothers and sisters come visit me. My dad is locked up in Florida for a **murder**. He was locked up in DC, but they closed DC up so he was in Kentucky, then West Virginia, and now Florida. I was like 13 or 12 the last time I saw him. I be here in my room thinking I'm just a juvenile. There are people in jail that are 15, 20, 17 years. I was writing to my dad's cellmate. He told me 80% of the kids here are going to be in prison, in **DOC**. You can lead a horse to the pond but you gotta wanna change. You gotta stay humble. I know I'm small, but my pride gets in the way sometimes. I gotta watch what I say. It only takes one minute to take somebody's life. I'm here 'cause I was defending my girlfriend. We were running, the dude hogged up a spit, pushed me out of the way, and his people started **jumping** me. I called my mom and she called the police. Police were everywhere 'cause it was a hood fight. Police were asking me questions, but I didn't wanna **snitch**. I called my peoples up later and they came. We were like 16 **deep** and they started shooting up his house. The police said I had a gun. I didn't have no gun, but the 15 other people did.

-U.L., Age 20

INTENSIVE BEHAVIOR REDIRECTION UNIT- an area of the facility that claims to provide more intensive treatment services for anti-social or violent youth, but in practice holds youth in conditions of solitary confinement.

ISOLATION- solitary confinement.

WILDIN' OUT- to act up, cause trouble, or behave outlandishly.

OPEN POP- short for open population, also known as gen pop or general population, refers to the main area of a detention or corrections facility where the majority of inmates are housed, i.e. not a special housing, maximum security, or solitary confinement unit.

MS 13- Mara Salvatrucha, a gang originating in Los Angeles.

BRACK- to strike.

MALICIOUS WOUNDING- in Virginia, the criminal act of shooting, stabbing, cutting, wounding, or causing bodily injury to another person with the intent to maim, disfigure, disable, or kill the other person in "malice," which is defined as the "state of mind which results in the intentional doing of a wrongful act without legal excuse or justification."

EARLY RELEASE DATE- the nearest date that an inmate could possibly be released depending on good behavior and a positive evaluation by the facility or parole board.

MURDER- "the unlawful killing of another human being without justification or excuse."

DOC- stands for Department of Corrections; the branch of government dealing with adult offenders.

JUMP- to attack, often with the intention of stealing the victim's belongings.

SNITCH- to tell on someone, specifically giving law enforcement or some other authority incriminating information; one who tells on others or gives authorities incriminating information.

DEEP- when used after a number, e.g. "eight deep," refers to how many people one is with.

I have been here 17 years. Kids are smaller now. Kids were larger, now they are smaller. I was 25 when I started in corrections. I was in the military before, in Desert Storm. Sometimes I can be their dad, best friend, officer. It depends on what they need at the time. It does help them. This is the **IBRU—Intensive Behavior Redirectional Unit**. Kids are in here from two weeks to months sometimes. It depends on the resident and how well he adapts to the program. Some of them don't work out. It depends on the nature of the charge they receive. It depends on if they learn to maintain their anger... if not they may be transferred. The other facility is supposed to take the more aggressive kids, older kids. I am a **JCO** senior. When we reorganize I'll be a resident specialist one or residential specialist two. It's still gong to be the same. We will still be right here with the kids. This is a difficult group of kids. They say we are going to have a three-month training. We go to the training facility and get paid while we are there. They say supposedly salary will change. I won't know until I get a phone call. It's just going to be what it's going to be for me. We used to have more of a correctional model of

shirts. Now they moved us to less aggressive uniforms. I can't explain what they are wearing or why. It's been about three months since they have been changing over. It's just another uniform to do a job. We work 12 hour shifts then often get drafted to do 4 hours overtime. That's 16 hours straight with a half hour for lunch.

-Juvenile Correction Officer, Age 42

INTENSIVE BEHAVIOR REDIRECTION UNIT- an area of the facility that claims to provide more intensive treatment services for anti-social or violent youth, but in practice holds youth in conditions of solitary confinement.

JCO- stands for juvenile corrections officer.

No matter what anybody says locked is locked. You try to pretend to make it something else. It's still the same thing. You have to change their way of thinking—"You want to be locked up or not locked up?"—these kids are not going home, they go to **gen pop**. They get used to it. They're still kids. You tell them something, they believe it. You make a promise, a kid expects you to come through. I don't believe in lying to people. I tell them they got a ways. "Least you can leave here is 14 days. You can be here in **IBRU** four to six months. Or you can redirect your behavior or your anger… but 14 days is the fastest anyone has got out of here." The people that normally come back are **lock babies**—residents that just can't function out there. They just like being in locked.

-Juvenile Correction Officer, female

GEN POP- short for general population, refers to the main area of a detention or corrections facility where the majority of inmates are housed, i.e. not a special housing, maximum security, or solitary confinement unit.

IBRU- stands for Intensive Behavior Re-direction Unit, an area of the facility that claims to provide more intensive treatment services for anti-social or violent youth, but in practice holds youth in conditions of solitary confinement.

LOCK BABIES- offenders who are always returning to the IBRU/SHU/solitary/isolation, intentionally or unintentionally.

SMOCK- also known as a turtle suit or suicide smock, these single piece tear-resistant garments are designed to be worn by
suicidal residents who, if wearing standard
facility uniforms, might use their clothing to
hang themselves.

72 HOURS- the standard minimum period
of time for a youth to be in solitary confinement for many facilities.

I'm 17 years old. I've been here four months. I've been in isolation four
months. I'm wearing a **smock** to prevent me from hurting myself. I hurt
myself. Why? I want to commit suicide. I don't talk to a therapist. They
ain't doin' no good. I spoke to her today for about five minutes. I've been
in here for six months. I was brought in for charges. I don't have a Dad.
My mom and my brothers live at home. There was emotional abuse at
home. I say I am going to hurt myself so they put me in a smock and I
have to wear a smock for **72 hours**. A couple of times I been wearing it.
It's comfortable. I got a 18 to 36 month sentence. If I show good behavior

I can get out in 18 months. We go to school in the building. We go the whole day. I can't have nothing. No books. I can't have nothing. I pass the time by just sitting here. No friends. I talk to the girl across the way. They allow me to talk to her. I get out of here for a hour a day. I sit and look and stare at space when they let me out. The red dots came from my head—it's blood. I just banged my head against the wall. I was mad at the staff. They wouldn't get me out of this smock.

-B.H., Age 17

I am 14 years old. D.X. is making that noise next door. He's in **IBRU**. My stuff is all outside my room, because my room got **sanitized**. You get no mattress or anything until they give it back to you. It's been like this for about two hours. They do that because I was banging my head. I was mad because I was getting new charges. I was standing at the door when I wasn't supposed to be. Also I had **contraband**. I had a broken spork. It's like, another item to do suicidal things with. I was sliding it out the door and one of them slid out the door and he got it. Both our doors were closed. I was just sliding all of them; I had two under the door and one got to him. I was 13 when I first came into the system. I turned 14 in here. My mom and my two sisters and my grandfather visit me. My dad is in Detroit. He works at Chrysler. I'm in for six to 12 months. I came here four months ago. I've been in **isolation** since 6:20 a.m. today. The most hours you can get for isolation is **72 hours**. I only have 23 hours for **attempting to circumvent security**. Circumventing is like a threat to security. I can lie down but there is no mattress. It's not comfortable. You get back pains and neck cramps. I'm in eighth grade. I'm in B cottage when I am not in here, it' down the hill. There are 18 kids in the cottage. They are from 15 to 20 years old.

-T.B., Age 14

IBRU- stands for Intensive Behavior Redirection Unit, an area of the facility that claims to provide more intensive treatment services for anti-social or violent youth, but in practice holds youth in conditions of solitary confinement.

SANITIZED- refers to a cell that has been emptied of all objects as a punishment.

CONTRABAND- object(s) or goods that confined offenders are prohibited from possessing.

ISOLATION- solitary confinement.

ATTEMPTING TO CIRCUMVENT SECURITY- trying to avoid, mislead, or undermine corrections officers in some way.

I'm 14. I've been here seven months. I was 12 when I first came in here. I came in for fighting my brother. My mom, dad, little brother, and sister visit. I'm in for 15-21 months. My oldest brother is home now. He was in **DOC**. I was physically and emotionally abused. My aunts hit me, foster people and stuff like that. I was in **foster homes** probably 2 years ago. I been in four or five foster homes. They just move us around and around. My little brother and little sister moved with me. My mom and dad used to fight so my mom had an **order** against my dad and he **violated** it so he got locked up... and my mom got on drugs. I went into foster care when I was like 7 or 8. My foster mom would push me around and hit me and stuff like that. I am here for **robbery** and **abduction**. I'm **on lock** so I wear orange. If you keep on getting **institutional charges** they put you on **IBRU**... it means 30 days lock or something like that. I got an extra charge for **destruction of state property**. I wrote on the floor. I used a pen and ink—I took the top of the pen off and blew the ink out of it. No, I don't think I'm an artist.

-D., Age 14

DOC- stands for Department of Corrections; the branch of government dealing with adult offenders.

ROBBERY- a crime of theft "by force or intimidation."

ABDUCTION- the crime of "restraining another through the use or threat of deadly force or through fraudulent persuasion."

FOSTER HOME- a single-family home placement in the child welfare system "in which a child is raised by someone other than their natural or adoptive parent" and lives with the caretaker's family.

RESTRAINING ORDER- "a command of the court issued upon the filing of an application for an injunction," which prohibits individuals from performing certain acts, such as carrying out threats or coming within a specific distance of an individual who feels threatened.

VIOLATION- generally refers to a probation or parole violation; see parole violation and probation violation.

ON LOCK- short for on lockdown, refers to being in secure housing/solitary confinement.

INSTITUTIONAL CHARGE- charges for offenses or rule breaking within a detention or corrections facility, which may or may mean charges in the court system.

IBRU- stands for Intensive Behavior Redirection Unit, an area of the facility that claims to provide more intensive treatment services for anti-social or violent youth, but in practice holds youth in conditions of solitary confinement.

DESTRUCTION OF STATE PROPERTY- the crime of willfully vandalizing or taking of state-owned property.

SECOND DEGREE MURDER- "a non-premeditated killing, resulting from an assault in which death of the victim was a distinct possibility."

"Diamond Level" is the highest level of achievement and privilege in C.C.'s facility.

CUSTODY- refers to the responsibility to care, control, and make decisions for a child; can also refer to being held by law enforcement (i.e. "in police custody").

SUSPENDED SENTENCE- an intermediate or community sentence, a sentence that does not require the offender be incarcerated, i.e. not an active sentence.

ACTIVE SENTENCE- a sentence that requires an individual to be incarcerated, unlike a suspended sentence.

FIRST DEGREE MURDER- "a premeditated, intentional killing, or results from a vicious crime such as arson, rape, or armed robbery," though exact definitions vary from state to state.

BENCH TRIAL- a trial in which there is no jury.

CHARGE AS AN ADULT- to charge a child as a criminal in adult court as opposed to a delinquent in juvenile court, typically justified by seriousness/circumstances of the offense and age at the time of the crime, which removes youth from the rehabilitation-focused juvenile system and places them in the punishment-focused adult system.

PAROLE- though youth may use the terms "parole" and "probation" interchangeably, parole refers to the court-ordered community supervision of individuals who have been released from confinement prior to the end of their original sentence.

DOC- stands for Department of Corrections; the branch of government dealing with adult offenders.

I've been here four years. I was 15 when I came up here for **second-degree murder**. My projected release date is 2023, but I have yearly reviews. I was sentenced for 12 years. Every time I go to review, I have the possibility of a release, or of getting some time knocked off. Being in the Diamond Level helps a lot. I've been in the Ad Design program for a while. We don't have access to the web. My aunt was my guardian. After I got locked up, my sisters moved with my aunt, and she got **custody** of me too. My mom didn't lose custody of me but they transferred it over to my aunt since she was taking both my sisters. This is my first charge. I was never in any trouble before. They took that a little bit into account but not that much. A weapon was involved. My family hunts a lot and they have weapons all over the house. It was never gang-related. I got 40 years sentenced with 28 **suspended**. They gave me 12 **active** years, six with and DJJ and six with DOC. I been doing really good since I've been here. I really didn't expect to get arrested 'cause it was an accident. They charged me with **first-degree** and then it got dropped down in the court system. The kid was 16. I didn't have no argument with him. I was playing with a gun. It was a **bench trial**; they **charged me as an adult**. The judge made a decision on the time and the charge. I didn't say nothing when he said 40 years; I thought I heard them wrong at first. I had a

paid lawyer. After the sentence, my lawyer explained it to me. He said first you have to wait two years and then every year after that you get reviewed. And when I'm out I'm just on indefinite **parole** for the rest of my life. If I could take it back I would, but I can't change anything about it, I just have to make my life as best as I can. I'd gladly help the other family if I could but I've been sentenced to no direct or indirect contact. The food here has its ups and downs. Sometimes it's alright, but last year, they started going by this calorie count. 600 for breakfast, 800 for lunch, and free for dinner. Once a month you can order out. Every month they pick a place. We have our own accounts to pay for it. A lot of kids only had nine dollars a month 'cause they don't get money from their parents. They used to have apprenticeship programs, you'd get two dollars an hour but after budget cuts they cut that down. So now we just work basically for free, for the experience. With Diamond Privilege you get unlimited phone calls, you get to order food every month, every Sunday you get to go watch the games or watch sports in a designated area. The hardest part is being away from your family, not being able help when your family needs it, and for me, me not knowing when I'm goin' home. If the judge releases me at my review I don't have to do those three years with **DOC**. Last two years, the **prosecution** stood up and said I should stay here and the judge said I'm staying here, but they tell me to keep up the good work. I only was in the courtroom for like a minute. The victim's family is there too. They don't say nothing.

-C.C., Age 19

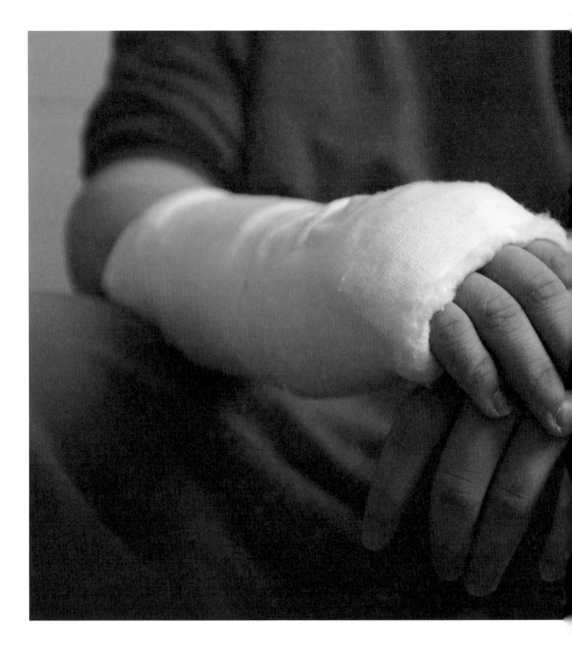

I am coming from **detention**. It's not fair; it's just how it's set up. When you get **committed** you come to **RDC**. I have no idea what RDC stands for. This is my first time here. I been here a week and five days. I don't know who else is here. I punched the wall in the **bullpen**. I'd been there for a while. I don't know. Like maybe an hour, maybe more. I got caught up in the wrong stuff. When you go into the courtroom, you stand in front of them and they basically say right there in front of you: "Guilty for this charge, you're going to **DJJ**." You're guilty of whatever charge they put on you like **assault**. This is my third month of being locked up. I went to see the judge and that's when I got committed to DJJ. I been here for almost two weeks. I most likely go home six months from now. At home, I've got my mama, my two brothers, and my grandma. My brothers are 14 and six. My dad is locked up. He's in for **armed robbery**. There's no man at home. My mom's boyfriend is locked up. He's in for a **probation violation**, I don't know what the original charges are. My mom's 33 or 34. My mom just got out, so she's looking for a job now. My mom was charged for **contributing to a minor**. Me and my friend were both **on the run**. She cut off his **bracelet**. So she got arrested for contributing. My original charge was

DETENTION- "Usually refers to the placement of a youth in a secure facility under court authority at some point between the time of referral to court intake and case disposition." Post-dispositional detention is at times necessary for reasons including "awaiting placement, short-term sentencing to detention, or being a danger to self or others."

COMMITTED- sentenced to time in a correctional facility, as opposed to detained, which is one's status prior to disposition or trial.

RDC- stands for Reception and Diagnostic Center, where newly committed youth are evaluated to determine what period of time and type of treatment is best suited for that child.

BULLPEN- a group holding cell where alleged offenders wait to go to court.

DJJ- stands for Department of Juvenile Justice; often used by youth to refer to commitment facilities.

ASSAULT- though what exactly constitutes an assault varies by jurisdiction, it generally refers to the crime of causing another fear that "he/she is about to suffer physical harm," with the degree of the assault depending on how much harm was caused.

ARMED ROBBERY- the crime of theft "by force or intimidation" with a deadly weapon; depending on jurisdiction may be charged as aggravated robbery.

PROBATION VIOLATION- failure to obey the conditions of one's probation as set forth by the court, which may result in new charges and/or detention.

Contributing to the Delinquency of a Minor- the crime of knowingly encouraging, causing, or aiding a child in delinquent acts as a person 18 years of age or older, including a parent.

ON THE RUN- avoiding contact with authorities; a term generally used for fugitives, synonymous with "on the lam."

BRACELET- refers to the electric monitoring device worn around the ankle, which is used to track the movement of individuals on house arrest, probation, or parole; see also Ankle Monitor.

MAIM- to unlawfully but not maliciously "shoot, stab, cut, or wound any person or by any means cause him bodily injury with the intent to maim, disfigure, disable, or kill."

GANG AFFILIATED- to be part of a gang, friends or family with someone in a gang, or to act for the benefit of a gang; to be declared gang affiliated by law enforcement can result in increased supervision in the streets or gang enhancement charges added onto other criminal charges.

MISDIMEANOR- "under federal law, and most state laws, any offense other than a felony."

MALICIOUS WOUNDING- the criminal act of shooting, stabbing, cutting, wounding, or causing bodily injury to another person with the intent to maim, disfigure, disable, or kill the other person in "malice," which is defined as the "state of mind which results in the intentional doing of a wrongful act without legal excuse or justification."

for **maiming**. I'm not **gang affiliated**. Maiming is when you fight somebody and break their bone. It can be different than an assault charge, like that can be an assault, but maiming is like a **misdemeanor** and there's a **malicious wounding**. It was gonna be jumped up to malicious wounding, but my lawyer got it dropped it down to a misdemeanor, so it's just a simple maiming. I was on the street when it happened. I haven't had one visit yet.

-E., Age 15

195

I been here four months. I have to stay here for one whole year. I haven't gotten any visits yet. I live with my mother, my stepfather, and my little brother. My dad's incarcerated for **child support**. He has other family too. My mother is a caregiver. My brother is eight. I think he's in first grade now. I'm in the ninth grade. I'm in special ed. The treatment here helps us figure out our cycle and how to not **reoffend**. I'm still doing my treatment. They give me drugs here. They give me Depakote, Adderall, and Risperdal. They have

me diagnosed as ADHD and bipolar too. They sentenced me for a year, then probation, but I don't know for how long. I like to rap. I rap right off the top. Sometimes I write out poems. My mother smokes and drinks and so does my stepfather—nothing excessive though. I used to smoke weed. I caught a couple of stealing charges, **assault** and **battery** and **malicious wounding**. I cut somebody with a piece of glass. With malicious wounding you have to draw blood to get the charge. It's a **felony**. I was 12 years old when I first came into the system.

-J.C., Age 16

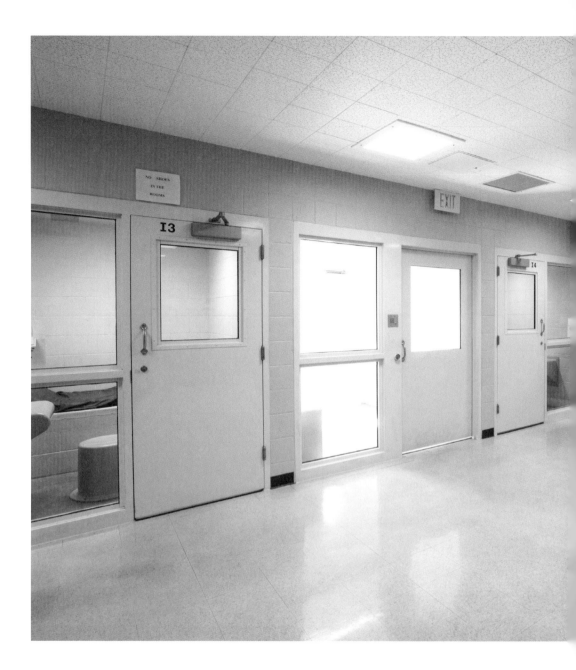

This is some noisy place. On this side we go to **canteen** every day. We can do more stuff. We have more freedom than the other side of the place. I'm 17. I been here about six months. I was 12 when I first went to juvie. I'm back for a **violation**. This is my second **commitment**. The first charge was a **possession of a firearm** and a **controlled substance**—weed, pills. Here, if you need more help for your work they have one-on-one help for your work. They work more directly with you. Teachers, counselors, staff all work with us. There are 11 kids in the unit. I've got friends here. My dad's incarcerated for drugs. I seen my father—he was around sometimes. I talked to him here now. My mom's **straight**, she's a private doctor. She's like a pediatric doctor. I'm in the 11th grade. I can get my hands on about anything on the streets.

-B.I., Age 17

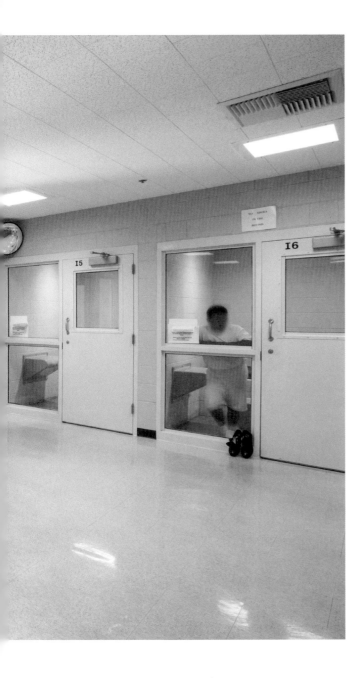

CANTEEN- a store within a confinement facility that sells hygiene items, snacks, paper, stamps, etc.; also known as a commissary.

VIOLATION- generally refers to a probation or parole violation; see parole violation and probation violation.

COMMITMENT- "A court order giving guardianship of a juvenile to the state department of juvenile justice or corrections. The facility in which a juvenile may be placed... may range from a secure correctional placement to a nonsecure or staff-secure facility, group home, foster care, or day treatment setting."

POSSESSION OF A FIREARM/DEADLY WEAPON- refers to the crime of carrying a gun or other object designed to inflict death, either because the defendant is a minor, on probation, or fails to follow a state's laws regarding legal gun possession (e.g. obtaining permits).

CONTROLLED SUBSTANCE- a drug or other substance for which its production and distribution is prohibited or regulated by the U.S. government.

STRAIGHT- clean cut, rule-abiding and/or sober.

IBRU- stands for Intensive Behavior Re-direction Unit, an area of the facility that claims to provide more intensive treatment services for anti-social or violent youth, but in practice holds youth in conditions of solitary confinement.

PROBATION VIOLATION- failure to obey the conditions of one's probation as set forth by the court, which may result in new charges and/or detention.

PROBATION- the status of a delinquent youth under court ordered supervision within the community, with specific conditions such as school attendance, the wearing of an electronic ankle monitor, refraining from interaction with other youth on probation, drug testing, etc. Failure to obey the conditions of probation may result in new charges and/or detention.

ASSAULT- though what exactly constitutes an assault varies by jurisdiction, it generally refers to the crime of causing another fear that "he/she is about to suffer physical harm," with the degree of the assault depending on how much harm was caused.

DETENTION- "Usually refers to the placement of a youth in a secure facility under court authority at some point between the time of referral to court intake and case disposition." Post-dispositional detention is at times necessary for reasons including "awaiting placement, short-term sentencing to detention, or being a danger to self or others."

MAJOR OFFENDER- one who has been convicted of a major charge.

HOUSE ARREST- "confinement to one's home or another specified location instead of incarceration in a jail or prison," most often enforced with an ankle monitor.

ANKLE BRACELET- refers to the electric monitoring device worn around the ankle, which is used to track the movement of individuals on house arrest, probation, or parole for the sake of supervision.

PROTECTIVE CUSTODY- the confinement of an individual to protect them from harm by the outside world or other inmates at a facility.

23 AND ONE- refers to conditions of solitary confinement in which inmates are confined to their rooms alone for 23 hours a day, with one hour allotted for large muscle movement outside of the cell.

HIT- an order to attack or kill someone, generally in organized crime.

GANG AFFILIATED- to be part of a gang, friends or family with someone in a gang, or to act for the benefit of a gang; to be declared gang affiliated by law enforcement can result in increased supervision in the streets or gang enhancement charges added onto other criminal charges.

GEN POP- short for general population, refers to the main area of a detention or corrections facility where the majority of inmates are housed, i.e. not a special housing, maximum security, or solitary confinement unit.

I'm 18 years old. I'm in solitary confinement. I been here about a month. I've been at this facility about nine months. I was 16 when I first went in to juvie. I originally went to juvie for **probation violation** on a fighting charge. It was a school incident. I was fighting in school; the judge gave me **probation**. There are lots of cops in school here. It was a minor fight but I still got an **assault** charge because you fightin' on school grounds and stuff. If your parents can't pick you up they take you to **detention** in cuffs. But nine times out of 10 if you get in a fight at school you gettin' suspended and a fighting charge. There were other charges too. I'm about to go back home. I live with my grandma and grandpa. My mom passed in a car accident—a head-on truck collision in 2005, 10 years ago. I was six or seven years old. I don't know where my dad is. I don't even know my dad's name. I'll be on probation for like six months since I'm not a **major offender**. I could be here for a year, but I think I am out after six months. **House arrest** is dumb, but cutting off **ankle bracelets** is dumb too. People been locked up for years and they just want a little more freedom so they cut them off. I think it's stupid to be on house arrest after being locked up for so long. I understand probation but house arrest is just dumb when you already got your punishment from your sentence. When I get out I want to go get a job as quickly as possible but being under house arrest I'll have to wait. When I get out I'm going to get my GED. In **protective custody**, it's like solitary but you get a little more privileges. The other kids had to stay in a room **23 and one**. I don't have a limit going out as long as everybody else gets in and out. I can't be out with the other kids because I got a **hit** on me and the investigator said there were too many hits out on me. People put hits out on other residents and stuff like that. A hitman is like the mafia but it's for kids out here. I don't know why they put it out on me, I get along with mostly everybody. I'm not **gang affiliated**. I don't really even know who the gangs are other than your Bloods and your Crips and whatever other gangs you got. I won't go to **gen pop** so I'll probably just go home in a bit cause it's safer. It's a win-win situation. My grandma and grandpa are my foster grandma and grandpa. They're like my real grandma and grandpa I been with them so long. Like 10 years. I been with them since my mom died. They're Indian and African-American if I'm correct. Like Native American. I never paid attention to my grandma when she told me that. I lost count the number of foster homes I been in, cause one it was me and my brother but then he left the foster house, he went to live with real people. We been through a lot.

-D.D., Age 18

I'm 19 years old, They would consider me gang affiliated. Mostly where I grew up there's like Bloods and Folk and Crip. They have me listed as a Blood member. It's mostly neighborhood gangs. I've been in my cell like a month and two weeks. I been here for about two years. I did two years in another insitution before I came over here. I came in when I was 14. I have three years mandatory **DOC time** as well. That's after I turn 21. But I'm supposed to go to court early so I could start my time early. They gave me **aggravated malicious wounding** and **use of a firearm**. My grandmother, my dad, and my sister come to visit. My dad's not affiliated but he was incarcerated before when he was younger. He's got really better, he's on his own with a job, he has steady work. He's good with his hands like construction and houses and stuff. He did five years and then he was going in and out. My grandmother has **custody** of me. My mother couldn't really

hold a steady job or anything like that, and right now she's incarcerated. She's emotionally unstable—she has a lot of mental problems but no drugs or alcohol involved. I don't know her sentence, but she's locked up for **child support**. When my grandmother took custody, my mother was supposed to pay child support, but she didn't. If I go to DOC now, I get out at 22 or 23. I'm over 18 so they'll put me in the adult facility since I'm 19. If I go over now I can get out in maybe three years. Maybe **DJJ** can advocate and DOC can say that I get to stay in a **DJJ** facility and then something else can happen but I don't know. It's mandatory. It depends on the laws right now. I could go over there and finish it up now. My father moved, he has my sister and she's doing really good, and my little brother's with my mom's boyfriend. From what I heard he's been in and out juvenile jail. He still off-track. When we were kids, my brother and I was molested by a family friend. I was about six or seven. Only a couple of the people in the facility know, just a couple of counselors but that's all. I've talked through a lot and gotten a lot of the anger and hate out of me so I don't see myself ever turning and doing that. I'm talking to my grandma now.

-E.D., Age 19

RAPED

There are cops sitting at my dining room table with my parents. My mom's crying, repeating hysterically, "I didn't know!!" What's going on?!" After a minute my mom comes in my room and tells me to go talk to the guys. I go out of the room and sit down. What I do I see? A file with my name on it.

"What's going on?" I asked. The guy across from me looks at me and reaches into the file and pulls out pictures, and shows them to me. The pictures are of me. Nude. In my grandma's bathroom, in my uncle's room; several of them had sex toys. Where'd they get these?!

"These photos are from a website full of known sex offenders. We know you've been raped. We suspect who it is. But can you solidify it for us? Who's doing this to you?"

"If you know, why ask?"

"Answer the question." I sit silently swallowing hard trying to rid the lump in my throat as I remember it all. Him giving me sex toys, him taking nude pictures of me, and, for the past two months, him trying to convince me to do a porn video. I swallow one more time.

"My uncle. Uncle E. That's who," I said in a small, husky voice.

"How long has this been happening?"

"Since I was eight and a half." I was going to turn thirteen in a month and a half.

"So... for five years?"

"Yeah."

"Thank you, B. Your uncle will be in custody tomorrow. He won't be able to hurt you for a long time," he said as my mom walked out of her room.

"Honey, are you okay?" My head was reeling so much I felt myself **tipping**. My vision started going, and the next thing I knew I was on the couch. The cop was telling my mom to make sure I got counseling, and if I remember anything that could put the perverted bastard behind bars longer, to call him. He looked over at me and told me that everything was going to be okay, and that he won't be able to get anywhere near me.

How did this happen? He was supposed to love me. I was adopted in, for god's sake! What he was doing to me was illegal, and now because of him, I'm addicted to having sex. That's great! A thirteen year old, going into **respite care** so I'll stop **running**, going into freshman year of high school. Being in this situation sucks. I still wonder to this day what would've happened if I would've reported this earlier. I guess I'll never know.

-B.S.

TIPPING- refers to being at ones emotional tipping point: feeling overwhelmed and unable to process what is happening.

RESPITE CARE- short-term, out-of-home placement for youth status offenders and children in need of services (CHINS).

RUNNING AWAY- a status offense that can bring a child into conflict with law enforcement, juvenile court, detention, or dependency court, depending on the runaway's circumstances; running away often leads children to commit more serious crimes in order to survive.

ADDICTED TO THE LIFESTYLE

I can't help but be addicted to **the lifestyle**. The only people I don't rip off or steal from is my family or friends. I admit I am not one to change. No matter how much people want me to. I can't help the fact that I'm addicted.

The drugs are hard, but I can't help but love them. I never get too sucked in by them. I always knew when to slow down. Never messed with a needle, always smoke or snort. My **DOC** is **crystal**. I never had to spend any of my money on drugs unless I was the **host**. Even then I was still getting **gifted**. People love me and practically worship me, doing anything to please me.

Robbing people is no biggie. Especially if you can tell their insurance will replace what was stolen. I've always been able to get my friends and I out of sticky situations. If I ever saw something that appealed to me, I would get it. We would drive around town at night looking for open garage doors or seeing who wasn't home. It was a new adventure every night!

I first started **walking the strip** when I was 16; that's when I learned how to speak for myself. I loved money and I don't like being ripped off. If someone **shorted** me, I would take their money and refuse to give them service unless they gave me full, plus tip for wasting my time. My body is mine, so I should be able to do with it what I want. So why did they charge me for prostitution? They say they don't want me to exploit myself like that. Well that will be on my record forever now, now everyone knows I'm a hoe. Not that I have shame. I love being the most wanted on **TNA**. All the men love me on there. I have no remorse for the wives or children whose husbands and fathers fell in love with me and my body. The men chose to be addicted to me. The same way I am addicted to the sex, money, and drugs. The lifestyle.

`-D.X.`

THE LIFESTYLE- can refer generally to life outside of the law, hustling, or can be used more specifically to refer to selling drugs, prostituting, participating in gangs.

D.X. never used drugs intravenously.

DOC- stands for "drug of choice."

CRYSTAL- slang for methamphetamine.

HOST- refers to being the host of a party in which one supplies drugs for their friends.

GIFTED- to be given drugs for free.

WALK THE STRIP- to prostitute oneself.

SHORT- to pay someone less than you owe them.

TNA- refers to a website where prostitutes can be contacted by johns to arrange a meeting.

THE BEGINNING

If you grew up in a place like me, you could understand why I'm here. It all started when I was eight. I grew up around a lot of **GZ.** When I was nine, I did my **first mission**; Me and E. remember like it was yesterday. I was walking to school; he rode up on the bike. He asked me, "Where you going D?" I said, "School." He said, "Bro, you want some money?" I said, "Hell yea." He said, "Come on." He put me on the handlebars and rode to a house. This was the start.

AT THE SPOT

If you are at the spot, you went from a young boy to a soldier. I became a soldier that day. It was real. I smoked until I couldn't move and had a good $200 in my pocket. I was becoming that guy. Growing up fast I lost my virginity at nine, by eleven it was really gone. Middle school was when I skipped, fought, and got expelled. That listed me under a gangbanger. As I hit 12 I wasn't in school at all. I was on the block, trapping and hitting licks. My thirteenth birthday was critical; the last cake I ever saw. My hood is where killings and shootings are a model for the young boys.

AT ****

I was coming from my brother's house. It's 3:00 and school got out. I was walking and saw my **old head**. We walked to the store. I saw a black charger across the street. I asked, "You think that's **the boys**?" He said, "Maybe, we don't got nothing." I walked in the store; that's when I grabbed a **dutch**. I looked; man was grabbing a soda and some munchies. I walked outside and two policemen asked us our names. Once I said "D," he told me to step to the wall; the black charger with the dark tints rode off. They said they're putting out **warrants** for our arrest and we have a **summons**. They took our names; 2 weeks later, one by one, we all were in detention waiting for a sentence for **burglaries**, **robberies** and **assaults**. I was thirteen. It was a nightmare.

DISAPPEARANCE

It was kind of a wreck growing up in a hood when a nigga doesn't have anything to live up to. Only thing you have is money, drugs, and respect. We were the type that takes all of it from you. We wanted control over everything; didn't matter what it was, we had to get it if we wanted clothes or food. So we robbed and took it from you. Yo, this is my story of a come up. A come up through the things I have done, I would have never thought that me being in a facility was one of the outcomes. I done hit so many licks that I thought I would never get caught. Once I got caught it was a hard way down. I mean, who wants to be in **the bean** eating peanut butter and jelly sandwiches? Not me. Well when you **hot**, everybody's hot.

THE RUN THAT CHANGED MY LIFE

Before I got caught, the hood was on fire. I will never forget this day. I was in front of the building chilling, talking about my boy and how

---

GZ- gangsters.

GET RIGHT- to get yourself in a better position that you previously were, specifically with money.

FIRST MISSION- refers to the first illegal thing one does/did.

SOLDIER- refers to a person who is in a war in the streets, surviving in violent surroundings.

GANG BANGER- active gang member.

TRAPPING- making money from selling drugs.

HIT LICKS- to rob a store or home, originally used specifically for robbing liquor stores, i.e. "hitting liquor stores."

OLD HEAD- an older person or adult who acts as a guiding force.

THE BOYS- the police.

DUTCH- refers to a cigar that is often emptied and refilled with marijuana.

WARRANT- "a written order issued by a judicial officer or other authorized person commanding a law enforcement officer to perform some act incident to the administration of justice... most commonly, police use warrants as the basis to arrest a suspect and to conduct a search of property for evidence of a crime."

SUMMONS- a legal document "that commands the defendant to appear before the court on a specific day to answer the complaint made by the plaintiff."

BURGLARY- "the criminal offense of breaking and entering a building illegally for the purpose of committing a crime."

ROBBERY- a crime of theft "by force or intimidation."

ASSAULT- though what exactly constitutes an assault varies by jurisdiction, it generally refers to the crime of causing another fear that "he/she is about to suffer physical harm," with the degree of the assault depending on how much harm was caused.

THE BEAN- a locked down facility.

HOT- being watched or monitored by law enforcement because they are suspicious of you.

ON THE RUN- avoiding contact with authorities; a term generally used for fugitives, synonymous with "on the lam."

FIEND- someone who is heavily addicted to drugs, e.g. fiending for a fix.

BASE- slang for crack-cocaine.

SLIPPING- not staying alert, not covering one's tracks, getting lazy.

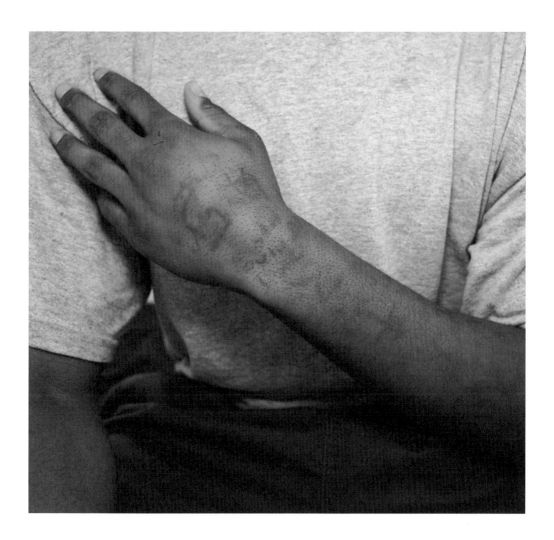

he got caught; laughing. I'm **on the run** at this time, everybody's saying, "Bro, you're getting caught next." I said, "Man I'm not worrying about nothing. How long I been on the run. Save it. I'm out here." Well I wish I never said that. I walked in the parking lot and a **fiend** called me. This was my new life, selling **base.** It wasn't good, but it was better than running in houses and getting caught like the others. Plus, it kept me out of trouble. I sold the base and took the 20 dollars. By the time I put it with the rest of the money, I heard, "Hey you. Come here." I was **slipping**. I heard keys. I said, "That's not the boys." I look back, it was them. I ran. He was on the heels of my Jordan's. I didn't know what to do. He was too slow, but close to me by trying to grab me and clench on. I tripped and looked up. The tazer was in my face. "Don't move; put your hands on the ground." I did. That's what got me where I'm at now; in a cell reading books, learning more, and becoming smarter too. Jail life is not for any one. Jail changed my life. The come ups have no love for anyone. This is a change to the come up. How to become better, improve yourself, and develop the skills needed to succeed in life.

-D.S.

MY HOME AWAY FROM HOME

I have been on **probation** since September of 2011. My original charges being two **misdemeanor** and a **status offense**: **Battery**, **Possession of a Controlled Substance**, and **Destruction of a Telephonic Device**. Since that day I have been back to **detention** twelve times, with stays as long as five months. As results of my many returns to detention I have been sent to four residential facilities, one of which I am still currently incarcerated in.

It was late July of 2012 when I was sent to a **group home** because my judge did not want to release me to my grand-parents' home, where I reside. I was at that group home for three weeks before I **dipped out**. Eventually, I turned myself in, and my judge then placed me in a substance abuse program that was inside of the **detention** center. I graduated that program early for good behavior. When I had gotten released that time it was early November of 2012, and I had been **caged** for a little over five months.

I relapsed on **spice** the day after being released.

I continued to use heavily and eventually started to get spun on crank. I did not fail a **UA** until late December of 2012. I went until February fifth, 2013 before I **got popped** again. That day in February I had initially gotten two **felonies**, a **status offense**, and a ticket; **GTA** and **Leaving the Scene of an Accident**, **Running Away**, and **Driving Without Privileges**. My GTA was reduced to a misdemeanor and my status offense dropped. I was then sent to a treatment facility. I was there for three months before being removed and sent back to another detention center; I had failed to complete the program.

I was in that detention center for 13 days before being committed to **DJC.** I arrived in **O&A** on May first and did not leave until July second. I had originally been referred and accepted another facility. After arriving to that facility the superintendent interviewed me and decided that facility would not be a good fit. I was then referred to another facility and ended up being denied there as well.

I am now incarcerated at the Department of Juvenile Corrections. I have currently been locked up for nine months and counting. I have 464 days over my head. My 15th and 16th birthdays have been spent incarcerated. All but four of my 20 high school credits have been earned while caged somewhere.

Recently, I was asked if I would be satisfied living my life in a prison. I could not respond, because I do not know. This has become a new way of life for me, my home away from home.

-H.N., Age 16

PROBATION- the status of a delinquent youth under court ordered supervision within the community, with specific conditions such as school attendance, the wearing of an electronic ankle monitor, refraining from interaction with other youth on probation, drug testing, etc. Failure to obey the conditions of probation may result in new charges and/or detention.

MISDEMEANOR- "under federal law, and most state laws, any offense other than a felony."

STATUS OFFENSE- "Conduct that is considered unlawful when committed by a minor (because of his/her childhood 'status'), but isn't criminal when committed by an adult." Such offenses include running away, truancy, violating curfew, possession of tobacco, etc.

BATTERY- an intentional act causing harmful, offensive or sexual contact with the body of another person.

POSSESSION OF A CONTROLLED SUBSTANCE- refers to the crime of carrying a controlled substance on your person and/or property.

DESTRUCTION OF A TELEPHONIC DEVICE- the crime of destroying a telephonic device that belongs to another person or the state, potentially as a means to prevent the summoning of law enforcement.

DETENTION- "Usually refers to the placement of a youth in a secure facility under court authority at some point between the time of referral to court intake and case disposition." Post-dispositional detention is at times necessary for reasons including "awaiting placement, short-term sentencing to detention, or being a danger to self or others."

GROUP HOME- an out-of-home placement for kids who have been removed from their home "which provides 24-hour non-medical care and supervision to children, provides services to a specific client group and maintains a structured environment, with such services provided at least in part by staff employed by the licensee."

DIPPED OUT- leaving without permission, in H.N.'s case, going AWOL from placement.

CAGED- incarcerated.

SPICE- refers to a wide variety of herbal mixtures and/or synthetic chemicals that produce mind-altering effects often likened to those of marijuana. Spice has been sold legally in its many variations with the label "not for human consumption."
H.N. began using methamphetamine.

UA- short for urine analysis test, the most prevalent form of drug testing.

GET POPPED- to get caught.

FELONY- a serious crime, characterized under federal law and many state statutes as any offense punishable by imprisonment in excess of one year.

GTA- stands for Grand Theft Auto, the crime of theft of an automobile, which is a felony in most states regardless of the car's value.

LEAVING THE SCENE OF AN ACCIDENT RESULTING IN INJURY OR DEATH- in Idaho, the charge given to a driver who leaves the scene of an accident they were involved in that likely resulted in injury.

RUNNING AWAY- a status offense that can bring a child into conflict with law enforcement, juvenile court, detention, or dependency court, depending on the runaway's circumstances; running away often leads children to commit more serious crimes in order to survive.

DRIVING WITHOUT PRIVILEGES- in Idaho, the crime of driving/controlling a motor vehicle without a license, or with a revoked/suspended/disqualified license.

DJC- in Idaho, stands for Department of Juvenile Corrections.

O&A- stands for Observation and Assessment, where one goes after being committed to be assessed psychologically, educationally, and physically to determine the best program for that youth.

LAST ENCOUNTER

I remember waking up to people yelling, I assumed it was my dad coming home wasted on palm wine as he always did. I wiped my sleepy eyes and staggered to the living room when all of a sudden two women pushed past me and bolted right out the front door. They both were completely naked and right behind them was my mom holding something that looked like a **swibe'** but then I realized it was an **obe'**. My dad was trying to catch up with my mom; he too was naked like both women. He managed to get a hold on my mom and pulled her back before she caught up with the woman closest to her.

All definitions of Nigerian terms were generously provided by J.O.

SWIBE'- a long, metal, spoon-like object used for stirring deep pans of food.

OBE'- a long-bladed kitchen knife that looks like a miniature machete, used in Nigeria for hacking into bone or cutting tough meat.

ASHAWO- elite prostitutes, mainly convinced to do sex work by madames as a means of getting off the street.

He stood in front of the door and blocked the way. He started apologizing saying he was drunk when he brought the **ashawos** home. My mom spat in his face. In Nigeria it's taboo for a female to spit in a male's face. He lunged at her and wrested her to the ground. She tried to free herself but all attempts failed. He slapped her so hard she passed out from the impact; he then ripped the **obe'** out of her hand and set it on the counter. It took my mom a couple of minutes to regain consciousness. All I could do was stare and listen to my mom cry.

I was overwhelmed by the feeling of hopelessness, but it was quickly replaced with anger. I ran towards my dad and bit him so hard I tasted blood. He cursed, and picked me up by the neck and threw me across the room. I landed on my butt, hitting my head on the breakfast table. This distraction gave my mom enough time to fully escape from his hold. She ran and grabbed the obe' sitting on the counter. My dad knew my mom would stab him if she had to. She loved me and would never let anything happen to me.

My mom had the knife pointed at him while she walked over to help me up. She told me to go outside and get in the car. I hesitated but then did as she asked. I was in a lot of pain, my sight was blurry and my head felt like it was about to explode. I limped through the backyard door, got in the car and locked it. It took my mom about 5 minutes to come out but it felt like hours. She came out of the house sprinting towards the car, so I quickly unlocked it. She got in the car and we peeled out of the drive way. I remember looking back at my dad's house. I saw him standing in the driveway with what looked like some type of assault rifle pointed at our car, but we were too far away for him to do any damage. I was only 4 when this took place and that was the last time I saw my dad.

-J.O., Age 11

213

THE DAY A PART OF ME LEFT FOREVER

I woke up and looked out the window; it was still dark outside. My stomach growled so I went downstairs. My mom was on the couch. She said "Go back upstairs. Now!" I asked no questions just went straight to the kitchen to grab a twinkie and a HoHo. Then I went back upstairs to eat my snacks and watch *Losing Isaiah* until I dozed off.

I felt someone shaking me so I woke up to my mom sitting on my bed with a glass of water. She said "Honey, wake up I have something to tell you." I stood up quickly. My mom said "You might want to sit down." I did, slowly and concerned.

Then I *really* woke and said to myself that it was only a dream. Then I had a flashback to what had happened that night...

I walked in the house speechless with blood all over me. I immediately ran straight to the bathroom and start screaming, "NOT RIGHT NOW! NOO GOD NOOO! IM DOING SO GOOD! WHYYY GOD!" Then I splashed my face with water and went to the kitchen to pour me a glass of water. I sat on the couch and cried silently to myself. My head felt like it was on fire and I felt like stamping out for good. My mom came in the living room and held me tightly in her arms. I felt warm and relaxed. I just felt like falling asleep in her arms forever.

A week later, I am dressed up in black from head to toe and walking in the church looking at all the family and **homies** crying and screaming loudly. I stood in line and made it halfway up to the casket and I got a tingling feeling in my stomach. I turned around and walked outside for fresh air. I sat on the ground next to my homie and took a few hits off his **square**. Then he asked, "Do you know who **noodled** him?" I said, "Don't you think if I knew who noodled him, I would have noodled them?!"

My lil **broskee** came outside and told me its time for me to sing. I went back inside and walked past the casket without looking at O. I grabbed the mic and started to sing "I Miss My Homies" by Master P. At the end of the song, me and D. took our black veils out our pockets and laid them on O. Then we sat down to listen to the preacher.

The preacher asked if anyone had something to say about O. I walked up to the mic and grabbed it and took it over to his casket. As I stared at his soulless body tears started to roll down my face. I said, "O. was a fighter and he died a fighter. Why? Because some **yonie** wanted his **shine** and someone in this damn church knows who that yonie is!" Then this dude in weird clothing stood up and said, "Fuck y'all." Then I took off out the church after him. I ran out the church and grabbed my **.40** out my pants, aimed it, then...

-J.C.

STAMPING OUT- dying.

HOMIES- close friends who have your back and are there for you in times of need.

SQUARE- a cigarette.

NOODLE- to shoot someone in the head.

BROSKEE- a friend who is more like your brother.

YONIE- a hater, i.e. a jealous, negative person or enemy.

SHINE- slang for wealth or success.

40- a term that technically refers to the width of ammunition required for certain guns, but is used in reference to the gun itself.

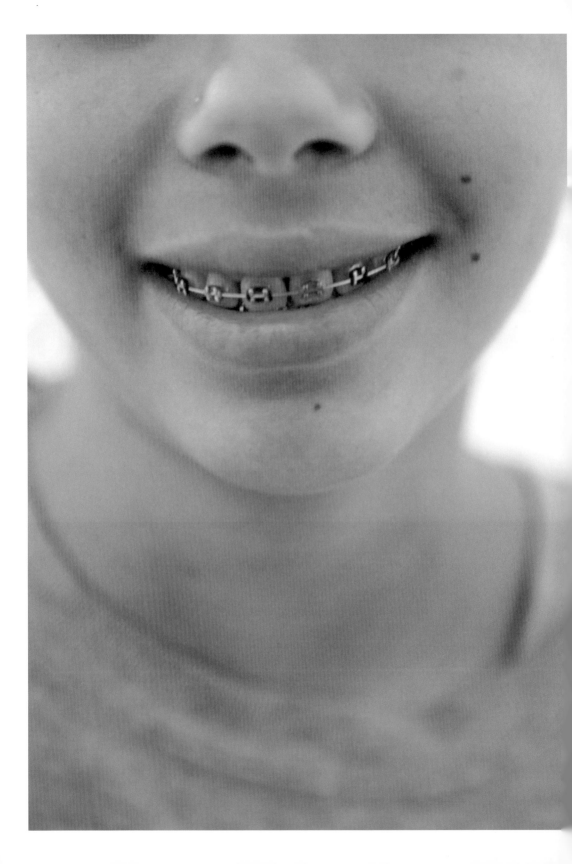

A PEEK INSIDE MY LIFE

When I was just seven years old I saw my mother get shot. My dad was nowhere to be found, so her so-called best friend took us in and abused us and allowed her husband to molest me and my little brother and sister.

When I turned eight years old my dad showed up and dropped us off in Florida with people we never meet. Helen, the lady we stayed with, did everything in her power to get money for us. She said she didn't want me because the older I get the less money comes in for me. Eventually she said I was poisoning her drinks and threatened me and said if I don't do as she said she was going to kill my little brother and sister, so I told the police I had done what I was being accused of.

I was placed in **detention** and was later placed on **probation**, then I got back in contact with my dad and for the first time in my whole life he explained why my mom had been shot. I hated him for it, but he told me it was my destiny. On my 12th birthday, instead of a birthday party, I was busy getting **jumped into** a gang that I really didn't want to be a part of. Two to three months later I found myself hanging out on the **pipeline**, where I began to sell my body and get hooked on drugs.

When I turned 13 I found out I was pregnant. My baby's father changed from being sweet and caring to abusive and when I was three months pregnant he pushed me down the stairs and started kicking me in the stomach. Because of his actions I had a miscarriage, so I began to do more drugs and started robbing people.

I got sent to a program where I began hitting staff, **cheating on meds** trying to overdose, and **cutting** myself. After I was discharged less than a month later, I was found in an abandoned house, drugged, laying with no clothes on and bleeding and sweating. I was admitted to detox. After I regained my strength I couldn't remember anything. When I did remember it wasn't a surprise that I had been raped again for the sixth time in my 15 years of living.

Around June 2010, I was found under the expressway and taken to the Mental Health Resource Center and they gave me a place to stay and something to eat. After three weeks I was placed in a **foster home**, at first I wanted to give it a try until my foster dad began coming on to me. I soon **ran away**. Finally, I found another foster home, where I became adopted and have a nice "mother" who gives me the family bond I never had as a child.

But that's just a peek; you don't know the half of my life story.

-K.R.

DETENTION- "Usually refers to the placement of a youth in a secure facility under court authority at some point between the time of referral to court intake and case disposition." Post-dispositional detention is at times necessary for reasons including "awaiting placement, short-term sentencing to detention, or being a danger to self or others."

PROBATION- the status of a delinquent youth under court ordered supervision within the community, with specific conditions such as school attendance, the wearing of an electronic ankle monitor, refraining from interaction with other youth on probation, drug testing, etc. Failure to obey the conditions of probation may result in new charges and/or detention.

JUMP IN- an initiation ritual for membership to a gang, which typically entails the inductee receiving a beating for a predetermined amount of time while remaining defenseless.

PIPELINE- where prostitutes wait for and solicit johns.

CHEAT ON MEDS- to not take and/or hide medications one has been prescribed.

CUTTING- a type of self-injury that is often the result of attempting to cope with intense emotions and problems for which the cutter doesn't have the skills to overcome alone.

FOSTER HOME- a single-family home placement in the child welfare system "in which a child is raised by someone other than their natural or adoptive parent" and lives with the caretaker's family.

RUNNING AWAY- a status offense that can bring a child into conflict with law enforcement, juvenile court, detention, or dependency court, depending on the runaway's circumstances; running away often leads children to commit more serious crimes in order to survive.

ESPN

It all started when I moved to the 1700 block of the Latrobe Homes projects on the eastside of Baltimore City. If you don't know anything about Baltimore, here is a quick lesson. Eastside is home to all the jails and downtown. You probably think it would be the calmest place in the city, but you're wrong. It's the worst, and Latrobe wasn't excluded. I was exposed to drugs and violence early; for me and my brother it was normal. If someone didn't get killed, or some **junkie** wasn't all over the playground, we thought the world was going to end.

The first thing that caught my eye was Ensor Street. On Friday nights anybody who was anybody could be found on Ensor Street. I had never been up close and personal with a **drug strip** and that's what Ensor was. The **corner boys** flooded the street. Most of them were my age. They were getting so much money without even moving or breaking a sweat and girls watched their every move. They had everything I wanted. I wanted to be a corner boy.

Before you cast judgment on me, I had my reasons for wanting to be a corner boy. After my father's death a year before, my mother struggled to support us and keep a roof over our heads. There were days we didn't have anything to eat, or our power was cut off. My mother was stranded with two bad kids and a dead end job at Mickey D's. All the stress led to cancer and cancer to her death. My brother and I were left to fend for ourselves. We jumped headfirst into **the game**.

What I realize after all these years is that the game is a world of its own and it's full of surprises. It can be your best friend or your worst enemy, but once you're in you're just like that junkie who keeps coming back—hooked. I earned my name by **putting in work** and the way I did it was monstrous. That was my setback. I caught three to five years for a gun charge. I left my brother alone in the game, but only for the moment.

Jail could have been my chance to change, but it's hard when you're hooked—addicted to money. The only thought on my mind was to **come up** at all costs. I refused to struggle any more. After serving three and a half years I was released. It took a cab and three buses to get me back into the city. I went to my brother's house and knocked on the door.

"Who is it?" he yelled.
"It's me, **broskee**!"
Before I could brace myself, he was bear hugging me.

I noticed a pistol on the floor that he probably answered the door with. That let me know how he was living.

We went in his room to talk. "You know," he said, "a lot has changed since you been gone. I run shit now. I want you with me like old times."

I thought maybe I could try to do right and get a job, something different, but **trapping** was the only thing I knew how to do.

My brother said, "You're the only one I trust to have my back 100 percent." That summed up my thinking. My brother needed me and I will always take care of my family no matter what. "I'm with you to the end, broskee."

We started getting money like it grew on trees. My first week home I made $10,000 by myself. The girls came with money and chased me. In three months I went from nothing to being a millionaire without working a single day. My whole life was drugs and money.

My brother called my phone. "Yo, we need to talk."

I said nothing so that he could say what he had to say.

"I'm done," he said.

"What you mean?"

"I've made enough. I'm out. You should, too."

I hung up the phone. I wasn't done. There was never too much money for me. I continued to trap. Why didn't I listen? Because I was hooked—addicted to the fast life. I should have changed while I still had the chance.

-M.D.

JUNKIE- a person who is heavily addicted to drugs, often used for intravenous users.

DRUG STRIP- a street or area that is a hub of illicit drug sales.

CORNER BOY- a young male in an urban area who hangs out with his friends on the street corners, often as a post for selling drugs.

THE GAME- similar to "The Life," refers to a number of underground industries depending on context, such as selling drugs, making music, prostitution, etc.

PUT IN WORK- to perform tasks (often illegal or dangerous) to gain respect in one's gang — for example, marking territory, attacking members of a rival gang, participating in a drug run, etc.

COME UP- to turn a profit; to gain something unexpected; to rise up financially.

BROSKEE- a friend who is more like your brother.

TRAPPING- making money from selling drugs.

HOW CAN YOU LOVE LIFE AT ITS WORST?

I'll tell you a story, what it's like in **the life**, this is untold, a period of strife.

I'd been sober four months, away from the monstrous drug that owned my soul.

I was healthy, happy; away from the man I loved but harmed me.

Professionals call it Stockholm Syndrome, I called it hard love. I see it now as manipulation.

They were looking for me, called it a **BP** hunt.

When we were together He would tell me, "You know I love you," and kiss me gently.

"You're worth good money, so do what you're good at and do as you're told."

I made more money for him, and then I got sold.

He cut the money different; I needed to be less selfish.

Real life sobriety was put on hold as the drugs took control.

I ran toward the pit of hell, this life consumed me.

Why'd I leave; it's all my fault. "Baby, I'm sorry... "

That was the worst He'd ever beat me.

"Shhh, hush Babygirl. Sleep softly."

I dreamed rapid fire, His words circled like a lost love of music in my bruised mind.

Too soon I woke by a tug of my body, too fast to cry, the pillow-case swallowed me.

Dazed and sore, four men took me out the door, forced me into a car restraining me.

I resisted hard, they yelled and pushed me.

"Shut the fuck up and settle the fuck down!"

Someone held my arms and grunted, "Hurry!"

I was tense, my veins were popping. Straight shot.

After that it's hard to say, warmth and a different kind of pleasure over took me.

Drifting from reality, they got me.

My body told my mind I was dreaming.

I'd done enough drugs to know how real fake things can feel.

At our destination, I was ushered out the car

I was barely complying we'd drove pretty far.

The snow was cold on my bare feet, as we walked to the house no girl lives to tell about.

Not sure how long but I lived in isolation. Tortured in my sleep I hear girls cry.

Now I understand, this is where I'll die.

My door opens, "Don't touch me." They mock me.

Sometimes in groups of five they rape me, even cut up my thigh.

Things become routine. My own makeshift IV. Not sure who used it before me.

Like strange men it almost never leaves my side.

Come, walk down the main hall. You'll see things done by the Devil himself.

THE LIFE- can refer generally to life outside of the law, hustling, or can be used more specifically to refer to selling drugs, prostituting, participating in gangs.

S.K. was no longer using meth and away from her pimp, who claimed to love her.

BP- stands for Baby Prostitute, an underage girl in sex work.

The pimp who claimed to love S.K. sold her to a different pimp.

S.K.'s new pimp took a greater share of the money she earned, justifying it by saying she needed to be less selfish.

S.K. was kidnapped in her sleep.
"This was the first time I shot up heroin; the needle was forced within me."

S.K. was being "warehoused" in isolation at a house where other girls were also being held.

S.K.'s captors cut her inner thighs with pocket knives and broken bottles as punishment for her failure to comply with their demands. "An old wire clothes hanger with a bag of mixed liquid drugs was forced upon me. I still have the scar on the top of my hand to remind me of this hell."

"I was forced to witness the murders of other girls. They were murdered for trying to escape or for not complying with the demands of our kidnappers."

This is His house, His jurisdiction.

And you'll see there is no God here.

The worst of days and ends, we'd group in the "living room" tied and gagged

Brutal examples and, dehumanizing murders took place.

This is my untold true story.

So can you love life at its worst?

I guess not in this case.

 -S.K.

UNFORGETTABLE FRIEND

I was nine years old when I met my unforgettable friend. I called him Shadow because we were both in a gang. We went through rough times and hard times. I remember we were walking down the street going to the market when, all of a sudden, a car full of **vatos** rolled up on us and asked us, "**What you bang?**" Shadow and I **threw up our hood**, but those guys were from different hoods and started **blasting** at us.

Shadow and I ran as fast as we could. We ran in some apartments to lose them, but they got out of the car and ran after us. Luckily, another of my **homies** lived in the apartments, and we started banging on his door. He opened the door, and we ran in. He asked us, "What is going on?" I told him, "Some **levas** are chasing us. They were shooting at us." My friend got his phone, called all my homies, and told them to get ready. My homie pulled out his **strap** and gave it to me.

Once all my homies arrived, they asked me, "What's happening?" I told them Shadow and I got hit up, and those guys started blasting at us once we told them what we banged. A couple of my homies and I went outside to see if those guys were still in the apartments. We walked to the market and saw the car parked there. I ran inside the store to see if they were in there. Once they saw me I said, "You lame punks!"

They all started to chase me again. Once they ran outside, my homies and I were waiting for them. I told them what we banged. They told me, "Let's get down one on one." After we fought, that guy didn't want to get back up so I kicked him in the face. His friends got mad so they pulled out pocket knifes and ran at me. Shadow ran in front of me and got **stuck** in his stomach three times. One of my homies started to shoot at those guys. He shot one of them in the arm and the other one in the leg. We rushed Shadow to a hospital. I thought to myself, "If it wasn't for him, I wouldn't be here to this day." He told me, after they let him out of the hospital that he would always be my brother, and that is what he is: My Unforgettable Friend.

-D.R.

VATO- guy, man, or homeboy in Spanish.

WHAT YOU BANG- a question asking about one's gang affiliation.

THROW UP THE HOOD- to show your gang sign, which is generally associated with a particular neighborhood or "hood."

BLAST- to shoot.

HOMIES- close friends who have your back and are there for you in times of need.

LEVA- a term used for traitors, snitches, sell outs, or people you don't respect in general in Spanish.

STRAP- a gun.

STICK- to stab.

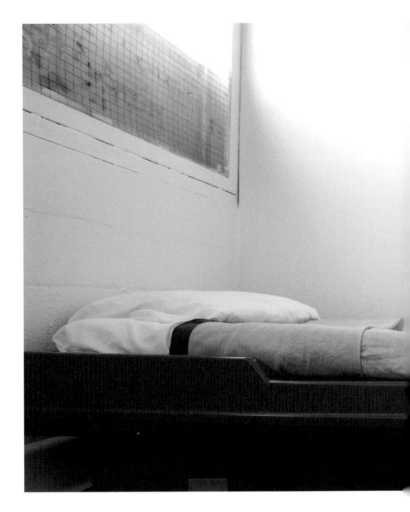

BLESSED IN- refers to becoming part of a gang without needing to work to be initiated, typically because one is family with high-ranking member(s) of the gang.

FOSTER CARE- "the informal and formal custodial care of children outside of their own biological family home when their parents are unable, unwilling, or prohibited from caring for them."

GROUP HOME- an out-of-home placement for kids who have been removed from their home "which provides 24-hour non-medical care and supervision to children, provides services to a specific client group and maintains a structured environment, with such services provided at least in part by staff employed by the licensee."

LOW KEY- uneventful, not wild or outlandish.

BIG HOMIE- a close friend or leader that you respect and look up to.

KNOW WASUP- to be aware of the reality of a situation.

THE SHU- stands for Secure Housing Unit, the wing of a corrections facility that houses inmates in solitary confinement/isolation.

THE HOLE- slang for solitary confinement/ isolation.

IMMIGRATION- refers to Immigration and Customs Enforcement, the arm of the United States Government most well-known for their role in responding to and deporting undocumented migrants.

SCRAP- a derogatory term for the Sureños used by their rivals, Norteños.

SNITCH- to tell on someone, specifically giving law enforcement or some other authority incriminating information; one who tells on others or gives authorities incriminating information.

I'm a **blessed in** child, I was born into this life not knowing what to expect or what I came into. My dad was 17 and my mom was 20. My mom just came up out of **foster care** or **group homes** along with my five tías. My dad was already running in the street. A couple months before I was born my dad's close friend got shot on the overpass next to the duplexes we used to live in. It was his 17th or 18th birthday. My dad went crazy. I was born months after that. My dad was there the whole time when I was born. I was his first child. My aunts all started working at age 14 and they bought me clothes to be while they wore whatever they could. You can say everything was **low key** until I was two years old. My dad, mom and me were walking over an overpass, my mom was carrying me and my dad was just wearing his Niner's jersey. They kept telling him to take it off, but he refused. He was supposed to be a man—a **big homie**. So they pointed the gun at me. He still didn't take it off. They ended up letting my mom and I go because they knew who my tío was. After that day my mom told my dad you either stick with us or run along with your friends. My dad walked out. We slept at a park for two weeks, until my tía took me in while my mom started working two jobs. When I was two, my mom had a boyfriend. When I was four she had my half brother. It hurt me cause she didn't wait. My dad was young; she shoulda **known wasup**. When I was eight I went over for father's day. My grandma said she needed to talk to me. We sat down and she said my dad's not

coming back, that he was in a cage for being a bad man. My dad always wrote to me; he'd tell me he got his diploma in **the SHU**. He'd draw me when he was in **the hole**. All that. The cops didn't like my dad but **immigration** came and took him to Mexico. Last time I seen him I was 12, and I saw him for an hour last year. I was going to see him this Saturday in TJ for his 35th birthday but I might not be able to no more. After that it was always trouble at home. I wanted my dad. My tío, the only one on my dad's side, became my everything until one year and four months ago he got shot in the head by **scraps**. My whole life was thrown away. Nobody sees me try, they all see me fail. It's like they don't wanna see me survive or rise above and show them I can be a successful Chicana. At age 12, I'd go to summer school and come home and babysit my brothers. At age 15, my uncle got shot in the head and everything fell apart for mi familia and I. He was the light to our day, he was our warrior, our shield, our protector, and he showed me everything I know today. From talking pain and knowing

how to deal with it, to street smarts and the culture we live in; to not talk, just sit and embrace what the slums has created. But do talk when needed to be heard cause closed mouths won't be heard nor fed. We aren't here to hurt. We're here to protect and carry on our culture, our people, our reason, and La Causa. Not many know what they're to stand for and represent. But we handle what needs to be handled when it's time—the right time. Not everybody sees what we do or why we do things. They only see what they want, what's convenient for them. They choose to blindfold the reasons we have. They give us that "why you do that for, that was wrong", "you should have thought about that before." But we don't tell, we don't **snitch**. We cover up and take time for others so they can continue the legacy and reasons for doing. Just open your eyes and realize.

-S.B., Age 16

I grew up in the streets just trying to make some **bands**
on that seminary block, where youngsters selling grams.
I ain't have no pops, my momma did what she can
but a woman can't teach a boy how to turn into a man.
I didn't understand if there really was a God why my pops
ain't have a chance.
I use to cry to God at night like why you breaking up my **fam**.
So I turned to the **hood**, the hood made me what I am.
They turned me to a monster, they turned me to a beast,
they turned me to somebody that I didn't want to be.
Cold nights at home I asked God why me,
why you take away my pops and leave me lonely in the streets,
why I had to be **grinding**, or my family couldn't eat.
My little brother only five and he looking up to me.
Every night I don't come home he say, "Mom, I miss C."
I'm only 17 but might be coming home at 23,
cause shit got real couple niggas, got killed
when you really in **the field**,
use yo gun as a shield, but that ain't okay.
I done seen lil niggaz get **murked** in broad day.
When Z. got killed I had to learn the hard way,
only 19 lost his life to gunplay.
But I ain't gon' sweat it 'cause the streets got hectic,
Yea they killed my big cousin so I was out here reckless,
tried to be a man but had to find a new plan.
And I ain't never had a good life.
I grew up **hustling** – making money and struggling, that's the hood life.
Family just trying to make it, barely getting by.
Shit was going downhill like a mudslide.
On Harmon, I was hungry at night
I lived with an Auntie who was in love with the pipe.
I ain't really understand she was destroying her life.
The only friends that I had was the roaches and that shit wasn't nice.
Can you believe how I feel my soul so dark, you'll think that I was ill.
I lost all my feelings when T. got killed.
The streets was under construction and my life was getting drilled.
So I had to take a kneel but I got talent that nobody could steal
Everybody want to rap or they just trying to sign a deal
But the bars that I spit give my listeners the chills.
Look me in my eyes, you'd probly feel how I feel.
Eleven years old, I seen my cousin get killed.
Done watched crackheads, overdose off a pill.
Yea I started from the bottom.
Now I'm climbing uphill.

-C.S., Age 17

BANDS- cash, more specifically one thousand dollars.

FAM- slang for family (biological or otherwise).

HOOD- the neighborhood one comes from and/or associates with.

GRIND- to work hard/make money.

THE FIELD- the area of the streets or the hood where everything goes down, generally a dangerous area.

MURK- to kill.

HUSTLING- making money by any means possible.

L.S.'s aunt was addicted to drugs.

MY STRUGGLE

My life begins like this: from birth I been homeless, living from motel to motel, until we would get kicked out. First we lived in a motel by a freeway and I would look out the window and cry because I couldn't believe this was my life, but something happened. We got put out. It wasn't nothing nice after that. My step-dad and my mama would decide on a place to park the van and we would just put the sheets up and go to sleep. Then three months later we found a motel in the 100's. It was nasty but it was a place to stay. The place was just nasty, it had mice and roaches. I would be on my way to school and I would step on mice tails. I hated the way my life was. I began to hate

my parents so I started looking for trouble... And I found it in my friend E. He showed me how to get money. When I moved to the nickel I was about nine, Then we went to the dubbz and it got **sick** after that. My life was just crazy so I came to the **JJC**. I been here six times. I was here on my 16th birthday; I thought I would get out before then. I regret even coming to court that day but I did and on the day of my birthday I tried to keep it together but I just couldn't and I had a panic attack. They made me take off my clothes and put on a **smock** in a **camera room** and I didn't get to put my clothes on 'til the next morning. I was so cold I couldn't get a blanket or nothing I was scared to use the restroom because of the camera and now I'm scared that I might have to turn 17 in a **group home** because I've been here a lot. They say I have family issues but I don't. But the judge don't see it that way. I go to court soon and my lawyer told me it's a wrap, they're sending me away from my family.

-T.W., Age 16

My full name is after someone in the bible. I've been here six weeks. I've been in this room for 15 minutes. I think it is time for me to come out. It is just a place where I can quiet down. Before this, I was at another level 14... but not a **lockdown**. I was there for a year and a half but I kept getting hospitalized for hurting myself. My mom lives in Las Vegas with a new husband. My mom has visited me. My dad abused alcohol, abused drugs, and abused me. He raped me when I was seven and kept doing it until I was 15. The neighbors finally heard me screaming and called the police. He never went to jail because he said I was lying. They took me to **DCFS** headquarters and then I was in a group homes ever since.

-M.A., Age 16

(interviewed and photographed in a DCFS psychiatric health facility)

LOCKDOWN TREATMENT- a secure residential placement for mental health or drug rehabilitation, in which youth are confined for the duration of their treatment.

DCFS- stands for Department of Child and Family Services, the governmental agency serving vulnerable children and families in some states.

I've been here three years. My sisters visit. I think I have a lot but I only know two. One is 23 the other 27. My mom doesn't visit—she's on **crack** and **heroin**. My dad is a **SO** and there is an **order** that he can't see me. It was between about six and 12 when he abused me. I told a **social worker** and they took me to a **foster home** when I was seven. My stepmom was married to my dad. She had a daughter who is my half-sister. I lived with her from when I was seven to ten—then they got rid of me. I started using drugs when I was ten. I got them from friends. I didn't go to school. I never went to school. I ended up in another foster home for two weeks and then I drank bleach. They sent me to a mental health hospital. I was there for two weeks. I was always trying to kill myself in there. Then I went to a **group home** with six kids. I was there two weeks then I left. When you **AWOL** you have to learn to read so you learn to read signs just to get around. I've been in two foster homes and four group homes. They I came here when I was 14. The food here is pretty nasty. I started cutting when I was six—when I was taken from my family. Most of my family doesn't like me. I don't have enough HS credits to even think of graduating. When I move to CTF metal is more available to cut. It's not easy to find here.

-E.L., Age 16

(interviewed in a DCFS psychiatric health facility)

CRACK- "a form of cocaine that has been processed to make a rock crystal (also called 'freebase cocaine') that can be smoked."

HEROIN- an extremely addictive opioid drug.

SO- stands for sex offender.

RESTRAINING ORDER- "a command of the court issued upon the filing of an application for an injunction," which prohibits individuals from performing certain acts, such as carrying out threats or coming within a specific distance of an individual who feels threatened.

FOSTER HOME- a single-family home placement in the child welfare system "in which a child is raised by someone other than their natural or adoptive parent" and lives with the caretaker's family.

GROUP HOME- an out-of-home placement for kids who have been removed from their home "which provides 24-hour non-medical care and supervision to children, provides services to a specific client group and maintains a structured environment, with such services provided at least in part by staff employed by the licensee."

AWOL- an acronym originating from the military meaning Absent Without Leave; in the context of dependency refers to a minor leaving their assigned placement without permission.

CTF refers to the less restrictive, "community treatment" branch of the institution, as opposed to the psychiatric treatment branch, where E.L. currently resides.

I've been coming here since I was 11. I am in for a **DV** with my mom. I thought when I first came here that jails were like I saw on TV. But this place, they are not here to hurt us. It's really cool. I first came here when I took something from my brother and he got mad and told my mom. She was tired from work so she burned me with cigarettes and hit me with an extension cord. I was seven years old. I can't talk about it without getting angry. I haven't seen her in eight years. I didn't know anything about **CPS**. My dad dropped out of the family completely. He was on **crack**. I was six years old when I was molested by my auntie's boyfriend. He put his finger in my vagina and my cousin's at the same time. He told my cousin that we couldn't tell anybody or he wouldn't give us candy. We didn't tell anybody for a while. It was my cousin's stepdad. When we told my auntie she wanted to tell the police but he said he would kill her if she did. We saw him with a gun and knew he would kill her. We went with my mom and she asked if everything went well and we told her that he touched us. Later, after he served five years, they took him in and expected everything to be normal. But I am still angry. Whenever I am out I guess my life is always in jeopardy. The only thing I know how to do is sell my body. I started prostitution because I needed some place to simply lay down my head. I was arrested in December in a hotel. I was with a friend who was 21 and helping me. They took me to **detention**. There you sleep all day. The only time out you get from it is to wash dishes. The staff talks about things they shouldn't been talking about with kids. I had to be willing to come here or else they wouldn't send me. My dad tried to help me but he was on crack. My grandmother can't help. Her life is messy. No one could see that I was suffocating. I don't have a pimp. I am doing it on my own. It's a rough world. I was having sex with police officers in Birmingham. I want to get out of here, get an apartment and get a singing career. The staff here, they are a blessing to me. They basically raised me. Last time I was in school I was 14. A lot of people know me as being a bad person... but it's because I have so much anger. I know that's no excuse. I want to go to community college. They are all okay here; it's different than other places. They know that they are here to help kids not hurt them. You don't have to punish kids to in order to help them. When kids have the attitude like "I will never make it in life because of what happened to me," they will never make it. People have to realize we are not bad kids just because we come from bad homes. We have made a bad decision somewhere along the way.

-B.W., Age 18

DV- stands for Domestic Violence, "any abusive, violent, coercive, forceful, or threatening act or word inflicted by one member of a family or household on another can constitute domestic violence."

CPS- Child Protective Services, the agency that in many states provides services in cases of child abuse or neglect.

DETENTION- "Usually refers to the placement of a youth in a secure facility under court authority at some point between the time of referral to court intake and case disposition." Post-dispositional detention is at times necessary for reasons including "awaiting placement, short-term sentencing to detention, or being a danger to self or others."

PROBATION- the status of a delinquent youth under court ordered supervision within the community, with specific conditions such as school attendance, the wearing of an electronic ankle monitor, refraining from interaction with other youth on probation, drug testing, etc. Failure to obey the conditions of probation may result in new charges and/or detention.

I've been out of **prison** 48 days. I was doing **20 split 5**. That means I did five and as long as I didn't get into trouble it stayed at 5. If you get into trouble it is another 15. I was in **county**. That's where they hold 16 and up. If you are involved in major crimes they **certify** you young as 16. I did juvenile so many times the juvenile court eventually got tired of me. I was 13 when I was first charged. I was well taken care of by my grandma. She is 72 or 73. My mom was incapable. She was an alcoholic. I barely knew my dad. **DHR** gave **custody** to my grandma. I think it was a **kin adoption**. My brothers and sisters were split up and went to different families. Seven of us went to grandma. I made some poor decisions as a kid. I wanted to be a grown man. I blame myself. From 13-17 I was in and out of here. Today I came through the front door. I was failing back then, but going through all this, everyone gets a sign. Some people don't pay attention. I got my GED and learned how to weld here. Now I work at Burger King for 21 days. I get minimum wage They know I have a **felony**—you can't lie about it. I applied for a lot of jobs and they all turned me down, but somebody gave me a chance. It's hard striving for success. Just because someone says no doesn't mean you don't keep trying; the next person can say yes. The Reverend has helped me get into Shelton State. Now I am staying with my sister. It's me, her, and her daughter. Prison was way more hard than here. **Detention** has a hands-off policy about kids here. Prison you get physically beat up. You have to learn to be a man in a hurry. You never know what can happen to you. People will pick fights. Here you get slapped on the wrist. Prison is hard-core. Only the strong survive there. I moved around so I could get certificates and try and get some education. I am working on getting my welding certificate now, but I have to go through so many people. I can't leave the state. If I get tools maybe I can do something. Religion is important to me. It is part of my life. I think everybody should get a second chance. Even someone who was charged with two **first degree robberies** and a shooting. It is a battlefield out there for kids. Now I have been working. It's a different environment. My sister works at a nursing home. She gets $16 an hour I think. I get minimum wage. Our apartment costs $320 a month. I trust my sister, my pastor and the assistant director here. These are people who have been around me most of my life. Mostly I didn't have to do what I did and I was with the wrong crowd. The others I was with are repeat offenders so I don't spend any time with them any more. Some are back on the inside.

-K.F., Age 23

PRISON- adult commitment facilities, correctional facilities that generally house individuals with sentences longer than one year.

20 SPLIT 5- refers to a blended sentence in which the first five years of the sentence are mandatory with 15 more to serve depending on one's behavior.

COUNTY- short for county jail, adult detention facilities.

CERTIFY- to deem a juvenile's case fit for adult criminal court and transferring it to adult criminal court due to the seriousness of the offense and/or the offender's age.

DHR- stands for Department of Human Resources, the department in Alabama's government dedicated to "the protection, well-being, and self-sufficiency of children and adults."

CUSTODY- refers to the responsibility to care, control, and make decisions for a child; can also refer to being held by law enforcement (i.e. "in police custody").

KIN ADOPTION- the adoption by the relative of a child.

FELONY- a serious crime, characterized under federal law and many state statutes as any offense punishable by imprisonment in excess of one year.

FIRST DEGREE ROBBERY- in Alabama, refers to a robbery committed with a deadly weapon or that resulted in serious physical injury to another.

This is the second time I've been here. I'm here for 10 days. First time I was here was for eight days. I had a **domestic violence** with my auntie. Another time it was **DV** and **shoplifting**, but my sister grabbed a jacket from the store and threw it to me. My mom has alcohol problems. My auntie has legal **custody**. My dad's deceased. He died of throat cancer. I was 12. I'm in eighth grade. I smoke now and then, even though my dad died of cancer. I'm here because I was in my room, I got angry and I put the dresser against the door and then I went into the closet and went to sleep. My auntie called the police and told them I was planning on killing my younger brother, but that's not true. I just wanted a quiet place to sleep so I went into the closet. But the police didn't believe me.

-L.Q., Age 14

DOMESTIC VIOLENCE- "any abusive, violent, coercive, forceful, or threatening act or word inflicted by one member of a family or household on another can constitute domestic violence."

DV- stands for Domestic Violence.

SHOPLIFTING- "theft of merchandise from a store or business establishment."

CUSTODY- refers to the responsibility to care, control, and make decisions for a child; can also refer to being held by law enforcement (i.e. "in police custody").

This is the second time I'm here. I've been here three months now. The first time I was 15 and here for a month. I got tired of the stuff at home so I **ran away**. I survived by breaking into houses. So I'm here mostly for **B&E** and **burglary**. I live with my mom and stepdad. My mom's about 40. My dad died of heart attack when I was four. My mom was doing **crack** and abandoned me and my sisters. I was staying in a **foster home** for two or three years. My little sisters and me were abandoned. We almost starved to death. And then I was staying with other relatives and a

hospital for two months. Then my mom got me back. She said she was clean but there were problems. I think she was on drugs again. I've never done drugs. They said I had behavioral problems and would break toys, push around my sisters, and go off by myself. I was so angry I would strip the bark off trees. They put me in children's hospital. I was angry at the situation and my mother. I sometimes don't want to see her—most times. She would badmouth my grandmother. Several times she would leave us all without food. I would get extra food at school for

the twins and I got in trouble for that. She would leave my eight-month-old sister unsupervised. They arrested my mom. She did nine months for a combination of drugs and child abuse. My stepdad was not in the picture until I was 10. There was really no support for my mom either. My mom's boyfriend would beat me and my younger sisters with a belt. Where was **CPS**? That's a question I ask myself but I don't know the answer.

-T., Age 16

I've been in the **timeout room** for two days. I've been in **detention** four times. The first time I was 13. I've been in **isolation** eight times. The longest time was two weeks. Any time they hear my name they lock me up. Any conflict or altercation, they lock me up. Doesn't matter who's to blame. They lock me up. They won't let me tell my side of the story. When I was 13 I got caught with a gun and some marijuana at the movies. I bought the gun for $60. I just wanted a gun so I can handle a situation myself. I got the $60 by **hustling**, just selling marijuana.

-D., Age 16

TIME-OUT ROOM- refers to solitary confinement.

DETENTION- "Usually refers to the placement of a youth in a secure facility under court authority at some point between the time of referral to court intake and case disposition." Post dispositional detention is at times necessary for reasons including "awaiting placement, short-term sentencing to detention, or being a danger to self or others."

ISOLATION- solitary confinement.

HUSTLING- making money by any means possible.

I'm in sixth grade but I've been held back. I was born in Fresno. I moved here when I was nine. There's a lot of **gangbanging** in Fresno. My auntie and cousins lived here and my mom decided to move here with my brother, sister and grandmother. My dad is deceased. He died of cancer when I was 5. I'm here because of a lot of suspensions and fighting. Kids were talking trash about my dad and telling me I'm a fat dumb ass. I've been here before for **trespassing** and **VP**. The original charge was **GTA**. This is my first time here. I thought I was going to get out tomorrow but I caught another charge with breaking the sink. I thought my mom wasn't coming to visit and I got mad and broke the sink off. My mom works as a teacher. My house is just me, mom, two brothers, and my sister.

-N.I., Age 13

GANG BANG- to participate in activities (often illegal) on behalf of a gang.

TRESPASSING- "the intentional and wrongful invasion of another's property," regardless of whether harm was caused during the invasion.

VP- Violation of Probation.

GTA- stands for Grand Theft Auto, the crime of theft of an automobile, which is a felony in most states regardless of the car's value.

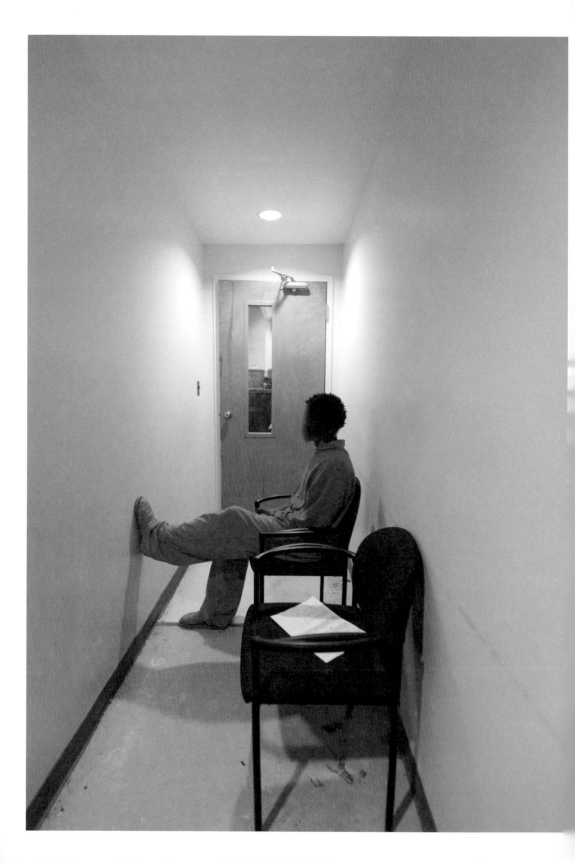

I'm getting my **72 hearing**. That's means I'm supposed to be heard within 3 days. I came in yesterday. I've been here three times before. First time I was 14. I live with my mom, stepdad, five brothers and three sisters. I stay with my dad sometimes. I've been suspended from school because I didn't do my work on time. I was suspended twice and then they put me in here. I'm hoping I get 28 days in **boot camp** and then can go home. I was in the county alternative school. It's a place to get your GED. I never got a chance to go to regular school. I stayed in alternative schools most of my life. I was originally charged with **DV**. I was with my sister who is 14 in her friend's mother's car. I was in the front seat and my sister wanted to get into the front seat, so she called the police because she knew I was on probation for my school suspension.

`-L., Age 15`

72 **HEARING**- refers to the initial court meeting defendants have within 72 hours of being brought into detention, which is mandated by law.

DV- stands for domestic violence, "any abusive, violent, coercive, forceful, or threatening act or word inflicted by one member of a family or household on another can constitute domestic violence."

247

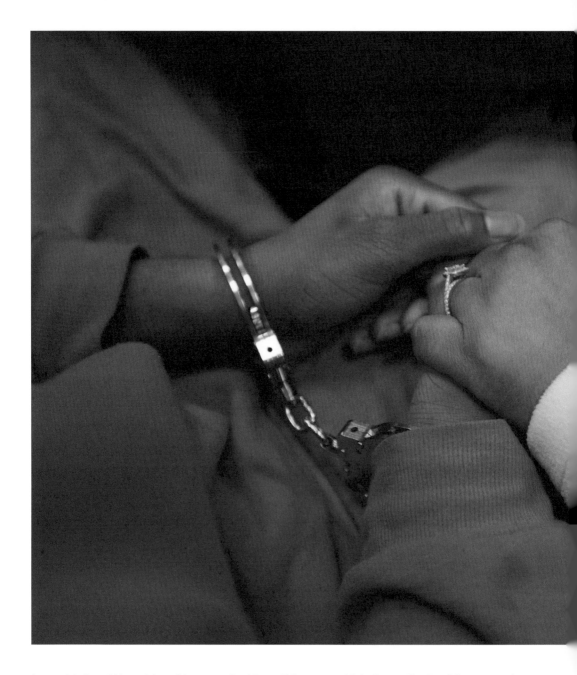

I was with three kids and they did an **armed robbery**. This was my third offense. They're giving me another chance. I'm moving across town. My mind is set on one thing and one thing only: to achieve my goals. I don't know how they got a gun and how it got into the robbery. But you can get a little gun here for $50 or $75. To get a gun you call a connect—someone who knows people. My **homeboy** got a revolver for cheap so you can sell it for cheap. I've been growing up since 11 or 12 knowing the streets but not running the streets. That means I was running with older kids. I've been smoking marijuana since I was 13. I live over on the West Side. My mom, my brother, and I live with my grandma who owns three houses. My brother just got out of **baby prison**. It's for 16 to 21. Detention is county. Prison is state. My dad was drinking a lot. I think he's working but I'm not sure. No there's never been any **domestic violence** in my house. When I have to go to drug classes there's a bus that picks me up or my mom drives me. I'm really a nice kid. They dropped the charges from **first degree robbery**

to third because I was telling the other kids not to do it. So you saw me in the courtroom. I won my trial. It wasn't really a trial. It was the **DA**, my **PO**, and my lawyer having to agree on something. They're giving me a little bit of string or rope to see if I'm going to hang myself. But I really believe they want me to succeed. If I don't I go to baby prison.

-M., Age 15

ARMED ROBBERY- the crime of theft "by force or intimidation" with a deadly weapon; depending on jurisdiction may be charged as aggravated robbery.

HOMEBOY- close male friends; see also Homies.

DOMESTIC VIOLENCE- "any abusive, violent, coercive, forceful, or threatening act or word inflicted by one member of a family or household on another can constitute domestic violence."

FIRST DEGREE ROBBERY- in most jurisdictions refers to the crime of robbery committed with a deadly weapon or that resulted in serious physical injury to another.

In the majority of jurisdictions, a crime committed in the first degree is the most serious form of that crime. By this classification, less serious forms of the crime have higher degree numbers.

DA- see District Attorney.

PO- Probation Officer.

I don't know where I go from here. I turn 18 in three weeks. Then I go to county, Men's Central. I'm **unfit**. I was found guilty but not sentenced yet. I'm from the City... Compton. In the house my life was not so good, y'know. My dad's an engineer for airplanes and my mom stays home and takes care of my grandma, mi abuela. I was doing bad in school. I'm really here 'cause I was angry. I was mad and upset. At 16 I got in an argument over a girl. She was my girlfriend for a year and eight months and then I wanted to break it off. You can read about it in the papers. I was in 11th grade when it happened... no maybe 10th. I'm not so good at school. My grandma doesn't know I'm locked up. She thinks I'm in Mexico, with my grandfather. I'm in here for two murders... the girls' parents that night. I was 14 or 15 when I started seeing her. I was 16 when the crime happened. No it's not about alcohol; I don't use alcohol and I don't use drugs. I guess I was in love too much. If I didn't have that hundred bucks for a gun, and I didn't have that friend, I wouldn't be here now. When I came here I was real scared, so I got on **suicide watch**. They said I have mental health issues; they did tests. My IQ is 57. That's what they told me. I don't now how to read or write. My name is all I can write. And I got to 11th grade. I go to school in here. Now I have 170 credits. I need 220 for a high school diploma. Now I've been here for a year and 9 months. Yea XX3 probation level means that staff is **sitting on** you 24 hours. I was **direct filed**. The judge is gonna give me too much time. They're gonna give me 30-to-life. They're gonna try to **wash** me.

-H.H., Age 17

UNFIT- refer's to ones status when their case has been ruled to warrant a trial in adult criminal court.

SUICIDE WATCH- a state of constant observation that may be ordered for a child if they are believed to be suicidal or are inflicting self-harm.

SITTING ON- observing or monitoring; most youth under observation are being watched 24 hours a day.

DIRECT FILE- "A prosecutor's discretion to bring charges against youth directly in adult criminal court instead of in juvenile court, without a prior certification hearing. States that permit this practice vary in what circumstances warrant it."

WASH- to wash away: one's identity, presence, and/or life outside of confinement due to an extremely long sentence.

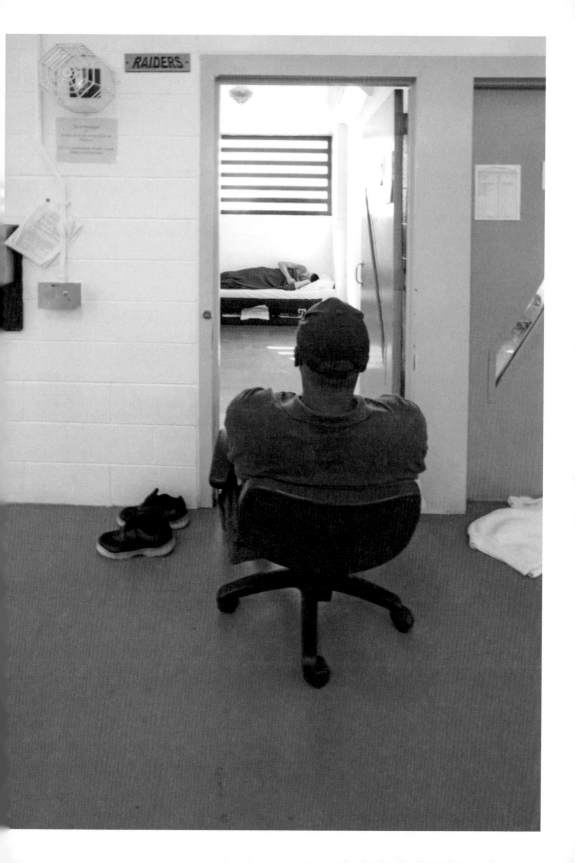

Glossary

AA - stands for Alcoholics Anonymous; a 12-step program that exists as an international mutual aid fellowship in which men and women meet regularly to share their experiences, help one another remain sober, and help other alcoholics achieve sobriety

Alcoholics Anonymous. Alcoholics Anonymous World Services, Inc. 2015. Available at http://juvie.us/0zl.

ACE - acronym standing for "adverse childhood experiences," originating from the Adverse Childhood Experiences Study's screening, designed to gather information on a youth's history of childhood maltreatment, trauma, and family dysfunction

Center for Disease Control and Prevention, National Center for Injury Prevention and Control, Division of Violence Prevention. "Ace Study." Atlanta, GA: CDC, 2014. http://juvie.us/lhq

ADA - stands for assistant district attorney

ARY - stands for at-risk youth, the status of a child after a request for services by the child's parent or guardian because the child has: been absent from the home for more than 72 consecutive hours without consent; is beyond parental control to the point that the behavior threatens health and safety; or has drug or alcohol abuse problems for which there are no pending criminal charges

"The Becca Laws." Prosecuting Attorney's Office. King County. December 27, 2012. Available at http://juvie.us/deb.

AS - stands for administrative segregation, which is the practice of confining inmates to their cells for 23 hours a day as a response to disruptive behavior; see Solitary Confinement

AWOL - an acronym originating from the military meaning Absent Without Leave; in the context of dependency refers to a minor leaving their assigned placement without permission

ABDUCTION - the crime of "restraining another through the use or threat of deadly force or through fraudulent persuasion"

"Abduction." West's Encyclopedia of American Law. 2005. Encyclopedia.com. Available at http://juvie.us/brt.

ABSCOND - "to hide, conceal, or absent oneself" from the jurisdiction or supervision of the court to avoid prosecution or supervision, e.g. failure to report to one's probation officer as assigned

"Abscond." West's Encyclopedia of American Law. 2005. Encyclopedia.com. (July 8, 2015). http://juvie.us/o8e

ACID - see "L.S.D."

ACTIVE SENTENCE - a sentence that requires an individual to be incarcerated, unlike a suspended sentence

"A Citizen's Guide to Structured Sentencing." The North Carolina Sentencing and Policy Advisory Commission. 2012. Available at http://juvie.us/4k7.

ADJUDICATION - "The hearing at which the judgment of whether the youth is or is not responsible for the offense he or she is charged with is made."

Justice Policy Institute. "The Costs of Confinement: Why Good Juvenile Justice Policies Make Good Fiscal Sense."

Washington, D.C.: Justice Policy Institute, 2009. Available at http://juvie.us/dba

ADULT HANGING - when a youth's sentence involves time in an adult facility that may or may not need to be served depending on behavior during juvenile sentence, as in adult time hanging over one's head; see also Blended Sentence

ADULT RECORD - the court's history of an individual's charges and convictions in adult criminal court

ADULT TRIAL - the practice of trying children in the adult criminal court, typically justified by seriousness/circumstances of the offense and age at the time of the crime, which removes youth from the rehabilitation-focused juvenile system and places them in the punishment-focused adult system

AFFILIATED - to be part of a gang, friends or family with someone in a gang, or to act for the benefit of a gang; to be declared gang affiliated by law enforcement can result in increased supervision in the streets or gang enhancement charges added onto other criminal charges

AGE OUT - refers to the point when a youth reaches an age where they are no longer eligible to receive services such as in the foster care or juvenile court system Aggravated Assault - "when a defendant intends to do more than merely frighten the victim" by "threat of bodily harm coupled with an apparent, present ability to cause harm," including "intent to kill, rob, or rape"

"Assault." West's Encyclopedia of American Law. 2005. Encyclopedia.com. (July 6, 2015). http://juvie.us/x5m

AGGRAVATED BATTERY- an intentional act causing harmful, offensive, or sexual contact with the body of another person, specifically with the intent to murder or cause serious harm

"Assault and Battery." West's Encyclopedia of American Law. 2005. Encyclopedia.com. (July 8, 2015). http://juvie.us/593

AGGRAVATED HUMAN TRAFFICKING - "recruiting, harboring, transporting, providing, or obtaining, by any means, a person under 18... to engage in forced labor, involuntary servitude or sexual gratification"

Human trafficking, 2014 Kansas Statutes 21-5426. Kansas State Legislature. 2014.

AGGRAVATED MALICIOUS WOUNDING - in Virginia, the criminal act of maliciously shooting, stabbing, cutting, wounding, or causing bodily injury to another person with the intent to maim, disfigure, disable, or kill, resulting in significant physical injury

Virginia Code § 18.2-51.2. Commonwealth of Virginia.

AGGRAVATED MURDER - the intentional killing of another human being under a number of aggravating circumstances that vary by jurisdiction, such as receiving payment for committing the murder, murder of an on-duty police officer, or killing someone under a specific age

"Aggravated murder defined." Oregon Revised Statutes Vol. 4 § 163.095. Oregon State Legislature. 2013.

AGGRAVATED ROBBERY - a crime of theft "by force or intimidation," with the use of a deadly weapon, infliction of serious bodily injury, or the presence of accomplices

FEENEY, FLOYD; KAHAN, DAN M.. "Robbery." Encyclopedia of Crime and Justice. 2002. Encyclopedia. com. (July 9, 2015). http://juvie.us/w51

AID AND ABET - a crime of assistance in committing a crime or helping a guilty party avoid law enforcement

"Aid and Abet." West's Encyclopedia of American Law. 2005. Encyclopedia.com. (July 9, 2015). http://juvie.us/vg8

ANKLE BRACELET - see Ankle Monitor

ANKLE MONITOR - refers to the electric monitoring device worn around the ankle, which is used to track the movement of individuals on house arrest, probation, or parole for the sake of supervision

ARMED - refers to the possession of a firearm, most often applied with another crime (e.g. armed robbery, armed carjacking) amplifying the seriousness of a violent crime and, subsequently, severity of the punishment significantly

ARMED ROBBERY - the crime of theft "by force or intimidation" with a deadly weapon; depending on jurisdiction may be charged as aggravated robbery

"Robbery." West's Encyclopedia of American Law. 2005. Encyclopedia.com. (July 9, 2015). http://juvie.us/bhs

ARSON - the crime of intentionally setting fire to a building or area

"Arson." Wex. Cornell University Law School Legal Information Institute. 2015. Available at http://juvie.us/xi5.

ASSAULT - though what exactly constitutes an assault varies by jurisdiction, it generally refers to the crime of causing another fear that "he/she is about to suffer physical harm," with the degree of the assault depending on how much harm was caused

Bergman, P. "Assault, Battery, and Aggravated Assault." The Nolo Network. Available at http://juvie.us/l45.

ASSAULT I - in Washington, the crime of assault performed with a deadly weapon or force likely to produce great bodily harm, causes great bodily harm, or exposes the victim to the human immunodeficiency virus

"Assault in the first degree." RCW 9A.36.011. Washington State Legislature. 1997.

ASSAULT II - in Oregon, the crime of assault while intentionally causing serious bodily injury with or without a deadly or dangerous weapon

"Robbery in the second degree." 2013 Oregon Revised Statutes, Vol. 4 § 163.175. Oregon State Legislature. 2013.

ASSAULT III - in Oregon, the crime of assault, either: of a victim under 10 years old; recklessly causing serious physical injury; committed with multiple people; etc.

"Robbery in the third degree." 2013 Oregon Revised Statutes, Vol. 4 § 163.165. Oregon State Legislature. 2013.

ASSAULT WITH A DEADLY WEAPON - the charge of assault aggravated by the use of a deadly weapon, such as a knife or gun, to commit the crime

ATTEMPTED MURDER - the crime of attempting to kill another person without cause or justification, proven by substantial steps being taken towards committing the crime

"Attempt to commit murder or manslaughter." 18 U.S. Code § 1113. United States Legislature. 2011.

ATTEMPTING TO CIRCUMVENT SECURITY - trying to avoid, mislead, or undermine corrections officers in some way

B&E - see Breaking and Entering

BP - stands for Baby Prostitute, an underage girl in sex work

BABY TIME - a short sentence

BACK UP - refers to the sentence one will have to serve if caught violating parole

BAD UA - a bad urine analysis test, meaning one tested positive for illicit substances

BANDS - cash, more specifically one thousand dollars

BANG - to participate in activities (often violent and criminal) on behalf of a gang

BASE - slang for crack-cocaine

BATTERY - the crime of intentionally causing harmful, offensive or sexual contact with the body of another person

"Battery." West's Encyclopedia of American Law. 2005. Encyclopedia.com. (July 6, 2015). http://juvie.us/mgp

BATTERY AGAINST A POLICE OFFICER - the crime of causing injury to a law enforcement officer, considered a much more serious crime than standard battery; if the battery results in serious injury, the sentence can be between five and 25 years depending on jurisdiction

Mince-Didier, A. "Battery Against a Police Officer." The Nolo Network. 2015. Available at http://juvie.us/9c8.

THE BEAN - a locked down facility

BECCA LAWS - refers to Washington State laws on truancy, at-risk youth (ARY), and children in need of services (CHINS), which are intended to ensure all youth receive education and protect children who are in danger or a danger to themselves

"Washington State Becca Task Force." Center for Children & Youth Justice. 2015. Available at http://juvie.us/p21.

BENCH WARRANT - a warrant issued by a judge when an individual fails to adhere to the rules of the court, e.g. not appearing to a court date or probation meeting, which enables an officer to immediately arrest an individual during a stop

"Bench Warrant." Wex. Cornell University Law School Legal Information Institute. 2015. Available at http://juvie. us/jlr.

BENCH TRIAL - a trial in which there is no jury

"Bench trial." Wex. Cornell University Law School Legal Information Institute. 2015. Available at http://juvie.us/xz2.

BIG HOMIE - a close friend or leader that you respect and look up to

BLAST - to shoot

BLENDED SENTENCE - a sentence that is outside of the court's "normal realm of consideration," whether juvenile or criminal. "For example, in some states a criminal court may impose a juvenile disposition for certain youth tried as adults... or a combined juvenile-and-adult sentence against an offender. While a court will impose an age-appropriate placement followed by a term in adult prison, the adult sentence is on hold pending a review of the youth's progress in the juvenile system."

Juvenile Law Center. "Commonly Used Terms." Philadelphia, PA: JLC, 2015. Available at http://juvie.us/b8f.

BLESSED IN - refers to becoming part of a gang without needing to work to be initiated, typically because one is family with high-ranking member(s) of the gang

BOUND OVER - in Ohio, transfer of a youth's case to adult criminal court

Beeler, J. letter to Senate Judiciary. "RE: The Adam Walsh Act and juvenile sex offenders." May 7, 2007. Available at http://juvie.us/wsu.

THE BOYS - the police

BOYS IN BLACK - correctional officers; a variation from the phrase "boys in blue," meaning law enforcement

BRACELET - refers to the electric monitoring device worn around the ankle, which is used to track the movement of individuals on house arrest, probation, or parole; see also Ankle Monitor

BRACK - to strike

BREAKING AND ENTERING - "the criminal act of entering a residence or other enclosed property through the slightest amount of force (even pushing an open door) without authorization"

Hill, G. and Hill, K. "Breaking and Entering." The People's Law Dictionary. MJF Books. 2002.

BROSKEE - a friend who is more like your brother

BULLPEN - a group holding cell where alleged offenders wait to go to court

BUNKED UP - to be share a cell and or bunk (slang)

BURGLARY - "the criminal offense of breaking and entering a building illegally for the purpose of committing a crime"

"Burglary." West's Encyclopedia of American Law. 2005. Encyclopedia.com. (July 8, 2015). http://juvie.us/rop

BURGLARY II - in Oregon, refers to the charge for the crime of burglary; see also Burglary

"Burglary in the second degree." 2013 Oregon Revised Statutes, Vol. 4 § 164.215. Oregon State Legislature. 2013.

CBT - stands for cognitive behavioral therapy; "a directive form of psychotherapy based on the theory that emotional problems result from distorted attitudes and ways of thinking that can be corrected... the therapist actively seeks to guide the patient in altering or revising negative or erroneous perceptions and attitudes."

"Cognitive Therapy." Miller-Keane Encyclopedia and Dictionary of Medicine, Nursing, and Allied Health, Seventh Edition. Retrieved July 10 2015 from http://juvie.us/06w

CIU - stands for Crisis Intervention Unit; refers to the unit where youth who are dealing with behavioral and mental health issues are sent, but is effectively solitary confinement in most cases

CO - stands for correctional officer

CPS - Child Protective Services, the agency that in many states provides services in cases of child abuse or neglect

CAGED - incarcerated

CANTEEN - a store within a confinement facility that sells hygiene items, snacks, paper, stamps, etc.; also known as a commissary

CAMERA ROOM - an observation room with security cameras, generally for youth entering a facility or youth who are considered a danger to themselves

CAMP - refers to juvenile boot camps, a type of juvenile

corrections facility

CAR HOP - to walk through an area of parked cars while checking if their doors are unlocked, and looting the car for valuables when unlocked cars are found

CARE WORKER - person who is employed to directly care for youth in a group home or emergency shelter

CARJACKING - "the criminal taking of a motor vehicle from its driver by force, violence, or intimidation"

"Carjacking." West's Encyclopedia of American Law. 2005. Encyclopedia.com. Available at http://juvie.us/eh8.

CASE MANAGER - "social worker whose role is to over-see and coordinate a client's (child/family) services in keeping with the client's goals and needs," such as identifying the most appropriate placement option for an abused child, or connecting a youth to mental health services

Garthwait , Cindy. "Case Worker." Dictionary of Social Work. University of Montana: Missoula, 2012.

CATCH A CASE - to be charged with a crime

CAUGHT UP - refers to getting caught by law enforce-ment, most often when the interaction results in charges

CERTIFY - to deem a juvenile's case fit for adult criminal court and transferring it to adult criminal court due to the seriousness of the offense and/or the offender's age

CHARGE - to formally accuse/a formal accusation within the legal system; does not necessarily indicate guilt

CHARGE AS AN ADULT - to charge a child as a criminal in adult court as opposed to a delinquent in juvenile court, typically justified by seriousness/circumstanc-es of the offense and age at the time of the crime, which removes youth from the rehabilitation-focused juvenile system and places them in the punish-ment-focused adult system

CHEAT ON MEDS - to not take and/or hide medications one has been prescribed

CHILD ENDANGERMENT - "an act or omission that renders a child to psychological, emotional, or physical abuse"

"Child Endangerment Law & Legal Definition." USLegal. 2015. Available at http://juvie.us/a9g.

CHILD SUPPORT - "a payment that a noncustodial parent makes as a contribution to the costs of raising his or her child"

"Child Support." West's Encyclopedia of American Law. 2005. Encyclopedia.com. Available at http://juvie.us/q4d.

CLAIM - to assert one's association to a location or membership in a group, such as a gang

CLIP - a device that holds multiple rounds of am-munition in one unit for facilitated insertion into a magazine or firearm

CODE OF CONDUCT - a set of behavioral expectations for youth held in a facility, which varies by institution and jurisdiction.

CODEFENDANT - "one of multiple defendants sued in the same civil action or formally accused of committing together the same crime"

"Co-defendant." Webster's New World Law Dictionary. Hoboken, NJ: Wiley Publishing, Inc , 2010.

COKE - slang for cocaine, a highly addictive stimulant drug

"Drug Facts: Cocaine." National Institute of Drug Abuse.

April 2013. Available at http://juvie.us/ysk.

COME UP - to turn a profit; gain something unexpected; to rise up financially

COMMISSARY - a store within a confinement facility that sells hygiene items, snacks, paper, stamps, etc.; also known as a canteen

COMMITMENT - "A court order giving guardianship of a juvenile to the state department of juvenile justice or corrections. The facility in which a juvenile may be placed... may range from a secure correctional placement to a nonsecure or staff-secure facility, group home, foster care, or day treatment setting."
US. Department of Justice, Office of Juvenile Justice and Delinquency Prevention. Glossary. Washington, D.C.: OJJDP, 2015. Available at http://juvie.us/4hq.

COMMITTED - sentenced to time in a correctional facility, as opposed to detained, which is one's status prior to disposition or trial

CONDITIONAL RELEASE - when used pre-adjudication in juvenile justice, refers to release of a child to a specific place (e.g. family home or group home) until their court date; when used post-adjudication in juvenile justice, refers to re-entry and aftercare programs for youth being release from commitment to assist in a successful reintegration to society
Sabonis , J. "The State Juvenile Justice System." Pine Tree Legal Assistance. April 27, 2011. Available at http://juvie. us/gom.

"Definitions." Juvenile Justice Chapter 985 § 3. The 2015 Florida Statutes.

CONSPIRACY - "the agreement between two or more persons to engage jointly in an unlawful or criminal act"
"Conspiracy." West's Encyclopedia of American Law. 2005. Encyclopedia.com. Available at http://juvie.us/a1m.

CONTINUATION SCHOOL - an alternative high school program "for students who are sixteen years of age or older, have not graduated from high school, are still required to attend school, and who are at risk of not graduating"
"Continuation Education." California Department of Education. 2015. Available at http://juvie.us/74z.

CONTRABAND - object(s) or goods that confined offenders are prohibited from possessing

CONTRIBUTING TO THE DELINQUENCY OF A MINOR - the crime of knowingly encouraging, causing, or aiding a child in delinquent acts as a person 18 years of age or older, including a parent
Code of Virginia § 18.2-371. Commonwealth of Virginia. 1950.

CONTROLLED SUBSTANCE - a drug or other substance for which its production and distribution is prohibited or regulated by the U.S. government
21 U.S. Code § 802. United States Legislature. 1970.

CONVICT (V.)- to find an individual guilty of an accused crime in a court of law
"Convict." West's Encyclopedia of American Law. 2005. Encyclopedia.com. (July 6, 2015). http://juvie.us/hgl

CORICIDIN - an over the counter cough/cold medication, sometimes referred to as "triple Cs," that is abused recreationally by ingesting quantities far above the directed dose
" Coricidin." Kaiser Permanente. September 2013. http://juvie.us/fwz.

CORNER BOY - a young male in an urban area who hangs out with his friends on the street corners, often as a post for selling drugs

COURT ORDER - "a formal statement from a court that orders someone to do or stop doing something"
"Court Order." Merriam-Webster.com. 2015. Available at http://juvie.us/xzi.

CRACK - "a form of cocaine that has been processed to make a rock crystal (also called 'freebase cocaine') that can be smoked"
"Drug Facts: Cocaine." National Institute of Drug Abuse. April 2013. Available at http://juvie.us/ysk.

CRACKHEAD - slang for a person who is heavily addicted to drugs, specifically crack

CREDIT CARD FRAUD - "a form of identity theft that involves the unauthorized taking of another's credit card information for the purpose of charging purchases to the account or removing funds from it
"Credit Card Fraud." Wex. Cornell University Law School Legal Information Institute. 2015. Available at http://juvie. us/ed5.

CRIMINAL DAMAGE - recklessly defacing, tampering, damaging, or destroying of any property of another person or of the state
"Criminal Damage to Property." USLegal , Inc. 2015. Available at http://juvie.us/2ro.

CRIMINAL INTENT - a factor in establishing that an action was criminal that "involves a conscious decision on the part of one party to injure or deprive another"
"What is Criminal Intent?" Black's Law Dictionary. 2015. Available at http://juvie.us/1dh.

CRIMINAL MISCHIEF I - in Oregon, the crime of intentionally damaging the property of another person under a variety of aggravating circumstances, including: causing damage in excess of $1,000; using an explosive or starting a fire; damaging a public utility or medical facility; etc
"Criminal mischief in the second degree." 2013 Oregon Revised Statutes, Vol. 4 § 164.354. Oregon State Legislature. 2013.

CRIMINAL MISCHIEF II - in Oregon, the crime in which "having no right to do so nor reasonable ground to believe the person has such right, the person intentionally damages the property of another, or, the person recklessly damages the property of another in an amount exceeding $500"
"Criminal mischief in the second degree." 2013 Oregon Revised Statutes, Vol. 4 § 164.354. Oregon State Legislature. 2013.

CRIMINAL THREATS - in California, the willful threatening to commit a crime which could cause great bodily injury or death
"Criminal Threats." CA Penal Code § 422.

CRYSTAL - slang for methamphetamine; see Methamphetamine

CURFEW TICKET - the summons given to minors found in public without a guardian after a certain time of night, which varies by jurisdiction; see also Status Offense

CUSTODIAL ASSAULT - in Washington, refers to the charge of assault in the first or second degree when the victim is a staff member, volunteer, service provider, or community correction officer at a corrections or detention facility

"Custodial Assault." RCW 9A.36.100. Washington State Legislature. 1988.

CUSTODY - refers to the responsibility to care, control, and make decisions for a child; can also refer to being held by law enforcement (i.e. "in police custody")

"Child Custody." West's Encyclopedia of American Law. 2005. Encyclopedia.com. Available at http://juvie.us/4rw

CUTTING - a type of self-injury that is often the result of attempting to cope with intense emotions and problems for which the cutter doesn't have the skills to overcome alone

Lyness , E. "Cutting." TeensHealth. The Nemours Foundation. June 2012. Available at http://juvie.us/drq.

DA - see District Attorney

DCFS - stands for Department of Child and Family Services, the governmental agency serving vulnerable children and families in some states

DHR - stands for Department of Human Resources, the department in Alabama's government dedicated to "the protection, well-being, and self-sufficiency of children and adults"

"Mission Statement." Alabama Department of Human Resources. 2015. Available at http://juvie.us/qvi.

DHS - stands for the Department of Human Services; the department of state/local government that exists to serve vulnerable children, adults, and families

DJJ - stands for Department/Division of Juvenile Justice, can be used to refer to the juvenile justice system in general or more specifically the juvenile corrections facility of a given jurisdiction

DJC - stands for Department of Juvenile Corrections

DOC - stands for Department of Corrections, the branch of government dealing with adult offenders; refers to an adult facility or the status of youth who have been tried as adults; also an acronym for "drug of choice"

DSD1 - stands for "down since day one," refers to a person who has been willing to be involved from the beginning

DUI - stands for Driving Under the Influence; the crime of driving while under the influence of alcohol or drugs

"DWI." West's Encyclopedia of American Law. 2005. Encyclopedia.com. Available at http://juvie.us/7tv.

DV - see Domestic Violence

DAY ROOM - name for the common area of a wing or unit in a facility

DEATH PENALTY - "the lawful infliction of death as punishment"

"Capital Punishment." West's Encyclopedia of American Law. 2005. Encyclopedia.com. Available at http://juvie. us/npa

DECLINE - in Washington state, to transfer a juvenile offender's case from juvenile court to the adult court system, i.e. a youth is "declined jurisdiction in the juvenile court"

Washington State Institute for Public Policy. "The Effectiveness of Declining Juvenile Court Jurisdiction of Youth." Olympia, WA: Washington State Legislature, 2013. Available at http://juvie.us/whz.

DEEP - when used after a number, e.g. "eight deep," refers to how many people one is with

DESTRUCTION OF A TELEPHONIC DEVICE - the crime of destroying a telephonic device that belongs to another person or the state, potentially as a means to prevent the summoning of law enforcement

DESTRUCTION OF STATE PROPERTY - the crime of willfully vandalizing or taking of state-owned property

DETAIN/DETENTION - "Usually refers to the placement of a youth in a secure facility under court authority at some point between the time of referral to court intake and case disposition." Post-dispositional detention is at times necessary for reasons including "awaiting placement, short-term sentencing to detention, or being a danger to self or others."

US. Department of Justice, Office of Juvenile Justice and Delinquency Prevention. Glossary. Washington, D.C.: OJJDP, 2015. Available at http://juvie.us/4hq.

DIPPED OUT - leaving without permission, in H.N.'s case, going AWOL from placement

DISTRICT ATTORNEY - "the lawyer who represents the state and brings a case against a defendant."

Juvenile Law Center. "Commonly Used Terms." Philadelphia, PA: JLC, 2015. Available at http://juvie.us/ b8f.

DIRECT FILE - "A prosecutor's discretion to bring charges against youth directly in adult criminal court instead of in juvenile court, without a prior certification hearing. States that permit this practice vary in what circumstances warrant it."

Juvenile Law Center. "Commonly Used Terms." Philadelphia, PA: JLC, 2015. Available at http://juvie.us/b8f.

DIRTY GUN - a gun that has previously been used in a murder or other serious crimes, lowering its value

DISORDERLY CONDUCT - "a crime that is charged when a person is being disruptive and disturbing the peace in which the public has gathered. Often, these types of crimes include the usage of alcohol."

The Zabriskie Law Firm. "Understanding Charges of Disorderly Conduct." HG.org. 2015. Available at http:// juvie.us/qp4.

DISPOSITION - "the stage of a delinquency proceeding comparable to the sentencing stage of an adult criminal trial."

Juvenile Law Center. "Commonly Used Terms." Philadelphia, PA: JLC, 2015. Available at http://juvie.us/b8f.

DISTRIBUTION - delivery of a controlled substance

"Food and Drugs." 21 U.S.C. § 802.11. 2012.

DISTRICT ATTORNEY - a public officer who is responsible for prosecuting crimes on behalf of the state

Hill, G. and Hill, K. "District Attorney." The People's Law Dictionary. MJF Books. 2002.

DISTURBING THE PEACE - a crime falling under the broader category of disorderly conduct, referring to conduct that compromises the safety, health, or overall peace of the public

DOC TIME - short for Department of Corrections' time, refers to part or all of a sentence that is in an adult corrections facility or counts towards a sentence from the adult criminal court

DOGGIE - a meth pipe

DOMESTIC VIOLENCE - "any abusive, violent, coercive, forceful, or threatening act or word inflicted by one member of a family or household on another can constitute domestic violence"

"Domestic Violence." West's Encyclopedia of American Law. 2005. Encyclopedia.com. Available at http://juvie. us/h91

DOWNER - any of a number of drugs that act as depressants

"Downer." American Heritage Dictionary of the English Language, Fifth Edition. Boston, MA: Houghton Mifflin Harcourt, 2015.

DRIVE-BY - to shoot at someone from a passing vehicle

DRIVING WITHOUT PRIVILEGES - in Idaho, the crime of driving/controlling a motor vehicle without a license, or with a revoked/suspended/disqualified license

"Motor Vehicles." Idaho Statutes § 18-8001. Idaho State Legislature. 1984.

DROP ONE'S FLAG - to stop representing and participating in the activities of a specific gang

DROP DIRTY - to fail a urine analysis test, to test positive for illicit substances

DRUG POSSESSION - the carrying of illicit drugs on your person and/or property

"Possession." West's Encyclopedia of American Law. 2005. Encyclopedia.com. (July 9, 2015). http://juvie.us/hqv

DRUG RECORD - one's history of drug use and drug offenses

DRUG STRIP - a street or area that is a hub of illicit drug sales

DRUG TRAFFICKING - the "global illicit trade involving the cultivation, manufacture, distribution and sale of substances which are subject to drug prohibition laws"

"Drug trafficking." United Nations Office on Drugs and Crime. 2015. Available at http://juvie.us/6dh.

DRY CELL - a cell without a toilet

DUAL/DUAL CUSTODY - the status of youth involved in both the dependency and delinquency systems (e.g. went from foster care to detention)

Juvenile Law Center. "Commonly Used Terms." Philadelphia, PA: JLC, 2015. Available at http://juvie.us/b8f.

EM - stands for electronic monitoring; see also "Ankle Monitor"

EARLY RELEASE DATE - the nearest date that an inmate could possibly be released depending on good behavior and a positive evaluation by the facility or parole board

ENGAGING IN CORRUPT ACTIVITY - in Ohio, a charge that can be brought onto someone who shows a pattern of engaging in crime, and has done so with more than one person

"Engaging in pattern of corrupt activity." Ohio Revised Code 2923 § 32. Ohio State Legislature.

ESCAPE - "the criminal offense of fleeing legal custody without authority or consent"

"Escape." West's Encyclopedia of American Law. 2005. Encyclopedia.com. Available at http://juvie.us/8s4

EXPUNGE - to remove or seal someone's arrest and conviction records, a practice that varies by age, type of crime, and jurisdiction; expungement is important because a criminal record can pose difficulties for ex-offenders seeking employment, residence, etc.

Bergman, P. "Expunging or Sealing an Adult Criminal Record." The Nolo Network. 2015. Available at http://juvie. us/max.

EXTRADITE - to "transfer an accused from one state or country to another state or country that seeks to place the accused on trial"

"Extradition." West's Encyclopedia of American Law. 2005. Encyclopedia.com. (July 10, 2015). http://juvie.us/vrb

FAILURE OF PLACEMENT - in the context of juvenile justice, refers to a violation of probation or a court order

Stewart, C., Giraldo , F., and Finley, M. "Using Data to Reduce Racial and Ethnic Disparities in Secure Detention." Presentation at the JDAI Conference, Kansas City, Missouri, October 5, 2010.

FALSE INFORMATION - the criminal offense of knowingly giving law enforcement false information concerning the commission of a crime

FAM - slang for family (biological or otherwise)

FEDERAL - short for federal prison; federal prisons are run by the Federal Bureau of Prisons (BOP) as opposed to state courts

"Terms & Definitions: State And Federal Prisoners And Prison Facilities." U.S. Department of Justice, Bureau of Justice Statistics. September 15, 2014. Available at http:// juvie.us/oir.

FEDS - short for federal law enforcement

FELONY - a serious crime, characterized under federal law and many state statutes as any offense punishable by imprisonment in excess of one year

West's Encyclopedia of American Law. 2005. Encyclopedia. com. 7 Jul. 2015. Available at http://juvie.us/vj8.

FELONY VANDALISM - "the intentional and malicious destruction of or damage to the property of another," which causes significant damage of which the cost to repair is above a certain value designated by the jurisdiction (e.g. more than $1,000)

"Vandalism." West's Encyclopedia of American Law, edition 2. 2008. The Gale Group, Inc.

THE FIELD - the area of the streets or the hood where everything goes down, generally a dangerous area

FIGHT FOR FITNESS - to attempt to keep a youth's case from being transferred out of juvenile court into adult criminal court.

FIRST DEGREE ASSAULT - in most jurisdictions refers to the crime of assault by means of a deadly weapon or assault resulting in serious physical injury

"Assault in the first degree." Alabama Code § 13A-6-20. Alabama State Legislature.

"Assault in the first degree." Revised Code of Washington § 9A.36.011. Washington State Legislature.

FIRST DEGREE MURDER - "a premeditated, intentional killing, or results from a vicious crime such as arson, rape, or armed robbery," though exact definitions vary from state to state

Hill, G. and Hill, K. "Second Degree Murder." The People's Law Dictionary. MJF Books. 2002.

FIRST DEGREE ROBBERY - in most jurisdictions refers to the crime of robbery committed with a deadly weapon or that resulted in serious physical injury to another

"Robbery in the first degree." Alabama Code § 13A-8-41. Alabama State Legislature.

FIRST MISSION - refers to the first illegal thing one does/did

FITNESS HEARING - in California, a hearing to

"determine whether the case warrants a trial in adult criminal court," based on the youth's age and seriousness of the offense.

The Superior Court of California, County of Orange. "Juvenile Court: Delinquency." Superior Court of Orange County. 2014. Available at http://juvie.us/v3t

FIXED SENTENCE - also known as a determinate sentence; a sentence of a specific length of time that is not subject to review, although it can be lengthened

"Determinate Sentence." Wex. Cornell University Law School Legal Information Institute. 2015. Available at http://juvie.us/214.

FLEEING STATE - to leave the state in an attempt to avoid a trial or prosecution for a crime, making the person a fugitive from justice.

FOSTER CARE - "the informal and formal custodial care of children outside of their own biological family home when their parents are unable, unwilling, or prohibited from caring for them"

CURRAN, LAURA. "Foster Care." Encyclopedia of Children and Childhood in History and Society. 2004. Encyclopedia. com. (July 10, 2015). http://juvie.us/gvc

FOSTER HOME - a single-family home placement in the child welfare system "in which a child is raised by someone other than their natural or adoptive parent" and lives with the caretaker's family

"Foster Home." Random House Dictionary. 2015. Webster's Unabridged Dictionary. http://juvie.us/e4z (accessed: July 10, 2015).

FULL CUSTODY - also known as sole custody, gives one parent or guardian the full responsibility of caring for a child, including making decisions about the child's welfare, education, medical care, and moral/religious development

"Types of Child Custody." Nolo. 2015. Available at http://juvie.us/xu9.

GZ - gangsters

GBI - see Great Bodily Injury

GPS - refers to electronic monitoring devices which must be worn by some probationers and parolees to monitor their whereabouts; see also Ankle Monitor

GTA - see Grand Theft Auto

G-CODED - refers to an inmate's file having a flag because he or she is homosexual, and therefore cannot have a cellmate

THE GAME - similar to "The Life," refers to a number of underground industries depending on context, such as selling drugs, making music, prostitution, etc.

GANG AFFILIATED - to be part of a gang, friends or family with someone in a gang, or to act for the benefit of a gang; to be declared gang affiliated by law enforcement can result in increased supervision in the streets or gang enhancement charges added onto other criminal charges

GANG BANG - to participate in activities (often illegal) on behalf of a gang

GANG BANGER - active gang member

GANG-ENHANCED FELONIES - serious crimes for which the severity of punishment has been increased due to the defendant's alleged commission of the crime in relation to a gang; see also Gang Enhancement, Felony

GANG ENHANCEMENT - refers to a set of laws allowing courts to increase the severity of a sentence due to a crime's perceived commission for the benefit of a gang. Gang enhancement charges can result in a youth's case being transferred to adult criminal court or time added to one's sentence

"Enhanced Penalties-Sentencing." Gang-Related Legislation by Subject. National Gang Center. 2015. Available at http://juvie.us/qgc

GANG INJUNCTION - "civil court orders that attempt to address crime... resulting in serious civil liberties violations. Law enforcement use them as a tool to label people gang members and restrict their activities in a defined area. Gang injunctions make otherwise legal, everyday activities—such as riding the bus with a friend or picking a spouse up from work late at night—illegal for the people they target."

"Gang Injunctions Fact Sheet." American Civil Liberties Union of Northern California. May 4, 2010. Available at http://juvie.us/kpg.

GANG UNIT - a specialized unit with a group of officers assigned to deal chiefly with gang-related issues, with the goal of reducing gang activity in the community.

"National Youth Gang Survey Analysis." National Gang Center. 2015. Available at http://juvie.us/f3m ,

GAY FOR THE STAY - a term for someone who is not homosexual outside of confinement, but during their time in confinement engages in homosexual relationships

GEN POP - short for general population, refers to the main area of a detention or corrections facility where the majority of inmates are housed, i.e. not a special housing, maximum security, or solitary confinement unit

GET POPPED - to get caught

GET RIGHT - to get yourself in a better position that you previously were, specifically with money

GIFTED - to be given drugs for free

GRAND THEFT AUTO - the crime of theft of an automobile, which is a felony in most states regardless of the car's value

Mince-Didier, A. "Grand Theft Auto." The Nolo Network. 2015. Available at http://juvie.us/74s.

GREAT BODILY INJURY - a charge of causing significant physical injury or injury that causes permanent damage, usually accompanied with another more general charge (i.e. assault with great bodily injury), and significantly increases the length of the sentence if convicted

Great Bodily Injury, CA Penal Code § 12022.7.

Washington Criminal Code, Revised Code of Washington § 9A.04.110.

GRIMEY - slang for wrong or unjust

GRIND - to work hard/make money

GROUP - short for group therapy, "a form of psychosocial treatment where small groups of people meet regularly to talk, interact, and discuss problems with each other and the group leader"

"Group Therapy." Miller-Keane Encyclopedia and Dictionary of Medicine, Nursing, and Allied Health, Seventh Edition. Retrieved July 10 2015 from http://juvie.us/xp7

GROUP HOME - an out-of-home placement for kids who have been removed from their home "which provides 24-hour non-medical care and supervision to children, provides services to a specific client group and maintains a structured environment, with such services provided at least in part by staff employed by the licensee." Some group homes have over 100 beds.

"Out-of-Home Care Facilities." DCFS Glossary. Los Angeles County Department of Child and Family Services. 2015. Available at http://juvie.us/dg5

GUARDIANSHIP - authority and responsibility held by a person who is legally appointed as the guardian of a minor, which grants the right to make decisions on the child's behalf including but not limited to residence, education, parental visitation, and medical treatment

"Legal Guardianship." DCFS Glossary. Los Angeles County Department of Child and Family Services. 2015. Available at http://juvie.us/dg5.

GUN SPECIFICATION - in Ohio, the mandatory imposition of an additional year to an offender's sentence because the offender possessed a firearm during the commission of a crime

"Firearm on or about offender's person or under offender's control specification." ORC 2941.141. Ohio State Legislature. 2011.

HRO - stands for high-risk offender, an individual who has been convicted of a very serious crime, such as murder or sex offenses, or is known to be violent.

HEROIN - an extremely addictive opioid drug

"Drug Facts: Heroin." National Institute on Drug Abuse. October 2014. Available at http://juvie.us/klg.

HIGH PROFILE CASE - a case that is well-known to the general public and/or has had a lot of media coverage. Because the judge wants to maintain a positive public image with the community, he may not release A. for fear of the negative repercussions in the next election. In some areas judges are appointed rather than elected, insulating them from the political repercussions of leniency

HIT - an order to attack or kill someone, generally in organized crime

HIT HOUSES - to rob a house

HIT LICKS - to rob a store or home, originally used specifically for robbing liquor stores, i.e. "hitting liquor stores"

HOLDING CELL - a courthouse cell where people awaiting to appear in court are held for short periods of time

THE HOLE - slang for solitary confinement/isolation

HOME DETENTION - the confinement of youth to their homes instead of a detention center when awaiting disposition or trial, requiring them to stay in the home either at all times or at all times besides when attending school or work, and enforced either through electric monitoring or frequent staff contacts

"Home Confinement and Electronic Monitoring." U.S. Department of Justice, Office of Juvenile Justice and Delinquency Prevention. Washington, D.C.: OJJDP, 2013. Home Detention Violation - to violate the terms of one's home detention, most likely resulting in the youth being placed in a confinement facility; see also Home Detention

HOME INVASION - the illegal, and often forceful, entry into a dwelling without the owner's permission; often charged as burglary

"Home Invasion Law & Legal Definition." USLegal. 2015.

Available at http://juvie.us/iag.

HOMEBOY - close male friends; see also Homies

HOMIES- close friends who have your back and are there for you in times of need

HOOD - the neighborhood one comes from and/or associates with

HOST - refers to being the host of a party in which one supplies drugs for their friends

HOT - being watched or monitored by law enforcement because they are suspicious of you

HOUSE ARREST - "confinement to one's home or another specified location instead of incarceration in a jail or prison," most often enforced with an ankle monitor

"House Arrest." West's Encyclopedia of American Law. 2005. Encyclopedia.com. Available at http://juvie.us/mtc

HUSTLING - making money by any means possible

IBRU - see Intensive Behavior Redirection Unit

IOP - stands for intensive outpatient program, a program most often used for drug dependency treatment for those who do not need medically-supervised detox, which allows patients to stay in their own homes while participating in a highly structured treatment program

"About the IOP Program." The Counseling Center. 2014. Available at http://juvie.us/7ob.

ILP - stands for Independent Living Program

IPS - short for Juvenile Intensive Supervision Program, assigned to juvenile offenders on conditional release or probation to provide structured and frequent contacts with an intensive supervision officer for youth who may otherwise be placed out of the home, as an alternative to incarceration

U.S. Department of Justice, Office of Juvenile Justice and Delinquency Prevention. "Juvenile Intensive Supervision: Planning Guide." NCJ 150065. Washington, D.C.: OJJDP, 1994. Available at http://juvie.us/8b7

ITP - stands for intensive treatment program; the maximum security area/program of the facility

Juvenile Treatment Centers. State of Oklahoma Department of Juvenile Justice, Office of Juvenile Affairs.

ICE - as a verb, slang for hanging out or "to chill;" as a noun, refers to methamphetamine

IDENTITY THEFT - "the assumption of a person's identity in order, for instance, to obtain credit cards from banks and retailers; to steal money from existing accounts;... or to establish accounts using another's name"

"Identity Theft." West's Encyclopedia of American Law. 2005. Encyclopedia.com. Available at http://juvie.us/el5

IMMIGRATION - refers to Immigration and Customs Enforcement, the arm of the United States Government most well-known for their role in responding to and deporting undocumented migrants

INDECENT LIBERTIES WITH A MINOR - in Kansas, soliciting or engaging in fondling or touching with a child 16 years of age or under

Sex Offenses, 2012 Kansas Statutes 21- 5506. Kansas Legislature. Updated 2012.

INDEPENDENT LIVING PROGRAM - a program providing "training, services, and programs to assist current and former foster youth achieve self-sufficiency prior to and after leaving the foster care system"

"Independent Living Program." California Department of Social Services. 2007. Available at http://juvie.us/fa2.

INDETERMINATE SENTENCE - "sentences in which an administrative agency, generally a parole board, has the authority to release an offender and determine whether an offender's parole will be revoked for violations of the conditions of release"

National Council on Crime and Delinquency. "National Assessment of Structured Sentencing." U.S. Department of Justice, Office of Justice Programs. NCJ 153853. 1996. Available athttp://juvie.us/abi.

INPATIENT - medical or rehabilitative treatment that requires the patient live on the premises of the care facility

"Inpatient." Random House Kernerman Webster's College Dictionary. Retrieved July 10 2015 from http://juvie.us/2dm

INSTITUTIONAL CHARGE - charges for offenses or rule breaking within a detention or corrections facility, which may or may mean charges in the court system

"Resident Handbook." Commonwealth of Virginia Department of Juvenile Justice. November 2013. Available at http://juvie.us/hpz.

INTAKE - "the process following arrest or referral to the juvenile court in which court personnel or the juvenile probation department investigates a youth's charges and background and decides whether to release the youth, channel the youth to a diversion program, or formally proceed against him/her in juvenile court." In certain jurisdictions intake may include a mandatory observation period (24-72 hours) during which the youth is held in isolation.

Juvenile Law Center. "Commonly Used Terms." Philadelphia, PA: JLC, 2015. Available at http://juvie.us/b8f.

INTENSIVE BEHAVIOR REDIRECTION UNIT - an area of the facility that claims to provide more intensive treatment services for anti-social or violent youth, but in practice holds youth in conditions of solitary confinement

"Resident Handbook." Commonwealth of Virginia Department of Juvenile Justice. November 2013. Available at http://juvie.us/hpz.

ISO - short for isolation; solitary confinement

ISOLATION - solitary confinement

JDC - Juvenile Detention Center

JCO - Juvenile Correctional Officer

JIP - short for Juvenile Intensive Probation Supervision, assigned to juvenile offenders on conditional release or probation to provide structured and frequent contacts with an intensive supervision officer for youth who may otherwise be placed out of the home, as an alternative to incarceration

U.S. Department of Justice, Office of Juvenile Justice and Delinquency Prevention. "Juvenile Intensive Supervision: Planning Guide." NCJ 150065. Washington, D.C.: OJJDP, 1994. Available athttp://juvie.us/8b7

JJA - stands for Juvenile Justice Authority, the operator of juvenile corrections facilities in the state of Kansas

JLWOP - see Juvenile Life Without Parole

JRA - in Washington, stands for Juvenile Rehabilitation Administration, the arm of the Washington State Department of Social and Health Services dealing with the highest-risk youth offenders

"About Juvenile Rehabilitation." Rehabilitation

Administration. Washington State Department of Social and Health Services. 2015. Available at http://juvie.us/r4v.

JUMP - to attack, often with the intention of stealing the victim's belongings

JUMP IN - an initiation ritual for membership to a gang, which typically entails the inductee receiving a beating for a predetermined amount of time while remaining defenseless

JUNKIE - a person who is heavily addicted to drugs, often used for intravenous users

JUVENILE CORRECTIONAL FACILITY - a secure residential facility "that is used for the placement, after adjudication and disposition, of any juvenile who has been adjudicated as having committed an offense, or of any other individual convicted of a criminal offense."

U.S. Department of Justice, Office of Juvenile Justice and Delinquency Prevention. Glossary. Washington, D.C.: OJJDP, 2015. Available at http://juvie.us/4hq.

JUVENILE CHARGES - charges that are litigated in juvenile court as opposed to adult criminal court

JUVENILE DETENTION CENTER - a secure residential facility that holds youth accused of delinquent or criminal activity while awaiting legal action, for the purpose of protecting both the detained youth and the community

Smith, S., and Stokes, T. "Juvenile Detention: A Nationally Recognized Definition." Journal for Juvenile Justice and Detention Services 14, no. 2. Richmond, KY: National Juvenile Detention Association, 1999.

JUVENILE LIFE WITHOUT PAROLE - "A prison sentence that comprises a person's entire natural life, without possibility of release, for an offense committed before the age of 18;" The mandatory sentencing of a juvenile to life without parole was declared unconstitutional in Miller v. Alabama (2012,) meaning a judge can still sentence those under 18 to life without parole, but must consider the circumstances of the case. The United States is the only country that sentences juveniles to life without parole.

Juvenile Law Center. "Commonly Used Terms." Philadelphia, PA: JLC, 2015. Available at http://juvie.us/b8f.

JUVENILE RECORD - "records kept by the juvenile court with information and documents relevant to a youth's delinquency charges"

Juvenile Law Center. "Commonly Used Terms." Philadelphia, PA: JLC, 2015. Available at http://juvie.us/b8f.

JUVIE LIFE - refers to a sentence lasting until the youth has reached the age limit for juvenile custody in a given jurisdiction (in some jurisdictions, youth can stay in a juvenile corrections facility until age 25); the maximum possible sentence in juvenile court

KICK IT - to spend time with, to hang out

KIDNAPPING - "the crime of unlawfully seizing and carrying away a person by force or fraud"

"Kidnapping." West's Encyclopedia of American Law. 2005. Encyclopedia.com. Available at http://juvie.us/qce

KIN ADOPTION - the adoption by the relative of a child

"Kinship Adoption." DCFS Glossary. Los Angeles County Department of Child and Family Services. 2015. Available at http://juvie.us/dg5

KNOW WHAT'S UP/KNOW WASUP - to be aware of the reality of a situation

KNOWN GANG MEMBER - a person who is known to be a gang member by law enforcement and, as a result, can be subject to increased observation on the streets and gang enhancement charges if convicted of a crime

LSD - Lysergic acid diethylamide, known on the street as "acid;" a schedule 1 controlled substance that produces powerful hallucinogenic effects

"Drug Facts: Hallucinogens – LSD, Peyote, Psilocybin, and PCP." National Institute of Drug Abuse. December 2014. Available at http://juvie.us/l6d

LUT - stands for lock-up threat; term for the status of youth who have been determined to be a danger to others and are for all intents and purposes placed in solitary confinement

"Classifications." Churchill County Juvenile Detention Facility Policy and Procedure Manual. Churchill County Department of Juvenile Justice. Date Unknown. Available at http://juvie.us/j02.

LEAVING THE SCENE OF AN ACCIDENT RESULTING IN INJURY OR DEATH - in Idaho, the charge given to a driver who leaves the scene of an accident they were involved in that likely resulted in injury

"Motor Vehicles." Idaho Statutes §18-8007. Idaho State Legislature. 1987.

LEVA - a term used for traitors, snitches, sell outs, or people you don't respect in general in Spanish

LEVELS - can refer to a number of different classifications depending on jurisdiction and context: levels as a hierarchy of privileges earned through good behavior; levels measuring how far you are in a program; levels as an indicator of a youth's mental health status; levels ranking how intensive the services are from facility to facility

THE LIFE/LIFESTYLE - can refer generally to life outside of the law, hustling, or can be used more specifically to refer to selling drugs, prostituting, participating in gangs

LOCK BABIES - offenders who are always returning to the IBRU/SHU/solitary/isolation, intentionally or unintentionally

LOCKDOWN - the confining of prisoners to their cells after a disturbance such as a riot or escape; can refer to solitary confinement when used by an individual

LOCKDOWN TREATMENT - a secure residential placement for mental health or drug rehabilitation, in which youth are confined for the duration of their treatment

LOCK-UP - refers to disciplinary detention in a segregated unit or wing of the facility, i.e. solitary confinement; also refers to incarceration in general

LOITERING - the crime of lingering or hanging around with no particular or legal purpose

"Loiter." Burton's Legal Thesaurus, 4E. 2007. Available at http://juvie.us/zxc.

LOITERING WITH INTENT TO COMMIT PROSTITUTION - the crime of lingering in an area for the purpose of engaging in prostitution, with intent being evidenced by behavior that "openly demonstrates the purpose of inducing, enticing, or soliciting prostitution"

California Penal Code § 653.22. California State Legislature. 2015.

LOOKOUT - a person who's job is to watch out for law enforcement or others while someone else or a group of people engage in some illicit activity, making them guilty by association

LOW KEY - uneventful, not wild or outlandish; also used before telling someone a piece of information that should be kept quiet to establish understanding that this is not public information

MIP - stands for minor in possession, the crime of having alcohol or a controlled substance on one's person or property while under the age of 21; see also Status Offense

"Underage Drinking: Possession/Consumption/Internal Possession of Alcohol." Alcohol Policy Information System. National Institute on Alcohol Abuse and Alcoholism. 2014. Available athttp://juvie.us/nvf.

MRT - see Moral Reconation Therapy ™

MAIM - in Virginia, to unlawfully but not maliciously "shoot, stab, cut, or wound any person or by any means cause him bodily injury with the intent to maim, disfigure, disable, or kill"

Code of Virginia § 18.2-51. Commonwealth of Virginia. 1975.

MAJOR - short for major charge, the term could be generally used to refer to more serious crimes, although seven specific major crimes have been designated by the FBI Uniform Crime Reporting System: homicide, rape, robbery, aggravated assault, burglary, larceny/theft, and vehicle theft

"Crime Statistics – Frequently Asked Questions." Seattle Police Department. 2015. Available at http://juvie.us/ec1.

MAJOR OFFENDER - one who has been convicted of a major charge

MALICIOUS HARASSMENT - the crime of intentionally injuring, damaging the property of, or threatening a person because of their race, color, religion, ancestry, national origin, gender, sexual orientation, or mental, physical, or sensory handicap

"Malicious harassment—Definition and criminal penalty." RCW 9A.36.080. Washington State Legislature. 2010.

MALICIOUS WOUNDING - the criminal act of shooting, stabbing, cutting, wounding, or causing bodily injury to another person with the intent to maim, disfigure, disable, or kill the other person in "malice," which is defined as the "state of mind which results in the intentional doing of a wrongful act without legal excuse or justification."

Koehler, Jamison. "Malicious Wounding in Virginia." Koehler Law. 2015. Available at http://juvie.us/17x

MANDATORY BIND OVER - in Ohio, refers to the mandatory (i.e. the judge has no discretion) transfer of a youth's case to adult criminal court for trial of certain offenses, and offenses committed by kids over a certain age

Beeler, J. letter to Senate Judiciary. "RE: The Adam Walsh Act and juvenile sex offenders." May 7, 2007.

MANSLAUGHTER - "the unjustifiable, inexcusable, and intentional killing of a human being without deliberation, premeditation, and malice," distinct from murder in that the act must not have been premeditated

"Manslaughter." West's Encyclopedia of American Law. 2005. Encyclopedia.com. Available at http://juvie.us/2z3

MATERIAL WITNESS - a witness who is believed to have information significant enough to affect the outcome of the case

MEASURE 11 - refers to Oregon Ballot Measure 11, passed in 1994, which applies mandatory minimum sentences for serious or violent crimes (e.g. a conviction of robbery in the first degree will result in a minimum sentence of seven years and six months, with the judge having no discretion to hand down a shorter sentence)

"Measure 11 Mandatory Minimum Sentencing." DOC Research and Statistics. Oregon Department of Corrections. Available at http://juvie.us/cr4.

MENACING - in Ohio, the crime of making someone believe that one will cause physical harm to a person, the person's property, or the person's immediate family

"Menacing." Ohio Revised Code § 2903.22.

METH - short for methamphetamine, also known as crystal meth, crystal, ice; an extremely addictive stimulant drug

"Methamphetamine." National Institute of Drug Abuse. Revised January 2014. Available at http://juvie.us/sml.

METH BABY - a child who was exposed to methamphetamine in the womb, which is linked to behavioral complications such as difficulty sustaining attention, anxiety, and a greater likelihood of aggressive behavior

"Prenatal Methamphetamine Exposure Linked With Problems." National Institute on Drug Abuse. December 21, 2012. Available at http://juvie.us/5qp.

MISDIMEANOR - "under federal law, and most state laws, any offense other than a felony"

"Misdemeanor." West's Encyclopedia of American Law, edition 2. 2008. The Gale Group 7 Jul. 2015 http://juvie. us/dfp

MISDEMEANOR THEFT - the crime of intentionally taking of personal property of another without permission, charged as a misdemeanor due to value of the property stolen; similar to petty theft

SCHWARTZ, LOUIS B. and KAHAN, DAN M. "Theft." Encyclopedia of Crime and Justice. 2002. Encyclopedia. com. Available at http://juvie.us/n7q.

MISUSE OF A CREDIT CARD - the charge given for a number credit card related crimes, such as using false information to obtain a credit card or intending to defraud a credit card to obtain property or services knowing that it was expired

"Misuse of credit cards." Ohio Revised Code 2913 § 21. Ohio State Legislature. 2011.

MOLLY - slang for MDMA in powder form

MORAL RECONATION THERAPY ™ - "a cognitive-behavioral counseling program that combines education, group and individual counseling, and structured exercises designed to foster moral development in treatment-resistant clients"

" Moral Reconation Therapy ™." Correctional Counseling, Inc. 2015. Available at http://juvie.us/dhq.

MURDER - "the unlawful killing of another human being without justification or excuse"

"Murder." West's Encyclopedia of American Law. 2005. Encyclopedia.com. Available at http://juvie.us/pn2.

MURK - to kill

NA - stands for Narcotics Anonymous, a program following the 12-step tradition developed by Alcoholics Anonymous that exists as an international mutual aid fellowship in which men and women meet regularly to share their experiences, help one another remain sober, and help other narcotics addicts achieve sobriety

"Information About N.A." Narcotics Anonymous World Services. 2015. Available at http://juvie.us/qdn.

NEGLECT - "the failure of a parent/guardian or caretaker to provide the care and protection necessary for a child's healthy growth and development. Neglect occurs when children are physically or psychologically endangered."

"Neglect." DCFS Glossary. Los Angeles County Department of Child and Family Services. 2015. Available at http://juvie.us/dg5

NON-CONTACT - refers to the status of two or more inmates who cannot come into contact with one another due to being codefendants, or a type of prison visitation in which contact is prohibited by a glass partition

O&A - stands for Observation and Assessment, where one goes after being committed to be assessed psychologically, educationally, and physically to determine the best program for that youth

OTP - stands for Orientation Training Phase in Colorado's Youthful Offender System; the first phase in YOS, which utilizes a militaristic, boot camp style approach to treatment

OBSTRUCTION OF JUSTICE - "a criminal offense that involves interference, through words or actions, with the proper operations of a court or officers of the court"

Franks, B.J. and Simpson, R.C. At Gun Point: Whistle Blowers' Point of View. AuthorHouse : Bloomington, 2012. p 593.

OFF PAPER - refers to the status of an individual who is out of the delinquency and dependency systems

ON LOCK - short for on lockdown, refers to being in secure housing/solitary confinement

ON THE LAM - avoiding contact with authorities; a term generally used for fugitives, synonymous with "on the run"

ON THE RUN - avoiding contact with authorities; a term generally used for fugitives, synonymous with "on the lam"

ONE-ON-ONE - 24-hour observation where a guard is appointed to constantly watch an inmate, typically assigned for youth who are perceived to be a liability to themselves

OPEN POP - short for open population, also known as gen pop or general population, refers to the main area of a detention or corrections facility where the majority of inmates are housed, i.e. not a special housing, maximum security, or solitary confinement unit

ORANGE - wearing orange, referring to the color of jumpsuit assigned to youth who have been tried in adult criminal court

OUT ON BOND - to be out of confinement due to one's bail being posted in the form of a bond, a guaranteed payment of bail that must be paid if the defendant fails to return to court for trial

"Glossary of Legal Terms." United States Courts. 2015. Available at http://juvie.us/cgr.

OUTPATIENT - medical or rehabilitative treatment that does not require the patient to live on the premises of the care facility

THE OUTS - short for "the outside," often used by people in locked institutions when referring to life outside of institutional settings

PV - Probation/Parole Violation

PO - Probation/Parole Officer

PC - protective custody

PC'D UP - to be under protective custody

PCP - Phencyclidine, also known as "angel dust;" a schedule II controlled substance that acts as a dissociative anesthetic and is known to cause many adverse psychological effects

"Drug Facts: Hallucinogens – LSD, Peyote, Psilocybin, and PCP." National Institute of Drug Abuse. December 2014. Available at http://juvie.us/l6d

PACK - to carry

PAPERS - refers to legal documentation that permits one to be in the country

PAROLE - though youth may use the terms "parole" and "probation" interchangeably, parole refers to the court-ordered community supervision of individuals who have been released from confinement prior to the end of their original sentence

"Parole." West's Encyclopedia of American Law. 2005. Encyclopedia.com. (July 9, 2015). http://juvie.us/d4u

PAROLE OFFICER - the public official supervising an individual on parole, with whom they have regular meetings

PAROLE VIOLATION - failure to obey the conditions of one's parole as set forth by the court, which may result in new charges and/or detention

PARTICIPATING IN A CRIMINAL GANG - the crime of participating in any criminal street gang with knowledge that its members have a pattern of engaging in criminal activity

"Gang Participation." Gang-Related Legislation by Subject. National Gang Center. 2015. Available at http://juvie.us/805.

PENITENTIARY - prison; when used by youth, often refers to adult correctional facilities

PEPPER SPRAY - "an aerosol spray that temporarily irritates the eyes and mucous membranes" used by law enforcement and correctional officers to incapacitate aggressive or unruly people

"Pepper Spray." Dictionary.com. Random House Dictionary. Random House, Inc. http://juvie.us/tab.

PETTY THEFT - theft of goods or money valued at less than a specific amount designated by the jurisdiction (e.g. less than $500)

SCHWARTZ, LOUIS B. and KAHAN, DAN M. "Theft." Encyclopedia of Crime and Justice. 2002. Encyclopedia. com. Available at http://juvie.us/n7q.

PIPELINE - where prostitutes wait for and solicit johns

PISA - Spanish word meaning countryman, often used to refer to Mexican immigrants who make little effort to assimilate to the culture of the U.S.

"Pisa." Urbandictionary.com. January 16, 2009. http:// juvie.us/l7f.

PLACEMENT - court ordered residential assignments in both the delinquency and dependency systems, which may "be secure and prison-like or have a more open setting, like group homes or foster care"

Justice Policy Institute. "The Costs of Confinement: Why Good Juvenile Justice Policies Make Good Fiscal Sense."

Washington, D.C.: Justice Policy Institute, 2009. Available at http://juvie.us/dba

PLEA BARGAIN/PLEA DEAL - "a plea agreement between prosecutor and defendant... the defendant agrees to plead guilty without a trial, and, in return, the prosecutor agrees to dismiss certain charges or make favorable sentence recommendations"

"Plea Bargaining." West's Encyclopedia of American Law. 2005. Encyclopedia.com. Available at http://juvie.us/hne

POD - term for a group of cells, similar to wing, unit, etc.

POOKIE - slang for meth pipe

POSSESSION - refers to the crime of carrying certain firearms, controlled substances, burglary tools, or other undesirable items on your person and/or property

"Possession." West's Encyclopedia of American Law. 2005. Encyclopedia.com. (July 9, 2015). http://juvie.us/hqv

POSSESSION OF A FIREARM/DEADLY WEAPON - refers to the crime of carrying a gun or other object designed to inflict death, either because the defendant is a minor, on probation, or fails to follow a state's laws regarding legal gun possession (e.g. obtaining permits)

Orlando, J. "Penalties for Illegal Handgun Possession." Connecticut General Assembly. August 7, 2012. Available at http://juvie.us/76q.

POSSESSION WITH INTENT TO DISTRIBUTE/SELL - the crime of not only being found in possession of a controlled substance, but intending to distribute the substance, which is determined by factors such as quantity of substance in question, presence of packaging materials, or large amounts of cash

"Possession with the Intent to Distribute." FindLaw. Thomson Reuters. 2015. Available at http://juvie.us/0iq.

PRIORS - refers to prior convictions; priors can result in harsher sentencing for a current charge

PRISON - adult commitment facilities, correctional facilities that generally house individuals with sentences longer than one year

PROBATION - the status of a delinquent youth under court ordered supervision within the community with specific conditions such as school attendance, the wearing of an electronic ankle monitor, refraining from interaction with other youth on probation, drug testing, etc. Failure to obey the conditions of probation may result in new charges and/or detention

Juvenile Law Center. "Commonly Used Terms." Philadelphia, PA: JLC, 2015. Available at http://juvie.us/b8f

PROBATION VIOLATION - failure to obey the conditions of one's probation as set forth by the court, which may result in new charges and/or detention

PROBATION OFFICER - the public official supervising youth on probation, with whom youth have regular meetings

PROMOTION OF PROSTITUTION - the charge for a wide variety of acts related to the facilitation of prostitution, including managing a house of prostitution, soliciting patrons, and recruiting prostitutes

"Promoting Prostitution." 2012 Kansas Statutes 21-6420. Kansas State Legislature.

PROP 21 - a California measure passed in 2001 that among other things, makes youth 14 years or older charged with certain felonies ineligible for juvenile court, automatically transferring them to adult criminal court; makes detention mandatory for 30 specific serious crimes; and increases sentences for gang-related crimes up to 10 years.

"Proposition 21." Legislative Analyst's Office of California. March 21, 2000. Available at http://juvie.us/6fw.

PROTECTIVE CUSTODY - the confinement of an individual to protect them from harm by the outside world or other inmates at a facility

"Protective Custody." Nolo's Plain-English Law Dictionary. The Nolo Network. 2015. Available at http://juvie.us/fbp.

PUBLIC INTOXICATION - also called drunk and disorderly or drunk in public, a charge alleging a person is drunk or intoxicated to the point of causing some disruption of public space

Portman, J. "Public Intoxication Laws and Penalties." The Nolo Network. 2015. Available at http://juvie.us/5l2.

PUT IN WORK - to perform tasks (often illegal or dangerous) to gain respect in one's gang – for example, marking territory, attacking members of a rival gang, participating in a drug run, etc.

PUT UP BOND - to guarantee, in the form of a bond, that the full bail amount will be paid if the defendant in question fails to attend scheduled court appearances, which allows a detained person to stay outside of confinement until trial or disposition

RE-ENTRY - the process of integrating back into society after confinement, or " reintegrative services that prepare out-of-home placed juveniles for re-entry into the community," also known as aftercare.

U.S. Department of Justice, Office of Juvenile Justice and Delinquency Prevention. "Aftercare Services." Juvenile Justice Bulletin. NCJ 201800. Washington, D.C.: September 2003.

RECEIVING STOLEN PROPERTY - "the offense of acquiring goods with the knowledge that they have been stolen, extorted, embezzled, or unlawfully taken in any manner"

"Receiving Stolen Property." West's Encyclopedia of American Law, ed. 2. 2008. Available at http://juvie.us/2lx.

RECIPROCITY - in this use refers to states acknowledging a person's status in the justice system across state borders, such as acknowledging the terms of one's parole in a state other than the state in which they were convicted and allowing them to complete parole in that state

RECKLESS BURNING - the crime of knowingly causing a fire, thereby recklessly placing a building or area in danger

"Reckless burning in the second degree." RCW 9A.48.050. Washington State Legislature. 2011.

RECORD SEALING - the practice of making one's delinquent/criminal record inaccessible to the public and eliminates the need for one's criminal history to be reported, e.g. to potential employers or landlords

Bergman, P. "Expunging or Sealing an Adult Criminal Record." Nolo. 2015. Available at http://juvie.us/max.

REGISTERED SEX OFFENDER - someone who has been convicted of a sexual offense that requires them to be placed on the Sexual Offender Registry due to federal, state, or local laws; being on the Sexual Offender Registry can create barriers for employment and residence

"What is a Registered Sex Offender?" Sex Crime Criminal Defense. 2015. Available at http://juvie.us/bw3.

RELAPSE PREVENTION - a plan of action for addicts

trying to prevent a drug relapse, including going to meetings, having a support network, and knowing what factors trigger one's addictive habits

REOFFEND - to commit another crime

REP - short for "represent"

REPRESENT - to express loyalty to a place or group

REPRESENTATION - refers to the attorney who defends and speaks on behalf of a client in court

Hirby , J. "What Is The Role Of A Defense Attorney?" The Law Dictionary. Available at http://juvie.us/8rj.

RESIDENTIAL TREATMENT CENTER - refers to any number of residential facilities for youth in both the juvenile justice and child welfare systems, including juvenile halls, detention centers, camps, emergency shelters, and group homes

"Residential Programs." U.S. Department of Justice, Office of Juvenile Justice and Delinquency Prevention. 2010. Available at http://juvie.us/lun.

RESISTING ARREST - the crime of obstructing a law enforcement officer's attempt to perform an arrest, which can range from running and hiding from officers to striking or pushing an officer during an arrest, unintentional or otherwise

White, C. "Resisting Arrest: Laws, Penalties, and Defense." The Nolo Network. 2015. Available at http://juvie.us/m70.

RESPITE CARE - short-term, out-of-home placement for youth status offenders and children in need of services (CHINS)

Edelman, P. and Watson, L." Improving the Juvenile Justice System for Girls: Lessons from the States. Georgetown Center of Poverty, Inequality, and Public Policy: Washington, D.C., 2012.

RESTITUTION - the payment of money and/or donation of services to the victims of a crime or society, with the intent of the restitution being to compensate damages caused by the crime

"Restitution." West's Encyclopedia of American Law. 2005. Encyclopedia.com. Available at http://juvie.us/xzg.

RESTRAINING ORDER - "a command of the court issued upon the filing of an application for an injunction," which prohibits individuals from performing certain acts, such as carrying out threats or coming within a specific distance of an individual who feels threatened

"Restraining Order." West's Encyclopedia of American Law. 2005. Encyclopedia.com. Available at http://juvie. us/1j9.

RICO CHARGES - refers to the Racketeer Influenced and Corrupt Organization Act (RICO) and the severe consequences that can be brought upon an individual who has engaged in a pattern of criminal activity as a member of a criminal enterprise

"RICO Charges." U.S. Attorney's Manual, CRM § 109. U.S. Department of Justice. 2015.

ROB II - in Oregon, the term used for robbery in the second degree, defined by the perpetrator of a robbery representing by words or conduct that they are armed with a dangerous weapon or the perpetrator is aided by another person

"Robbery in the second degree." 2013 Oregon Revised Statutes, Vol. 4 § 164.405. Oregon State Legislature.

ROBBERY - a crime of theft "by force or intimidation"

"Robbery." West's Encyclopedia of American Law. 2005. Encyclopedia.com. (July 9, 2015). http://juvie.us/bhs

"ROMEO AND JULIET" LAWS - a set of laws that lessen the severity of—but don't eliminate—punishment for consensual sex between minors when one partner is 19 years or younger and the other partner's age is within four years; for example, in Kansas the law "upholds the illegality of consensual sex between an older male and a younger female but offer lesser sentences (typically 1-4 years) as a result of this legislative compromise"

"A Guide to the Romeo and Juliet Laws." Laws.com. Available at http://juvie.us/vsf.

RUNNING AWAY - a status offense that can bring a child into conflict with law enforcement, juvenile court, detention, or dependency court, depending on the runaway's circumstances; running away often leads children to commit more serious crimes in order to survive

Mince-Didier, A. "Runaway Teenagers." The Nolo Network. 2015. Available at http://juvie.us/alm.

RUN RECORD - one's history of running away from placements (most common) or home

SB 163 - refers to California Senate Bill 163, which allows for youth who would otherwise be placed in a group home to remain in the family home with expanded family-based services that work with families to address issues

County Wrap-Around Services Pilot Project, CA Senate Bill no.163. October 9, 1997.

THE SHU - stands for Secure Housing Unit, the wing of a corrections facility that houses inmates in solitary confinement/isolation

SO - stands for sex offender

SANCTIONS HOUSE - in Kansas, a locked facility—most often a juvenile detention facility—where the judge might place a youth for a number of days (called a "sanction") "in addition to a sentence like probation, or as a consequence of violating probation"

"Juvenile Crime and Consequences in Kansas: An information booklet for juveniles." Kansas Legal Services, Inc. September 2011. Available at http://juvie.us/521.

SCRAP- to fight with hand-to-hand combat; also a derogatory term for the Sureños used by their rivals, Norteños

SECOND DEGREE COMMERCIAL BURGLARY - in California, burglary of commercial spaces, i.e. not residential spaces, is charged as second degree burglary; see also Burglary

CA Penal Code § 460.

SECOND DEGREE MURDER - "a non-premeditated killing, resulting from an assault in which death of the victim was a distinct possibility"

Hill, G. and Hill, K. "Second Degree Murder." The People's Law Dictionary. MJF Books. 2002.

SECTION 8 - refers to the Housing Choice Vouchers Program, which "provides qualifying families with assistance in paying the monthly rental fee for homes and apartments that are located anywhere, not just in subsidized housing projects"

"What is Section 8?" GoSection8.com. 2015. Available at http://juvie.us/z9x.

SECURE COMMUNICATION - communication, via face-to-face visits or letters, that has not been interfered with or detected by the staff of a facility

SEVERANCE - the decision to try multiple defendants' cases separately

"Severance." West's Encyclopedia of American Law. 2005. Encyclopedia.com. Available at http://juvie.us/5ty

SEX OFFENSE - refers to a number of crimes related to knowingly subjecting someone to unwanted or illegal sexual contact, including sexual assault, child pornography, and in some cases, sexting

"What is a Registered Sex Offender?" Sex Crime Criminal Defense. 2015. Available at http://juvie.us/bw3.

SEX TRAFFICKING - "recruitment, harboring, transportation, provision, or obtaining of a person for the purpose of a commercial sex act"

"Victims of Trafficking and Violence Protection Act." H.R. 3244, § 103.8A 106 th Cong. (2000). Available at http://juvie.us/38w.

SEXUAL HARASSMENT - harassment based on a person's sex, unwelcome sexual advances, requests for sexual favors, and other forms of verbal or physical sexually motivated harassment

"Sexual Harassment." U.S. Equal Employment Opportunity Commission. 2015. Available at http://juvie.us/y0n.

SHACKLES - a device with two cuffs connected by a chain, used on the ankles, wrists, and occasionally connecting the ankles to the stomach, used to severely limit the movement of prisoners

SHELTER CARE - refers to emergency shelter care in the child welfare system, temporary placements or drop-in facilities for youth who must be immediately removed from their home or current placement; these facilities generally have a 30-day maximum stay by law

"Out-of-Home Care Facilities." DCFS Glossary. Los Angeles County Department of Child and Family Services. 2015. Available at http://juvie.us/dg5

SHOPLIFTING - "theft of merchandise from a store or business establishment"

"Shoplifting." West's Encyclopedia of American Law. 2005. Encyclopedia.com. Available at http://juvie.us/ecd.

SHORT - to pay someone less than you owe them

SHOWING COLORS - to represent a gang; gangs are often associated with a specific color that indicate one's loyalty when worn

SITTING ON - observing or monitoring; most youth under observation are being watched 24 hours a day

SLIPPING - not staying alert, not covering one's tracks, getting lazy

SMACK - disrespectful comments or gossip; slang for heroin

SMOCK - also known as a turtle suit or suicide smock, these single piece tear-resistant garments are designed to be worn by suicidal residents who, if wearing standard facility uniforms, might use their clothing to hang themselves

SNITCH - to tell on someone, specifically giving law enforcement or some other authority incriminating information; one who tells on others or gives authorities incriminating information

SOCIAL SERVICES - refers to the department of state/local government that exists to serve vulnerable children, adults, and families; also known as the department of health and human services or the department of human services in certain jurisdictions

SOCIAL WORKER - in the context of youth in the delinquency and dependency systems, most often refers to a case manager in investigations of child abuse and neglect; see also Case Manager Soldier - refers to a person who is in a war in the streets, surviving in violent surroundings

SPICE - refers to a wide variety of herbal mixtures and/or synthetic chemicals that produce mind-altering effects often likened to those of marijuana. Spice has been sold legally in its many variations with the label "not for human consumption."

NDA for Teens: The Science Behind Drug Abuse. "Spice." National Institute on Drug Abuse. May 2015. Available at http://juvie.us/qxj.

SPONSOR - in the context of addicts and addiction recovery, refers to a recovering addict who shares their knowledge of fighting addiction with a less experienced addict and provides one-on-one support in times of weakness

"Recovery and Sponsorship." Alcoholrehab.com. Available at http://juvie.us/836.

SSI CHECK - stands for Supplemental Security Income check, a federal income supplement for aged, blind, and disabled people or those with little to no income, including minors

"Supplemental Security Income Home Page." Social Security Administration. 2015. Available at http://juvie.us/6nm.

STAR COURT - in Los Angeles County, stands for Succeeding Through Achievement and Resilience Court, a specialized court that provides multidimensional intervention services for underage victims of sex trafficking

"Succeeding Through Achievement and Resilience (STAR) Court." Los Angeles Superior Court. Judicial Council of California. 2015. Available at http://juvie.us/prw.

STATUS OFFENSE - "Conduct that is considered unlawful when committed by a minor (because of his/her childhood 'status'), but isn't criminal when committed by an adult." Such offenses include running away, truancy, violating curfew, possession of tobacco, etc.

Juvenile Law Center. "Commonly Used Terms." Philadelphia, PA: JLC, 2015. Available at http://juvie.us/b8f.

STATUTORY RAPE - a general term for the crime of engaging in sexual activity with a minor. The age restrictions that define the crime vary widely from state to state.

U.S. Department of Health and Human Services. "Statutory Rape: A Guide to State Laws and Reporting Requirements." U.S. Department of Health and Human Services. Available at http://juvie.us/tqa.

STICK - to stab

STRAIGHT - clean cut, rule-abiding and/or sober

STRAP - a gun

SUICIDE BED - a bed engineered to prevent the possibility of its occupant committing suicide, which is not bunked and built with as few pieces as possible, if not a single plastic piece

SUICIDE WATCH - a state of constant observation that may be ordered for a child if they are believed to be suicidal or are inflicting self-harm

SUMMONS - a legal document "that commands the defendant to appear before the court on a specific day to answer the complaint made by the plaintiff"

"Summons." West's Encyclopedia of American Law. 2005. Encyclopedia.com. Available at http://juvie.us/3x6.

SUPERPREDATOR - a term coined by scholar John Dilulio , Jr. in the early 1990's as part of the "super predator theory" to describe a speculated "new breed" of juvenile offender, "kids that have absolutely no respect for human life and no sense of the future. . . . These are stone-cold predators!" The term was used by the mass media to support the argument for a new wave of "tough on crime" policies that condemned youth to punishments once reserved only for adult criminals instead of rehabilitation. Many of the policies that resulted from publicizing the "super predator theory" are still in place today, though the theory itself has long since been disproved.

"The Superpredator Myth, 20 Years Later." Equal Justice Initiative. April 7, 2014. Available at http://juvie.us/2qp.

SUSPENDED SENTENCE - an intermediate or community sentence, a sentence that does not require the offender be incarcerated, i.e. not an active sentence

"A Citizen's Guide to Structured Sentencing." The North Carolina Sentencing and Policy Advisory Commission. 2012. Available at http://juvie.us/4k7.

TNA - refers to a website where prostitutes can be contacted by johns to arrange a meeting

TAG/TAGGING - the practice of quickly marking a signature, symbol, or sign in public spaces akin to graffiti, which can sometimes be used to mark territory

TAKE THE RAP - to take the blame

TAKEDOWN - a restraint technique for aggressive or unruly youth in a crisis situation that "redirects a youth to the ground in a controlled manner in order to limit the youth's physical resistance and to facilitate the application of a restraint device"

Florida Department of Juvenile Justice. "Florida Administrative Code Rule 63H-1.002." Rehired Employee Training Vol. 39, 151. August 5, 2013. http://juvie.us/9jd

THE TANK - intake

TENNER - 10 dollars worth of something, most often some kind of drug

THROW UP THE HOOD - to show your gang sign, which is generally associated with a particular neighborhood or "hood"

TIME HANGING - when a youth's sentence involves time in an adult facility that may or may not need to be served depending on behavior during juvenile sentence, as in time hanging over one's head. See also Blended Sentence

TIME SERVED - refers to the practice of applying the time spent in detention to the eventual sentence that is handed down, e.g. if someone was detained pre-trial for six months and receives a sentence of four years, the six months served counts toward the four years with time served

TIME-OUT ROOM - refers to solitary confinement

TIPPING - refers to being at ones emotional tipping point: feeling overwhelmed and unable to process what is happening

THEFT - includes a number of crimes involving the intentional taking of personal property of another without permission

SCHWARTZ, LOUIS B. and KAHAN, DAN M. "Theft." Encyclopedia of Crime and Justice. 2002. Encyclopedia. com. Available at http://juvie.us/n7q.

THROW THE BOOK AT - to impose the most severe punishment, with the word "book" referring to mean the collection of laws and penalties of a jurisdiction

THROW UP THE HOOD - to show your gang sign, which is generally associated with a particular neighborhood or "hood"

TRANSFER OF JURISDICTION - the court-approved transfer of a probationer or parolee to another juris-diction than that in which the case was processed

TRAPPING - making money from selling drugs

TRESPASSING - "the intentional and wrongful invasion of another's property," regardless of whether harm was caused during the invasion

"Trespass." West's Encyclopedia of American Law. 2005. Encyclopedia.com. Available at http://juvie.us/8gi

TRIBAL COURT - "a Court of Indian Offenses, a court established and operated under the code or custom of an Indian tribe, or any other administrative body of a tribe which is vested with authority"

"Definitions." 25 United States Code § 21.1903.

TRIBAL COUNCIL - the legislative body of a tribe

"Frequently Asked Questions." U.S. Department of the Interior, Indian Affairs. 2015. Available at http://juvie.us/sg8.

TRIPLE C - see Coricidin

TRUANCY - the status offense of repeated absence from school, which breaks compulsory education laws in the U.S.

Juvenile Law Center. "Commonly Used Terms." Philadelphia, PA: JLC, 2015. Available at http://juvie.us/b8f.

TRY AS AN ADULT - the practice of trying children in the adult criminal court, typically justified by seri-ousness/circumstances of the offense and age at the time of the crime, which removes youth from the rehabilitation-focused juvenile system and places them in the punishment-focused adult system

TWEAKER- slang for a person who is heavily addicted to drugs

UA - short for urine analysis test, the most prevalent form of drug testing

UNFIT - refer's to ones status when their case has been ruled to warrant a trial in adult criminal court

UNLAWFUL USE OF A WEAPON - refers to any number of crimes involving the possession of a lethal weap-on with intent to use it unlawfully or the discharging of a lethal weapon in public spaces

UPPER - a drug that acts as a stimulant

"Upper." The Oxford Pocket Dictionary of Current English. 2009. Encyclopedia.com. Available at http://juvie.us/zdx

USE - refers to using drugs

USE OF A FIREARM IN COMMITTING FELONY - the crime of using or attempting to use a firearm while committing a felony

Virginia Code § 18.2-53.1. Commonwealth of Virginia.

VP/VOP - Violation of Parole/Probation

VANDALISM - "willful or malicious destruction or defacement of public or private property"

"Vandalism." Merriam-Webster.com. 2015. http://juvie.us/1us.

VATO - guy, man, or homeboy in Spanish

VEHICULAR ASSAULT - the causing of significant bodily harm to another because one is driving recklessly

Izzi , M. "Vehicular Assault Laws." LegalMatch. August 19, 2014. Available at http://juvie.us/eit.

VEHICULAR HOMICIDE - the killing of a person with a vehicle, whether inside or outside the vehicle, intentionally or unintentionally

"Homicide." West's Encyclopedia of American Law. 2005. Encyclopedia.com. Available at http://juvie.us/jom.

VIOLATION - generally refers to a probation or parole violation; see parole violation and probation violation

VIOLATION OF PROBATION - see Probation Violation

VOLUNTARY PLACEMENT - "an out-of-home placement of a minor by or with participation of a State agency, after the parents or guardians of the minor have requested the assistance of the agency and signed a voluntary placement agreement"

Child Welfare Policy Manual § 8.3A.13. U.S. Department of Health and Human Services. 2015.

WAIVER HEARING - a hearing to determine whether or not a youth's case should be tried in adult criminal court, taking into consideration the youth's age and seriousness of the offense

U.S. Department of Justice, Office of Juvenile Justice and Delinquency Prevention. Glossary. Washington, D.C.: OJJDP, 2015. Available at http://juvie.us/4hq.

WALK THE STRIP - to prostitute oneself

WARRANT - "a written order issued by a judicial officer or other authorized person commanding a law enforcement officer to perform some act incident to the administration of justice... most commonly, police use warrants as the basis to arrest a suspect and to conduct a search of property for evidence of a crime."

"Warrant." West's Encyclopedia of American Law. 2005. Encyclopedia.com. Available at http://juvie.us/obs.

WASH - to wash away: one's identity, presence, and/or life outside of confinement due to an extremely long sentence

WEIGHT - slang for a high volume of drugs

WET CELL - a cell with a toilet and/or sink inside

WHACK - slang for uncool, undesirable, or unfair

WHAT YOU BANG - a question asking about one's gang affiliation

WILDIN ' OUT - to act up, cause trouble, or behave outlandishly

WORK RELEASE - "a program in which certain prisoners are permitted to leave a penal institution for a specified time in order to hold jobs, prior to their full release"

"Work-release." Webster's New World College Dictionary. Wiley Publishing, Inc : Cleveland, 2010.

WRAPAROUND SERVICES - "a youth-guided, family-driven team planning process that provides coordinated and individualized community-based services for youths and their families to achieve positive outcomes"

"Wraparound Process." U.S. Department of Justice, Office of Juvenile Justice and Delinquency Prevention. OJJDP: Washington, D.C., 2013.

XANAX - a prescription drug in the benzodiazepine

family used to treat anxiety and panic disorders; one of the most abused prescription drugs with potential for addiction

"Xanax." Drugs.com. 2015. Available at http://juvie.us/c4d.

YIR - stands for Youth Incident Report, a reporting mechanism for youth who commit offenses within a facility

YOS - stands for Youthful Offender System, the branch of the Colorado juvenile justice system that acts as a middle tier between youth corrections and adult criminal corrections

"Youthful Offender system." Colorado Department of Corrections. Available at http://juvie.us/yjg.

YWTP - stands for Young Women's Transition Program, a program for girls transitioning out of Oregon juvenile correction facilities that teaches independent living and social skills and prepares them for a successful reintegration to society

"Corvallis House." Oregon Youth Authority. Oregon State Government. August 2007. Available at http://juvie.us/ulw.

THE YARD - the exercise area of a facility, generally outdoors

YOUTH PRISON - juvenile correctional facility

ZERO DAY - a military-originating term for the first day of one's training, in which one must complete a series of tasks intended to physically and mentally challenge the person, usually with the aim of "breaking" them

11550- refers to California Health and Safety Code section 11550, which states that it is against the law to "use or be under the influence of any controlled substance"

Using and/or Being Under the Influence of Drugs, California Health and Safety Code § 11550 HS.

20 SPLIT 5 - refers to a blended sentence in which the first five years of the sentence are mandatory with 15 more to serve depending on one's behavior

211 - refers to California Penal Code section 211, pertaining to the felony of robbery

Robbery, California Penal Code § 211 PC.

.22 - a term that technically refers to the width of ammunition required by certain guns, but is used in reference to the gun itself

23 AND ONE - refers to conditions of solitary confinement in which inmates are confined to their rooms alone for 23 hours a day, with one hour allotted for large muscle movement outside of the cell

25-TO-LIFE - a life sentence with a chance of parole at 25 years

300 - refers to section 300 of the California Welfare and Institutions Code which states that children who have been subject to abuse and neglect can be taken into the custody of the dependency court

California Welfare and Institutions Code § 300. California State Legislature. 2015.

.40 - a term that technically refers to the width of ammunition required for certain guns, but is used in reference to the gun itself

50-TO-LIFE - a life sentence with a chance of parole after 50 years

602 - refers to section 602 of the California Welfare and Institutions Code, which states that kids who break the law, if found guilty, can become a ward of the court

California Welfare and Institutions Code § 602. California State Legislature. 2015.

72 HEARING - refers to the initial court meeting defendants have within 72 hours of being brought into detention, which is mandated by law

Pandullo , M. "Explaining the 48 hour hearing and the 72 hour hearing." Pandullo Law Criminal Defense. May 23, 2014. Available at http://juvie.us/mfb.

72 HOURS - the standard minimum period of time for a youth to be in solitary confinement for many facilities

–